THE STATE OF THE WORLD'S LAND AND WATER RESOURCES FOR FOOD AND AGRICULTURE

Managing systems at risk

publishing for a sustainable future

Published by:
The Food and Agriculture Organization of the United Nations
and
Earthscan

First published 2011 with FAO by Earthscan
2 Park Sq. Milton Park, Abingdon, OX14 4RN
Simultaneously published in the US and Canada by Earthscan
711 Third Avenue, New York, NY 10017
Earthscan is an imprint of the Taylor & Francis group, an informa business

The designations employed and the presentation of material in this information product do not imply the expression of any opinion whatsoever on the part of the Food and Agriculture Organization of the United Nations (FAO) concerning the legal or development status of any country, territory, city or area or of its authorities, or concerning the delimitation of its frontiers or boundaries. The mention of specific companies or products of manufacturers, whether or not these have been patented, does not imply that these have been endorsed or recommended by FAO in preference to others of a similar nature that are not mentioned.

ISBN 978-1-84971-326-9 (hdk)
ISBN 978-1-84971-327-6 (pbk)
FAO ISBN: 978-92-5-106614-0 (pbk)

Library of Congress Cataloging-in-Publication Data
The state of the world's land and water resources for food and agriculture : managing systems at risk. -- 1st ed.
p. cm.
1. Agricultural productivity. 2. Agricultural productivity--Water-supply.
3. Agricultural ecology. 4. Crops and climate. I. Earthscan.
S494.5.P75S73 2011
338.1'6--dc23
2011027406

Recommended citation for this book:
FAO. 2011. The state of the world's land and water resources for food and agriculture (SOLAW) – Managing systems at risk. Food and Agriculture Organization of the United Nations, Rome and Earthscan, London.

Contents

Foreword

This edition of *The State of the World's Land and Water Resources for Food and Agriculture* (SOLAW) fills an important thematic gap in FAO's flagship publication series, and presents objective and comprehensive information and analyses on the current state, trends and challenges facing two of the most important agricultural production factors: land and water.

Land and water resources are central to agriculture and rural development, and are intrinsically linked to global challenges of food insecurity and poverty, climate change adaptation and mitigation, as well as degradation and depletion of natural resources that affect the livelihoods of millions of rural people across the world.

Current projections indicate that world population will increase from 6.9 billion people today to 9.1 billion in 2050. In addition, economic progress, notably in the emerging countries, translates into increased demand for food and diversified diets. World food demand will surge as a result, and it is projected that food production will increase by 70 percent in the world and by 100 percent in the developing countries. Yet both land and water resources, the basis of our food production, are finite and already under heavy stress, and future agricultural production will need to be more productive and more sustainable at the same time.

A major objective of this publication is thus to build awareness of the status of land and water resources, and inform on related opportunities and challenges. Across the years, FAO has established itself as a unique source for a variety of global data on land and water. These data have been fully exploited in the preparation of this book, presenting the most comprehensive and up-to-date global overview of the availability of land and water resources, their use and management, as well as related future trends and developments. This further takes into consideration major drivers of global change, including demands driven by demographics, changing consumption patterns, biofuel production and climate change impacts.

The variety of situations that characterize the world's agricultural landscapes is at the core of SOLAW. It identifies geographic zones with high population densities, where rainfed and irrigated crop production systems are under increasing pressure and are at heightened risk of reaching limits to increased production and productivities. These 'systems at risk' are drawn to the attention of the global community for concerted and timely remedial intervention, including through investments and international cooperation, not only on a global scale but locally, where the consequences of lack of action on agricultural livelihoods are likely to be greatest.

SOLAW also highlights the essential but often understated contribution that appropriate policies, institutions and investments make in assuring equitable access to resources and their sustainable and productive management, while assuring acceptable levels of economic development. It also discusses options and strategies for addressing evolving issues such as water scarcity and land degradation.

SOLAW contains numerous examples of successful actions undertaken in various parts of the world, which illustrate the multiple options available that are potentially replicable elsewhere. The necessary planning and negotiating mechanisms for doing so are highlighted. Given increasing competition for land and water resources, choices of options inevitably require stakeholders to evaluate trade-offs among a variety of ecosystem goods and services. This knowledge would serve to mobilize political will, priority setting and policy-oriented remedial actions, at the highest decision-making levels.

Jacques Diouf
Director-General
Food and Agriculture Organization
of the United Nations (FAO)

Preface

Feeding a growing population

Land and water resources and the way they are used are central to the challenge of improving food security across the world. Demographic pressures, climate change, and the increased competition for land and water are likely to increase vulnerability to food insecurity, particularly in Africa and Asia. The challenge of providing sufficient food for everyone worldwide has never been greater.

The world's population continues to rise. Today's population of around 7 billion is expected to increase to about 9 billion by 2050 (United Nations, 2009). By this time, another one billion tonnes of cereals and 200 million extra tonnes of livestock products will need to be produced every year (Bruinsma, 2009). The imperative for such agricultural growth is strongest in developing countries, where the challenge is not just to produce food but to ensure that families have access that will bring them food security.

Today almost 1 billion people are undernourished, particularly in Sub-Saharan Africa (239 million) and Asia (578 million). In developing countries, even if agricultural production doubles by 2050, one person in twenty still risks being undernourished – equivalent to 370 million hungry people, most of whom will again be in Africa and Asia. Such growth would imply agriculture remaining an engine of growth, vital to economic development, environmental services and central to rural poverty reduction.

For nutrition to improve and for food insecurity and undernourishment to recede, future agricultural production will have to rise faster than population growth. This will have to occur largely on existing agricultural land. Improvements will thus have to come from sustainable intensification that makes effective use of land and water resources as well as not causing them harm.

The policies, practices and technologies needed to boost production and strengthen food security have long been discussed. Institutional mechanisms, the development of trade and markets and the financial facilities needed to raise productivity in a sustainable way have been negotiated at the international level. At national level, measures to raise output and strengthen food security are being put in place, including investment in pro-poor, market-friendly policies, institutions and incentives, as well as the infrastructure and services needed to improve productivity. Yet the challenge still remains.

Increased competition for land and water

And there are warning signs. Rates of growth in agricultural production have been slowing, and are only half the 3 percent annual rate of growth seen in developing countries in the past. In 2007 and 2008, any complacency was jolted by food price shocks, as grain prices soared. Since then, the growing competition for land and water are now thrown into stark relief as sovereign and commercial investors begin to acquire tracts of farmland in developing countries. Production of feedstock for biofuels competes with food production on significant areas of prime cultivated land. A series of high profile floods, droughts and landslides further threaten the stability of land and water resources.

Deeper structural problems have also become apparent in the natural resource base. Water scarcity is growing. Salinization and pollution of water courses and bodies, and degradation of water-related ecosystems are rising. In many large rivers, only 5 percent of former water volumes remain in-stream, and some rivers such as the Huang He no longer reach the sea year-round. Large lakes and inland seas have shrunk, and half the wetlands of Europe and North America no longer exist. Runoff from eroding soils is filling reservoirs, reducing hydropower and water supply. Groundwater is being pumped intensively overpumped and aquifers are becoming increasingly polluted and salinized in some coastal areas. Large parts of all continents are experiencing high rates of ecosystem impairment, particularly reduced soil quality, biodiversity loss, and harm to amenity and cultural heritage values.

Agriculture is now a major contributor to greenhouse gases, accounting for 13.5 percent of global greenhouse gas emissions (IPCC, 2007). At the same time, climate change brings an increase in risk and unpredictability for farmers – from warming and related aridity, from shifts in rainfall patterns, and from the growing incidence of extreme weather events. Poor farmers in low income countries are the most vulnerable and the least able to adapt to these changes.

The steady increase in inland aquaculture also contributes to the competition for land and water resources: the average annual per capita supply of food fish from aquaculture for human consumption has increased at an average rate of 6.6 percent per year between 1970 and 2008 (FAO 2010a), leading to increase demand in feed, water and land for the construction of fish ponds.

The deteriorating trends in the capacities of ecosystems to provide vital goods and services are already affecting the production potential of important food-producing zones. If these continue, impacts on food security will be greatest in developing countries, where both water and soil nutrients are least abundant. Yet in some locations, better technology, management practices and policies (which take into consideration the need for appropriate tradeoffs between environmental needs and agricultural production) have arrested and reversed negative trends and thus indicate pathways towards models of sustainable intensification. The risks, however, are considerable. On present trends, a series of major land and water systems and the food outputs they produce are at risk.

Scope of the book

This book deals primarily with the issue of land and water for crops. It examines the kinds of production responses needed to meet demand. It also assesses the potential of the world's land and water resources to support these desired increases in output and productivity. Risks and tradeoffs are examined, and options reviewed for managing these without harm to the resource base.

While the use of land and water for forestry and livestock is briefly discussed in Chapter 1, these subjects have been addressed in greater detail in two earlier FAO reports to which the reader is referred: *The State of the World's Forests* (FAO, 2009a) and *The State of Food and Agriculture* (FAO, 2009b). Similarly, more detailed analyses of trends and challenges on inland fisheries and aquaculture are provided in the recent FAO, report *The State of World Fisheries and Aquaculture* (FAO, 2010a). These global reports are supplemented by comprehensive analysis of gender in agriculture in FAO and World Bank reports (FAO, 2011a; World Bank, 2009b).

Chapter 1 analyses the current status of land and water resources together with trends. It assesses the biophysical and technical aspects of the resources and their use, and presents projections for the year 2050. Chapter 2 reviews current institutional arrangements, and assesses socio-economic and environmental impacts of current land and water management. Chapter 3 reviews current and future threats to land and water and their implications for a series of major systems at risk. Chapter 4 examines requirements and options to achieve the necessary levels of output and productivity required in a sustainable way. Chapter 5 assesses the institutional responses at local, national and international levels, with an analysis of lessons for the future. Finally, Chapter 6 draws conclusions and advances policy recommendations. These centre on the pragmatic step by step approaches towards a new paradigm of more sustainable, lower-carbon intensive agricultural production, based on more ecologically-sensitive management of land and water by farmers, supported by policies, institutions and incentives from national governments and the global community.

Acknowledgements

The preparation of the SOLAW report has benefited from the support and input of a number of individuals and specialized institutions:

Conceptualization and overall supervision: P. Koohafkan.

Coordination: H. George.

SOLAW Preparation core group: H. George, J-M. Faurès, J. Burke, N. Forlano, F. Nachtergaele, P. Groppo, S. Bunning, P. Koohafkan and P. Steduto.

External reviewers and advisers: H. P. Binswanger, R. Conant, P. Mahler, R. Stewart and R. Brinkman.

Summary report writing team: C. S. Ward (independent consultant) and J. Pretty (University of Essex).

Preparation and review of thematic reports and SOLAW chapters:

D. Bartley, C. Batello, M. Bernardi, R. Biancalani, H. P. Binswanger, J. Bonnal, J. Bruinsma, S. Bunning, J. Burke, C. Casarotto, N. Cenacchi, M. Cluff, R. Cumani, J. De la Cruz, C. De Young, O. Dubois, T. Facon, J. M. Faurès, N. Forlano, G. Franceschini, K. Frenken, T. Friedrich, A. Fynn, J. Gault, H. George, P. Gerber, P. Grassini, P. Groppo, T. Hofer, J. Hoogeveen, B. Huddleston, W. Klemm, P.K. Koohafkan, R. Lal, D. Lantieri, J. Latham, C. Licona Manzur, L. Lipper, M. Loyche-Wilkie, J. Mateo-Sagasta, P. Mathieu, G. Munoz, F. Nachtergaele, C. Neely, D. Palmer, M. Petri, T. Price, T. Robinson, S. Rose, M. Salman, V. Sadras, S. Schlingloff, P. Steduto, L. Stravato, P. Tallah, L. Thiombiano, J. Tranberg, F. Tubiello, J. Valbo-Jorgensen and M. van der Velde.

Institutions involved in the preparation of the thematic reports:

- **IIASA** (International Institute for Applied Systems Analysis) – G. Fischer, E. Hizsnyik, S. Prieler and D. A. Wiberg.

- **IFPRI** (International Food Policy Research Institute) – R. Meinzen-Dick, E. Nkonya and C. Ringler.

- **IIED** (International Institute for Environment and Development) – L. Cotula.

- **CDE** (Centre for Development and Environment, University of Berne) – G. Schwilch, C. Hauert and H. Liniger.

- **University of Bonn, Germany/University of Frankfurt** – S. Siebert.

- **Geodata Institute** (University of Southampton).

- **AGTER** (Association the Governance of Land, Water and Natural Resources).

Preparation of statistics and maps: K. Frenken, H. George, J. M. Faurès, J. Hoogeveen, L. Peiser, M. Marinelli, M. Petri and L. Simeone, with assistance from R. Biancalani, J. Latham and R. Cumani.

SOLAW website: H. George, L. Peiser and S. Giaccio, with assistance from G. Lanzarone, M. Fani, D. Lanzi, M. Marinelli, B. Mukunyora, F. Snijders and K. Sullivan.

Publishing arrangements and graphic design: N. Forlano, R. Tucker and J. Morgan, with assistance from G. Zanolli, M. Umena and P. Mander.

Secretarial assistance: M. Finka.

List of abbreviations

AEZ	agro-ecological zoning
AGTER	Association for the Governance of Land, Water and Natural Resources
AgWA	Partnership for Agricultural Water in Africa
APFAMGS	Andhra Pradesh Farmer Managed Groundwater Systems
AQUASTAT	FAO's global information system on water and agriculture
ARID	Association Régionale de l'Irrigation et du Drainage en Afrique de l'Ouest et du Centre (West Africa)
ASEAN	Association of Southeast Asian Nations
AU	African Union
CA	conservation agriculture
CAADP	Comprehensive Africa Agriculture Development Programme
CBD	United Nations Convention on Biological Diversity
CBO	community-based organization
CCX	Chicago Climate Exchange
CDE	Centre for Development and Environment
CDM	Clean Development Mechanism
CEC	cation exchange capacity
CEOS	Committee on Earth Observation Satellites
CGIAR	Consultative Group on International Agricultural Research
DFID	UK Department for International Development
EIA	environmental impact assessments
EMBRAPA	Empresa Brasileira de Pesquisa Agropecuária
ENSO	El Niño southern oscillation
ESA	European Space Agency
EU	European Union
FAO	Food and Agriculture Organization of the United Nations
FAOSTAT	FAO statistical database
FCT	Forest Carbon Tracking Task
FDI	foreign direct investment
FIVIMS	Food Insecurity and Vulnerability Information and Mapping Systems
FLO	Fairtrade Labelling Organizations International
GAEZ	Global Agro-Ecological Zones
GEF	Global Environment Facility
GEO	Group on Earth Observations

GEOSS	Global Earth Observation System of Systems
GHG	greenhouse gas
GIAHS	Globally Important Agricultural Heritage Sites
GIS	geographical information system
GIZ	Deutsche Gesellschaft für Internationale Zusammenarbeit (GIZ) GmbH
GLADIS	Global Land Degradation Information System
GLASOD	Global Assessment of Soil Degradation
GTOS	Global Terrestrial Observing System
GWP	Global Water Partnership
HASHI	Hifadhi Ardhi Shinyanga (Shinyanga Land Rehabilitation Programme, Tanzania)
IDA	International Development Association (World Bank)
IEA	International Energy Agency
IFAD	International Fund for Agricultural Development
IFPRI	International Food Policy Research Institute
IIASA	International Institute for Applied Systems Analysis
IIED	International Institute for Environment and Development
IMAWESA	Improved Management of Agricultural Water in Eastern and Southern Africa
IMT	irrigation management transfer
INM	integrated nutrient management
IPM	integrated pest management
IPCC	Intergovernmental Panel on Climate Change
IPPC	Integrated Pollution and Prevention Control (Directive)
IRWR	internal renewable water resources
IWMI	International Water Management Institute
LADA	Land Degradation Assessment in Drylands
LCBC	Lake Chad Basin Commission
LIFDC	low-income food-deficit countries
M&E	monitoring and evaluation
MASSCOTE	Mapping System and Services for Canal Operation Techniques
MDG	Millennium Development Goal
MEA	Millennium Ecosystem Assessment
MICCA	Mitigation of Climate Change in Agriculture
NGO	non-governmental organization
NPK	nitrogen, phosphorus, potassium (fertilizer)
OAS	Organization of American States
ODA	official development assistance
OECD	Organisation for Economic Co-operation and Development

PES	payment for environmental services
PIM	participatory irrigation management
PNTD	participatory and negotiated territorial development
PPP	public–private partnership
PRA	participatory rural appraisal
PRODEBALT	Lake Chad Basin Sustainable Development Program
RAE	Rehabilitation of Arid Environments
REDD+	Reducing Emissions from Deforestation and Forest Degradation and the enhancement and conservation of forest carbon stocks and sustainable management of forests in developing countries
SADC	Southern African Development Community
SARIA	Southern Africa Regional Irrigation Association
SLM	sustainable land management
SLWM	sustainable land and water management
SNIF	National Land Reclamation Society (Romania)
SOLAW	State of the World's Land and Water Resources for Food and Agriculture
SRI	system of rice intensification
UNCCD	United Nations Convention to Combat Desertification
UNCTAD	United Nations Conference on Trade and Development
UNDP	United Nations Development Programme
UNEP	United Nations Environment Programme
UNFCCC	United Nations Framework Convention on Climate Change
UN-REDD	United Nations Collaborative Programme on Reducing Emissions from Deforestation and Forest Degradation in Developing Countries
WFD	Water Framework Directive (EU)
WFP	World Food Programme
WOCAT	World Overview of Conservation Approaches and Technologies
WTO	World Trade Organization
WUA	water user association
WWAP	World Water Assessment Programme
WWC	World Water Council

List of tables

List of boxes

List of figures

List of maps

WHAT SOLAW SAYS

The world's cultivated area has grown by 12 percent over the last 50 years. The global irrigated area has doubled over the same period, accounting for most of the net increase in cultivated land. Meanwhile, agricultural production has grown between 2.5 and 3 times, thanks to significant increase in the yield of major crops.

However, global achievements in production in some regions have been associated with degradation of land and water resources, and the deterioration of related ecosystem goods and services. These include biomass, carbon storage, soil health, water storage and supply, biodiversity, and social and cultural services. Agriculture already uses 11 percent of the world's land surface for crop production. It also makes use of 70 percent of all water withdrawn from aquifers, streams and lakes. Agricultural policies have primarily benefited farmers with productive land and access to water, bypassing the majority of small-scale producers, who are still locked in a poverty trap of high vulnerability, land degradation and climatic uncertainty.

Land and water institutions have not kept pace with the growing intensity of agricultural development and the increasing degree of interdependence and competition over land and water resources. Much more adaptable and collaborative institutions are needed to respond effectively to natural resource scarcity and market opportunities.

Towards 2050, rising population and incomes are expected to call for 70 percent more food production globally, and up to 100 percent more in developing countries, relative to 2009 levels. Yet the distribution of land and water resources does not favour those countries that need to produce more in the future: the average availability of cultivated land per capita in low-income countries is less than half that of high-income countries, and the suitability of cultivated land for cropping is generally lower. Some countries with rapidly growing demand for food are also those that face high levels of land or water scarcity. The largest contribution to increases in agricultural output will be most likely to come from intensification of production on existing agricultural land. This will require widespread adoption of sustainable land management practices, and more efficient use of irrigation water through enhanced flexibility, reliability and timing of irrigation water delivery.

The prevailing patterns of agricultural production need to be critically reviewed. A series of land and water systems now face the risk of progressive breakdown of their productive capacity under a combination of excessive demographic pressure and unsustainable agricultural practices. The physical limits to land and water availability within these systems may be further exacerbated in places by external drivers, including climate change, competition with other sectors and socio-economic changes. These systems at risk warrant priority attention for remedial action simply because there are no substitutes.

The potential exists to expand production efficiently in order to address food security and poverty while limiting impacts on other ecosystem values. There is scope for governments and the private sector, including farmers, to be much more proactive in advancing the general adoption of sustainable land and water management practices. Actions include not just technical options to promote sustainable intensification and reduce production risks, they also comprise a set of conditions to remove constraints and build flexibility. These include (1) the removal of distortions in the incentives framework, (2) improvement of land tenure and access to resources, (3) strengthened and more collaborative land and water institutions, (4) efficient support services (including knowledge exchange, adaptive research and rural finance), and (5) better and more secure access to markets.

Widespread adoption of sustainable land and water management practices will also require the global community to have the political will to put in place the financial and institutional support to encourage widespread adoption of responsible agricultural practices. The negative trend in national budgets and official development assistance allocated to land and water needs to be reversed. Possible new financing options include payments for environmental services (PES) and the carbon market. Finally, there is a need for much more effective integration of international policies and initiatives dealing with land and water management. Only by these changes can the world feed its citizens through a sustainable agriculture that produces within environmental limits.

EXECUTIVE SUMMARY

In a crowded world with populations still rising and consumption patterns changing, humankind has not done enough to plan and manage the future development of land and water resources. After decades of underinvestment, poor management and lack of governance, the evidence is widely apparent. From dramatic mudslides on slopes too steep to bear human settlement, to unprecedented inundation of whole river basins, the impact on human lives from extreme meteorological events makes the news. What does not, though, is the creeping degradation of the land and water systems that provide for global food security and rural livelihoods. In some regions, whole systems are now at risk. Urgent steps need to be taken to reverse trends in their degradation while maintaining their integrity and productivity.

There is no doubt that access to and management of land and water resources need to improve markedly. Projected demands for food and agriculture production have to be met, malnutrition and rural poverty still have to be addressed, and competing demands for land and water must be reconciled with concerns over rapid degradation of natural systems. This calls for improved governance of land and water resources and a closer integration of policies, combined with increased and more strategic investment targeting food security and poverty alleviation.

This book presents the state of land and water resources for food production, and analyses threats to food security and sustainable development. The threats result not just from the relative physical scarcity of land and water. Trends in population growth, and changes in diets and climate present a complex set of challenges to which agricultural practices must adapt. The potential of the world's land and water systems to meet these challenges is examined in this context. Options for managing some of the 'systems at risk' to achieve sustainable levels of output are explored together with the attendant risks and trade-offs. The book discusses required institutional and policy changes, and technical approaches needed in the specific environments. The main findings and recommendations are presented below.

The challenge of land and water

The availability of land and water to meet national and global demands for food and agriculture production have been put into sharp relief following the recent rise in commodity price levels (and associated volatility) and increased large-scale land acquisition. The social impacts of rapid food price inflation have hit the poorest hardest. The buffering capacity of global agricultural markets to absorb supply shocks and stabilize agricultural commodity prices is tied to the continued functioning of land and water systems. At the same time, climate change brings additional risks and further unpredictability of harvests for farmers due to warming and related aridity, shifts in rainfall patterns, and the frequency and duration of extreme events. While warming may extend the limit of agriculture in the northern hemisphere, it is anticipated that key agricultural systems in lower latitudes will need to cope with new temperature, humidity and water stresses.

Status and trends in the use of land and water resources

Over the last 50 years, land and water management has met rapidly rising demands for food and fibre. In particular, input-intensive, mechanized agriculture and irrigation have contributed to rapid increases in productivity. The world's agricultural production has grown between 2.5 and 3 times over the period, while the cultivated area has grown only by 12 percent. More than 40 percent of the increase in food production came from irrigated areas, which have doubled in area. In the same period, the cultivated area of land per person gradually declined to less than 0.25 ha; a clear measure of successful agricultural intensification. Agriculture currently uses 11 percent of the world's land surface for crop production, and accounts for 70 percent of all water withdrawn from aquifers, streams and lakes.

The distribution of land suitable for cropping is skewed against those countries that have most need to raise production. Cultivated land area per person in low-income countries is less than half that in high-income countries, and its suitability for agriculture is generally lower. This is a troubling finding, given that the growth of demand for food production, as a function of population and income, is expected to be concentrated in low-income countries. The main implication is that a global adjustment of agricultural production will need to be anticipated in order to compensate for these facts of geography.

Rainfed agriculture is the world's predominant agricultural production system, but also hosts the majority of the rural poor. The large swathes of temperate cereal production in the northern hemisphere will continue to supply global markets, and may even see a northward expansion, nudged by global warming. Instead, in the dry tropics and subtropics, rainfed production is held hostage by erratic precipitation. Unpredictable soil moisture availability over the course of a growing season reduces nutrient uptake and, consequently, yields. Taken with low soil fertility and carbon content of tropical soils, yields in rainfed systems are little more than half the achievable potential in many low-income countries. While improved land and nutrient management can result in higher yields, these can prove difficult to sustain if the threat of erratic rainfall remains. The rural poor on marginal lands with limited access to improved seed, fertilizer and information remain vulnerable.

The tendency to locate high-input agriculture on the most suitable lands for cropping relieves pressure on land expansion, and limits encroachment on forests and other land uses. The steady trend towards precision agriculture and commercialization of all types of food and industrial crops is clear. Since 1961, while total cultivated land has shown a net increase of 12 percent to 2009, land under irrigation has more than doubled. While much of the prime agricultural land suitable for irrigation has been developed, the call for on-demand, just-in-time water services is rising, and the global area equipped for irrigation continues to expand at a rate of 0.6 percent per year. Groundwater use in irrigation is expanding quickly, and almost 40 percent of the irrigated area is now reliant upon groundwater as either a primary source or in conjunction with surface water. This pattern of intensification, through a concentration of inputs, has offset expansion of rainfed cultivation for staple cereals and established guaranteed supply chains for a wide range of agricultural products into urban centres.

In too many places, however, achievements in production have been associated with management practices that have degraded the land and water systems upon which the production depends. In some of these areas, the accumulation of environmental impacts in key land and water systems has now reached the point where production and livelihoods are compromised. Intensive agricultural practice has, in some cases, resulted in serious environmental degradation, including the loss of biodiversity, and surface and groundwater pollution from the improper use of fertilizers and pesticides.

Irrigation has had direct benefits in terms of production and incomes, and indirect benefits in terms of reduced incidence of downstream flood damage. However, there have also been associated impacts for which the costs may at times outweigh the benefits of production. Impacts may include reduction in environmental flows, changes in downstream access to water, or reduction of the extent of wetlands that have important ecological functions of biodiversity, nutrient retention and flood control. The accumulation of environmental impacts in key land and water systems has reached the point where, in some cases, production and livelihoods are compromised.

While the intensive exploitation of land and water, particularly in large-scale agriculture, has potential to protect forests by reducing pressure on land, it could also cause broader ecosystem deterioration, including loss of climatic buffering and carbon storage from forest biomass when cleared, loss of biodiversity, and loss of amenity, tourism and cultural heritage values. Unsustainable management practices on small-scale farms could also cause degradation (e.g. nutrient mining, erosion), as well as contributing to greenhouse gas emissions. Often, such practices are the result of unfavourable socio-economic conditions (e.g. insecure land tenure, lack of incentives, lack of access to markets or appropriate technologies, use of marginal lands).

Water availability to agriculture is a growing constraint in areas where a high proportion of renewable water resources are already used, or where transboundary resource management cannot be negotiated. Overall, increasing water scarcity constrains irrigated production, particularly in the most highly stressed countries and areas. In low- to medium-income countries with fast population growth, the demand for water is outstripping supply. Rising demand from both agriculture and other sectors is leading to competition for water, resulting in environmental stress and socio-economic tension. Where rainfall is inadequate and new water development is not feasible, agricultural production is expected to be constrained more by water scarcity than land availability.

Groundwater abstraction has provided an invaluable source of ready irrigation water, but has proved almost impossible to regulate. As a result, locally intensive groundwater withdrawals are exceeding rates of natural replenishment in key cereal-producing locations – in high-, middle- and low-income countries. Because of the dependence of many key food production areas on groundwater, declining aquifer levels and continued abstraction of non-renewable groundwater present a growing risk to local and global food production.

There is a strong linkage between poverty and the lack of access to land and water resources. Worldwide, the poorest have the least access to land and water, and are locked in a poverty trap of small farms with poor-quality soils and high vulnerability to land degradation and climatic uncertainty. Technologies and farming systems within reach of the poor are typically low-management, low-input systems that can contribute to land degradation or buffer rainfall variability. Highest trends in land degradation are associated with the poor.

Policies, institutions and investments in land and water

The lack of clear and stable land and water rights, as well as weak regulatory capacity and enforcement, have contributed to conflict over land access and competition for water use. In particular, the systematic inclusion of customary and traditional use rights in national legislation is a necessary first step in order to protect rural livelihoods and provide incentives for responsible land and water use.

Agricultural development policies have tended to focus on investments in high-potential areas and on irrigation, mechanization and crop specialization (mono-cropping) for marketed commodities and export crops. Their benefits have accrued to farmers with productive land and access to water, machinery and capital, largely bypassing the majority of smallholders, who are constrained by generally poor and vulnerable soils under typically low-management, low-input systems. Such policies have often prioritized short-term economic gains, ignoring long-term resource degradation and impacts on ecosystem services. Rural livelihoods and cultures have also been impacted as these new agricultural systems have been adopted.

Land and water use in agriculture is caught in a policy trap. On one hand, agricultural policies have been effective in responding to increasing demand, but on the other hand they have resulted in a set of unintended consequences, including over-application of fertilizer and pesticides, and depleted groundwater storage. Equally, water policies have driven expansion of water supply and storage, but in some water-short areas, this has created excess demand and 'constructed' scarcity. Low tariffs for irrigation water services have also encouraged its inefficient use.

In many river basins, the rate of socio-economic change and the accumulation of environmental problems have outpaced institutional responses. Environmental policy has had some influence in high-income countries, but has had far less effect so far on the development agenda of poorer countries.

Effective collaboration between land and water institutions has lagged behind patterns of use and consumption. Although land and water function as an integrated system, many institutions deal with them separately. While the legal decoupling of land and water is deliberate to avoid resource grabbing, the growing intensity of river basin development, and the degree of interdependence and competition over land and water resources, require more adaptable and collaborative institutions that can respond effectively to natural resource scarcity and changing market opportunities. Even institutions that are dedicated to integrated regional or basin management deal primarily with either land or water resources and their respective multiple uses, rather than with land and water jointly. National and local institutions regulating land and water use in many countries have come under growing pressure to arbitrate between different uses as competition for land and water has increased. The absence or weakness of transboundary cooperation frameworks (both within federated states and between riparian countries) have led to sub-optimal investment and tensions between upstream and downstream users.

Levels of public and private investment in basic agricultural infrastructure and institutions have declined over the past two decades. Agricultural infrastructure (rural roads, irrigation schemes, storage and marketing chains) has become increasingly unresponsive to changing markets and inefficient in delivering high-quality produce. Renewed but smarter investment in modern agriculture is now seen as a vital component of global recovery to give more overall stability in food supply. The growing interdependence and competition over land and water resources in intensively used river basins indicates that this stability will not be achieved without more effective natural resource allocation and environmental regulation. Existing land and water systems that are threatened by depletion and degradation of natural resource endowments will be a priority target.

Large-scale land acquisitions are on the increase in parts of Africa, Asia and Latin America, where land and water resources appear abundant and available. They are driven by concerns about food and energy security, but other factors such as business opportunities, demand for agricultural commodities for industry and recipient country are also at play. Although large-scale land acquisitions remain a small proportion of suitable land, in any one country, contrary to widespread perceptions there is very little 'empty' land as most remaining suitable land is already used or claimed, often by local people. While they offer opportunities for development, there is a risk that the rural poor could be evicted or lose access to land, water and other related resources. Many countries do not have sufficient mechanisms to protect local rights and take account of local interests, livelihoods and welfare. A lack of transparency and of checks and balances in contract negotiations could promote deals that do not maximize the public interest. Insecure local land rights, inaccessible registration procedures, vaguely defined productive use requirements, legislative gaps and other factors too often undermine the position of local people.

Perspectives for land and water use towards 2050

By 2050, rising population and incomes are expected to result in a 70 percent increase in global demand for agricultural production. From a 2009 baseline this will need to be a 100 percent increase in low- and middle-income countries. This implies a global annual growth rate of 1 percent, and up to 2 percent in low- and middle-income countries. Increased production is projected to come primarily from intensification on existing cultivated land. Expansion will still be possible in sub-Saharan Africa and Latin America. In the longer run, climate change is expected to increase the potential for expansion in some temperate areas.

Both irrigated and rainfed agriculture will respond to rising demand. A doubling of current production could be derived from already developed land and water resources. Some further land and water resources could be diverted to crop production, but in most cases they already serve important environmental and economic functions. Possible conversion to crop production would require prior evaluation of the trade-off between production benefits, and loss of their current ecological and socio-economic services.

Most future growth in crop production in developing countries is likely to come from intensification, with irrigation playing an increasingly strategic role through improved water services, water-use efficiency improvements, yield growth and higher cropping intensities. Both irrigated area and agricultural water use are expected to expand rather slowly: land under irrigation will increase from 301 Mha in 2009 to 318 Mha in 2050, an increase of 6 percent. However, any expansion will require trade-offs, particularly over intersectoral water allocation and environmental impacts. Considerable growth of supplemental and pressurized irrigation is likely on private farms. On the basis of existing trends in agricultural water-use efficiency and yield gains, it is projected that agricultural withdrawals will need to increase to more than 2 900 km^3/yr by 2030 and almost 3 000 km^3/yr by 2050. This indicates a net increase of 10 percent between now and 2050.

As land and water resource scarcity becomes apparent, competition between municipal and industrial demands will intensify and intrasectoral competition will become pervasive within agriculture – between livestock, staples and non-food crops, including liquid biofuels. Municipal and industrial water demands will be growing much faster than those of agriculture, and can be expected to crowd out allocations to agriculture. Meanwhile, the levels of soil management and precision application of water will need to rise to meet agricultural productivity increases. This will involve intrasectoral competition for scarce land and water, and the ultimate source of naturally available freshwater – groundwater – will be hit hard.

Climate change is expected to alter the patterns of temperature, precipitation and river flow upon which agricultural systems depend. While some agricultural systems in higher latitudes may gain net benefits from temperature increases as more land becomes suitable for crop cultivation, lower latitudes are expected to take the brunt of the negative impacts. Global warming is expected to increase the frequency and intensity of droughts and flooding in subtropical areas. Deltas and coastal areas are expected to be impacted negatively by sea-level rise. Mountain or highland systems and irrigated systems that rely on summer snowmelt are also expected to experience long-term changes in base flows. Adaptation and mitigation strategies should focus on increasing resilience of farming systems to reduce current and likely risks, such as droughts, excessive rainfall and other extreme events. These strategies should also mitigate the negative impacts of climate change on agricultural production.

Land and water systems at risk: what and where

Across the world, a series of agricultural production systems are at risk due to a combination of excessive demographic pressure and unsustainable agricultural practices. Global figures on the rate of use and degradation of land and water resources hide large regional discrepancies in resource availability. Land and water constraints are expected to compromise the ability of key agricultural production systems to meet demand. These physical constraints may be further exacerbated in places by external drivers, including climate change, competition with other sectors and socio-economic changes. These systems at risk warrant attention for remedial action since they cannot be replicated.

In SOLAW, a production system is considered 'at risk' where the current local availability and access to suitable land and water resources are constrained. In addition, local scarcity of land and water resources may be further constrained by unsustainable agricultural practices, growing socio-economic pressures or climate change. Systems at risk occur within the nine major categories of global agricultural production systems mapped in SOLAW.

Land and water for sustainable intensification

More than four-fifths of agricultural production growth to 2050 is expected to come from increased productivity on presently cultivated land. A variety of agronomic and technical approaches are available to achieve higher output, overcome constraints and manage risks. These will need to be accompanied and guided by increasingly effective and collaborative land and water institutions – public and private, formal and informal.

Land and water productivity gaps: an untapped potential

Land productivity is generally low on rainfed croplands, because of low inherent soil fertility, severe nutrient depletion, poor soil structure and inappropriate soil management practices. This is particularly the case in sub-Saharan Africa, where yields are often below 1 t/ha. Sustainable land and water management techniques can increase productivity through integrated soil fertility management where rainfall is reliable.

Integrated rainfed production practices, such as conservation agriculture, agroforestry and integrated crop–livestock systems, or integrated irrigation and aquaculture, combine best management practices that are adaptable to the local ecosystems, cultures and to market demand. Pesticide use and risks can be minimized by integrated pest management (IPM). Integrated soil fertility management, combined with rainwater harvesting, and soil and water conservation on slopes, could improve rainfed yields. By focusing on nitrogen and carbon cycles, these practices can also enhance carbon sequestration and mitigate greenhouse gas (GHG) emissions.

These approaches have proven to be successful when they form part of a rural development and livelihoods improvement strategy that includes support services and better market access. Education, incentives and farmer field schools speed the transition to more productive and resilient land-use systems. However, risk and initial low profitability can inhibit the adoption of these techniques. Overall, feasibility and risk assessments are needed to evaluate socio-economic constraints and formulate effective incentive packages for farmers to adopt appropriate management approaches, and adapt techniques and practices to their specific farming situation.

Most irrigation systems across the world perform below their capacity and are not adapted to the needs of today's agriculture. The low level of water productivity associated with their management translates into lost opportunities for resource use efficiency and economic returns. The scope for increase in water supply for irrigation is now limited in many water-scarce regions. Some additional irrigation water is likely to come from large multipurpose hydropower schemes. Small-scale water storage projects are also expected to boost supply, and some new groundwater development is anticipated. But water demand management will become increasingly important. A combination of improved irrigation scheme management, investment in modern technology, knowledge development and training can substantially increase water-use efficiency and improve supply to the often poor tail-end users. It can also improve water management where there is collective interest in maintaining aquifer function and services. The highest gains are possible in sub-Saharan Africa and parts of Asia.

To raise land and water productivity on larger irrigation schemes, an integrated modernization package of infrastructure upgrades and management system improvements is required, together with an economic environment providing undistorted incentives, manageable allocation of risk and market access. There is also scope for improving irrigation efficiency and productivity in small-scale and informal irrigation. This requires mechanisms to ensure the availability of knowledge, technology and investment support, adapted to the local management practices and socio-economic context.

Recycling and re-use of water is another option, but only with effective regulation can water be safely derived from drainage, saline and treated wastewater. On-site and off-site risks from salinization and waterlogging require careful drainage planning, investment and management in many irrigation projects. Salt and water balance studies, and a regulatory and monitoring system, are required.

National support for sustainable land and water management
The world's farmers will continue to be the prime agents of change, and their perspective has to count. Farmers are necessarily engaged in the planning and sustainable management of land and water, but many are forced into unsustain-

able practices by poverty and lack of aligned incentives, insecure land tenure and water-use rights, lack of adequate local organizations, and inefficient support services (including rural credit and finance, markets and access to technology and knowledge). Here, public resources can be allocated more strategically, together with mechanisms to engage private sector financing, both at the national level and through credit mechanisms at the local level. This should translate into a higher share of public investments in agriculture. Within countries, three principal areas of investment are vital. (1) At the national level, governments will need to invest in public goods such as roads, storage, land and water resource protection works and to facilitate private investment. (2) Investment is needed in the institutions that regulate and promote sustainable land and water management: research and development, incentives and regulatory systems, and land use planning and water management. (3) At basin or irrigation scheme level, an integrated planning approach is needed to drive a sequenced programme of land and water investments. For irrigation schemes, a focus on modernization of both infrastructure and institutional arrangements is needed.

Land and water administration institutions can be strengthened to improve systems for land and water rights where shortcomings inhibit improved productivity. Common-property systems can be adapted to provide secure land tenure by legal recognition and protection, or by negotiated and legalized conversion to individual rights. Land markets can be promoted and regulated to improve allocation efficiency and equity.

Multilevel stakeholder participation across land and water systems can greatly enhance water productivity and reduce stress by improving allocation efficiency among sectors, and by introducing technologies and a governance structure promoting efficient water use. Examples are participatory collective irrigation or groundwater management. Cooperation in transboundary water management, starting from the technical level, can promote optimal, multi-objective investment and basin-wide benefit-sharing. Future institutional development is likely to increasingly reflect participatory and pluralistic approaches, with growing devolution and accountability at local levels. Irrigation reforms would build on the movement of governments to decentralize control over irrigation and to seek greater responsibility from irrigating farmers. Basin management approaches reflect best practice in devolving land and water management to the lowest geographic unit, and in involving stakeholders in planning and decision-making.

In particular, the need to address trade-offs will centre on the level and modalities of intensification, protection and conservation, the balances between commercial farming and staple production and between growth and income distribution, the level of national food security, and the sharing of costs and benefits between urban and rural populations. What is vital is that the analysis should be explicit and decisions taken in the broader public interest. Participatory processes and transparency are thus important.

Improving the application of technology for sustainable land and water management requires the integration of knowledge from research with local diagnosis and adaptation. There is an extensive research basis for most land and water systems, but research and extension need to be equipped to offer adapted technology on demand. Outreach programmes such as Farmer Field Schools, in partnership with local farmer groups, NGOs and the private sector have proved successful in promoting a range of sustainable technologies and practices, including pressurized irrigation, conservation agriculture or product certification.

SOLAW has revealed a number of gaps and inconsistencies in existing databases and information systems. These gaps should be filled by further inventories of land and water resources to help guide choices and implementation. Further research on the main existing farming systems will be essential to determine conservation and intensification strategies. Methods of assessing and valuing ecosystem services, including land and water audits, should be developed to provide the tools that are needed to value development options and help make informed decisions. Networks and modern media need to become more effective in exchanging and disseminating knowledge, and for identifying and filling knowledge gaps.

A first step to manage land and water more efficiently is removing distortions that encourage land and water degradation, such as cheap energy prices that drive inefficient, energy-intensive farming or groundwater depletion. An incentive structure including price incentives and regulatory measures can then be designed to promote better practice. Payments for environmental services may rebalance costs incurred by farmers and benefits to other sectors of society.

The recent trend in land acquisition needs to be addressed through appropriate regulations, and through well-informed agricultural and food policies that take more account of land availability and access rights. Developing guidelines for land governance, or a code to regulate international investments backed up by capacity building at all levels, would be useful to improve decision-making and negotiations.

Requirements for international cooperation and investment

There is an urgent need for better and more effective integration of international initiatives dealing with land and water management. International cooperation on sustainable land and water management has become a high priority in many institutions because of concerns about food security, poverty reduction, environmental protection and climate change. Several international agreements contain principles of conservation of natural resources, including land and water, but these have rarely been translated into substantive action on the ground or national codes of conduct or practice, and a consolidated agreement and framework for action on sustainable land and water management is not yet in place.

Several organizations and programmes, including the Global Environment Facility (GEF), have been raising awareness and prompting action on sustainable land and water management, and some have strengthened institutions and governance. However, different organizations often work in the same field, which reduces focus and impact, and approaches remain largely sectoral rather than integrated.

A number of recent initiatives and partnerships from civil society and the private sector (such as Fairtrade, environmental certification or organic labelling) may also have positive effects on sustainable land and water management. They should be promoted and guided through better knowledge and monitoring mechanisms. Large-scale agriculture, in particular, also has the potential to reduce transactions costs associated with carbon trading, thereby providing incentives for sustainable management.

Global investment in land and water management remains below the levels necessary to address persistent food insecurity and deal with natural resource scarcity. Gross investment requirements between 2007 and 2050 for irrigation development and management are estimated at almost US$1 trillion. Moreover, land protection and development, soil conservation and flood control will require around US$160 billion. New financing options include PES and the carbon market. Global-level financing should complement public and private finance at the national level. To effectively attract and absorb these higher levels of investment, nations need to develop favourable policies, institutions and incentives, along with a strong monitoring and evaluation mechanism that addresses the social, economic and environmental dimensions of sustainability.

Financial resources to promote sustainable land and water management will need to be sourced and disbursed through existing funds and/or from private and market sources. A dedicated fund to support sustainable land and water management by smallholders could be set up within the context of global climate change negotiations over carbon sequestration financing, with a focus on the multiple benefits of raising soil carbon storage, reducing losses of soil nutrients and controlling runoff from farmers' fields. Programmes could then provide incentives to promote local-level adoption of sustainable land and water management practices, and also to promote global goods such as reforestation and carbon capture, and to reduce negative environmental impacts. Programmes adopting the concept of PES could facilitate adoption of such initiatives by farmers.

Land and water management offers important opportunities for synergies between climate change adaptation and mitigation. Agriculture and deforestation together account for up to a third of total anthropogenic GHG emissions. At the same time, climate change is expected to impact patterns of land and water use for agriculture. However, many of the sustainable land and water management practices that are recommended to increase resilience and reduce vulnerability to climate change also contribute to mitigation, largely through carbon sequestration. In addition to its contribution as a carbon sink, increasing the storage of organic matter in the soil provides many further benefits, including improvement of soil water storage and retention of soil nutrients. These benefits can reduce fertilizers requirements and enhance their uptake. This contribution of improved land and water management to mitigating climate change may mean that developing countries should be able to attract financial support based on the carbon sequestration value of their sustainable land and water management.

Meeting the challenges – business as usual is not enough

The over-riding challenges faced by agriculture are: to produce at least 70 percent more food by 2050; to improve food security and livelihoods of the rural poor; to maintain the necessary ecosystem services; and to reconcile the use of land and water resources among competing uses. All these challenges will need to be addressed together with the anticipated impacts of climate change where they have a net negative impact on agricultural production. These challenges will not be met *unless*:

- Existing agricultural practices can be transformed to reduce pressure on land and water systems.

- Negative impacts of intensive production systems are reduced markedly, and increased food production is aligned with poverty alleviation, food and livelihood security diversification and the maintenance of ecosystem services.

- Negative impacts of smallholder agriculture associated with high population density, widespread poverty, and lack of secured access to land and water resources, are reduced.

- Agricultural systems at risk are addressed as a priority and progress in redressing risks is monitored.

- Investment, economic and trade policies favour sustainable agriculture and balanced rural development.

- Sustainable intensification can be implemented through integrated planning and management approaches that can be scaled up from local levels to address systems at risk and mainstream climate change mitigation and adaptation simultaneously.

The principles and practices around which major initiatives for sustainable land and water management can be built are:

- Broad adoption of participatory and pluralistic approaches to land and water management, with growing devolution and local accountability.

- Increasing investment for improvement of essential public good infrastructure related to the whole market chain from production to consumer.

- Appraisal of ecosystem services, including land and water audits, developed to frame planning and investment decisions.

- A review of the mandates and activities of existing global and regional organizations for land and water, with a view to promote collaboration, if not integration.

- International trade agreements that favour a 'green economy' approach and contribute to sustainable agriculture overall.

- Cooperative frameworks and basin-wide management institutions that can work together to optimize economic value and ensure equitable benefit sharing in international river basins.

- A dedicated fund to support sustainable land and water management by smallholders. Incentive programmes such as PES for watershed management and clean water, biodiversity and sustainable production schemes could then promote adoption of sustainable land and water management practices, capturing carbon and reducing negative environmental impacts.

Conclusion

The land and water systems, underpinning many key food-producing systems worldwide, are being stressed by unprecedented levels of demand. Climate change is expected to exacerbate these stresses in some key productive areas.

There is scope for governments and the private sector (including farmers) to be much more proactive in enabling and promoting the general adoption of more sustainable land and water management practices. These have the potential to expand production efficiently in order to address food insecurity while limiting impacts on other ecosystem values. However, this will require profound changes in the way land and water are managed. Global and national policies will need to be aligned and institutions transformed to become genuine collaborators in applying knowledge and in responsible regulation of the use of natural resources. Business as usual, with or without some marginal adjustments, will not be enough.

The status and trends of land and water resources for food and agriculture described in SOLAW provide a basis for designing and prioritizing regional programmes and financing, to enhance sustainable management of land and water and address the systems at risk.

Chapter 1
STATUS AND TRENDS IN LAND AND WATER RESOURCES

The world's land and water resources are finite and under pressure from a growing population. Global figures show a relatively low share of land and water actually used by agriculture, but these figures hide major regional variations and a series of locally important imbalances between demand and supply. Demand for land and water from non-agricultural sectors, and a growing recognition of the need to meet environmental requirements further intensifies competition. This chapter reviews current status and trends of land and water resources, their geographical distribution and their use in agriculture. It presents projections for future agricultural demands towards 2050, and analyses its implication both for rainfed and irrigated agriculture.

The present status of land and water

The world's net cultivated area has grown by 12 percent over the last 50 years, mostly at the expense of forest, wetland and grassland habitats. At the same time, the global irrigated area has doubled. The distribution of these land and water assets is unequal among countries. Although only a small proportion of the world's land and water is used for crop production, most of the easily accessible and (thus economic) resources are under cultivation or have other ecologically and economically valuable uses. Thus the scope for further expansion of cultivated land is limited. Only parts of South America and sub-Saharan Africa still offer scope for some expansion. At the same time, competition for water resources has also been growing to the extent that today more than 40 percent of the world's rural population is now living in water-scarce regions.

Land distribution, use and suitability

The global land area is 13.2 billion ha. Of this, 12 percent (1.6 billion ha) is currently in use for cultivation of agricultural crops, 28 percent (3.7 billion ha) is under forest, and 35 percent (4.6 billion ha) comprises grasslands and woodland ecosystems. Low-income countries cover about 22 percent of the land area (Table 1.1).

Land use varies with climatic and soil conditions and human influences (Map 1.1). Figure 1.1 further shows the dominant land use by region. Deserts prevail across much of the lower northern latitudes of Africa and Asia. Dense forests predominate in the heartlands of South America, along the seaboards of North America, and across Canada, Northern Europe and much of Russia, as well as in the tropical

TABLE 1.1: REGIONAL DISTRIBUTION OF MAIN LAND USE CATEGORIES (2000)

Country category	Global share of land, %	Share of global population, %	Cultivated land Mha	%	Forest land Mha	%	Grassland and woodland ecosystems Mha	%	Sparsely vegetated and barren land Mha	%	Settlement and Infrastructure Mha	%	Inland water bodies Mha	%
Low-income	22	38	441	15	564	20	1 020	36	744	26	52	1.8	41	1.4
Middle-income	53	47	735	11	2 285	33	2 266	33	1 422	21	69	1	79	1
High-income	25	15	380	12	880	27	1 299	39	592	18	31	1	123	4

Source: adapted from Fischer et al. (2010)
Note: The extents of land cover classes were extracted from a dataset used for global agro-ecological modelling. Owing to different dates of data acquisitions, spatial resolutions, definitions and processing techniques, the estimates in this table may differ somewhat from those of other more recent sources. For example, the global extent of forest land is reported in FAO (2010d) as 4 billion ha versus approximately 3.7 billion ha reported here. See Annex A1 for the definition of regional and subregional country groupings.

belts of Central Africa and Southeast Asia. Cultivated land is 12 to 15 percent of total land in each category. Grasslands and woodlands (33 to 39 percent) and forest land (20 to 33 percent) dominate land use and cover in all three country income categories.

Cultivated land is a leading land use (a fifth or more of the land area) in South and Southeast Asia, Western and Central Europe, and Central America and the Caribbean, but is less important in sub-Saharan and Northern Africa, where cultivation covers less than a tenth of the area.

The global area of cultivated land has grown by a net 159 Mha since 1961 (Table 1.2 and Figure 1.2). This increase, however, includes a larger area of land newly brought

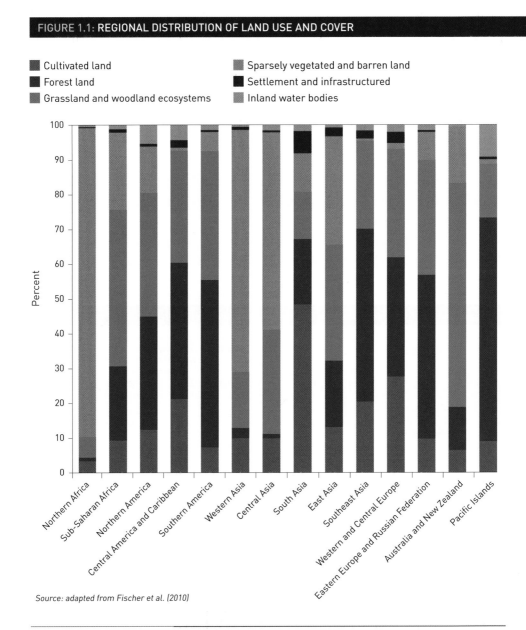

FIGURE 1.1: REGIONAL DISTRIBUTION OF LAND USE AND COVER

- Cultivated land
- Forest land
- Grassland and woodland ecosystems
- Sparsely vegetated and barren land
- Settlement and infrastructured
- Inland water bodies

Source: adapted from Fischer et al. (2010)

MAP 1.1: DOMINANT LAND COVER AND USE

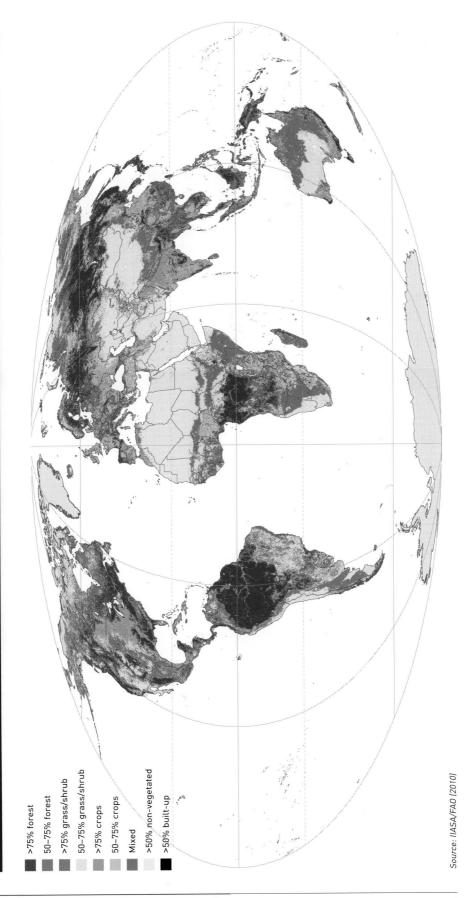

>75% forest
50–75% forest
>75% grass/shrub
50–75% grass/shrub
>75% crops
50–75% crops
Mixed
>50% non-vegetated
>50% built-up

Source: IIASA/FAO (2010)

Chapter 1. Status and trends in land and water resources

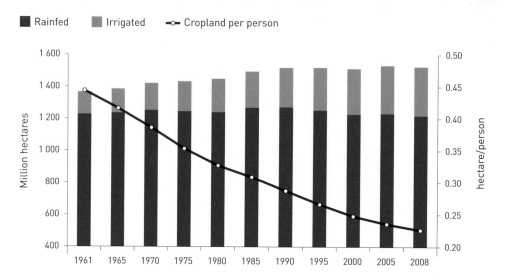

FIGURE 1.2: EVOLUTION OF LAND UNDER IRRIGATED AND RAINFED CROPPING (1961–2008)

Source: FAO (2010b)

TABLE 1.2: NET CHANGES IN MAJOR LAND USE (Mha)

	1961	2009	Net increase 1961–2009
Cultivated land	1 368	1 527	12%
• rainfed	1 229	1 226	−0.2%
• irrigated	139	301	117%

Sources: FAO (2010b,c)

into cultivation, while over the same period previously cultivated lands have come out of production. All of the net increase in cultivated area over the last 50 years is attributable to a net increase in irrigated cropping, with land under rainfed systems showing a very slight decline. Irrigated area more than doubled over the period, and the number of hectares needed to feed one person has reduced dramatically from 0.45 to 0.22 ha per person (FAO, 2010b).

Methods for forest inventory, forest definitions and the geographical extents of assessments change over time, rendering comparisons difficult. Nonetheless, a decline of about 135 Mha (3.3 percent) in forested area between 1990 and 2010 suggests that the expansion in the cultivated area and the replacement of degraded arable land with new cultivated land have been partly achieved through conversion of previously forested areas (FAO, 2010d).

Globally, about 0.23 ha of land is cultivated per head of the world's population. High-income countries cultivate more than twice the area per capita (0.37 ha) than low-income (0.17 ha) countries, while middle-income countries cultivate 0.23 ha per capita (Table 1.3).

FAO defines land suitability for agriculture in terms of capacity to reach potentially attainable yields for a basket of crops (Box 1.1). Assuming well-adapted production systems are used, currently cultivated land is mostly of prime (28 percent of the total) or good quality (53 percent). The highest regional proportion of prime land currently cultivated is found in Central America and the Caribbean (42 percent), followed by Western and Central Europe (38 percent) and Northern America (37 percent). For high-income countries as a whole, the share of prime land in currently cultivated land is 32 percent (Table 1.3). In low-income countries, soils are often poorer and only 28 percent of total cultivated land is classed as prime (Figure 1.3).

FIGURE 1.3: TOTAL EXTENT OF CULTIVATED LAND BY LAND SUITABILITY CATEGORY FOR EACH GEOGRAPHIC REGION

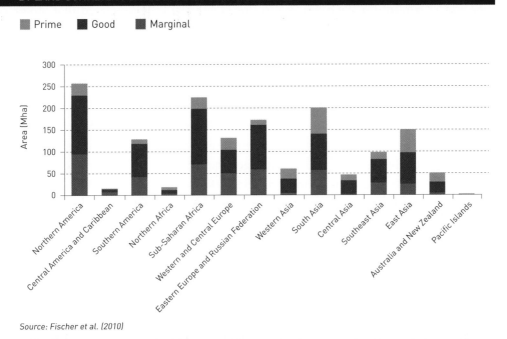

Source: Fischer et al. (2010)

TABLE 1.3: SHARE OF WORLD CULTIVATED LAND SUITABLE FOR CROPPING UNDER APPROPRIATE PRODUCTION SYSTEMS

Regions	Cultivated land (Mha)	Population (million)	Cultivated land per capita (ha)	Rainfed crops (%)		
				Prime Land	Good Land	Marginal Land
Low-income countries	441	2 651	0.17	28	50	22
Middle-income countries	735	3 223	0.23	27	55	18
High-income countries	380	1 031	0.37	32	50	19
Total	1 556	6 905	0.23	29	52	19

Source: adapted from Fischer et al. (2010)

Water use, withdrawals, scarcity and quality

Through the global hydrological cycle, renewable water resources amount to 42 000 km³/yr. Of this, about 3 900 km³ is withdrawn for human uses from rivers and aquifers: some 2 710 km³ (70 percent) is for irrigation, 19 percent for industries and 11 percent for the municipal sector (Table 1.4). It is estimated that more than 60 percent of all water withdrawals flows back to local hydrological systems by return flows to rivers or groundwater. The remaining part is considered consumptive water use through evaporation and plant transpiration.

With the doubling of the global irrigated area over the last 50 years, withdrawals for agriculture have been rising. Globally, total water withdrawals still represent only a small share – about 9 percent of internal renewable water resources (IRWR) (Table 1.4), but this average masks large geographical discrepancies. The rate of withdrawal varies greatly by country or region. Europe withdraws only 6 percent of its internal resources and just 29 percent of this goes to agriculture. The intensive agricultural economies of Asia withdraw 20 percent of their internal renewable resources, of which more than 80 percent goes to irrigation. In many of the low rainfall regions of the Middle East, Northern Africa and Central Asia, most of the exploitable water is already withdrawn, with 80–90 percent of that going to agriculture, and thus rivers and aquifers are depleted beyond sustainable levels.

About 40 percent of the world's population lives in transboundary river basins, and more than 90 percent live in countries with basins that cross international borders (Sadoff and Grey, 2005). These 263 international water basins account for about 50 percent of global land area and 40 percent of freshwater resources (Giordano and Wolf, 2002). Many of these transboundary rivers are among the largest flows of water globally. The growth in water withdrawals, primarily by agriculture, has brought about the need for collaboration among countries, through treaties and agreements between riparian countries, the formulation of international agreements such as the 1997 UN Convention on the Law of the Non-navigational Uses of International Watercourses and regional initiatives such as the Southern African Development Community (SADC) Protocol on Shared Water Resources.

TABLE 1.4: WATER WITHDRAWAL BY MAJOR WATER USE SECTOR (2003)

Continent Regions	Total withdrawal by sector						Total water withdrawal *	Total freshwater withdrawal	Freshwater withdrawal as % of IRWR
	Municipal		Industrial		Agricultural				
	km³/yr	%	km³/yr	%	km³/yr	%	km³/yr	km³/yr	
Africa	21	10	9	4	184	86	215	215	5
Northern Africa	9	9	5	6	80	85	94	94	201
Sub-Saharan Africa	13	10	4	3	105	87	121	121	3
Americas	126	16	280	35	385	49	791	790	4
Northern America	88	15	256	43	258	43	603	602	10
Central America and Caribbean	6	26	2	11	15	64	24	24	3
Southern America	32	19	21	13	112	68	165	165	1
Asia	217	9	227	9	2 012	82	2 456	2 451	20
Western Asia	25	9	20	7	227	83	271	268	55
Central Asia	5	3	8	5	150	92	163	162	61
South Asia	70	7	20	2	914	91	1 004	1 004	57
East Asia	93	14	150	22	434	64	677	677	20
Southeast Asia	23	7	30	9	287	84	340	340	17
Europe	61	16	204	55	109	29	374	374	6
Western and Central Europe	42	16	149	56	75	28	265	265	13
Eastern Europe and Russian Federation	19	18	56	51	35	32	110	110	2
Oceania	5	17	3	10	19	73	26	26	3
Australia and New Zealand	5	17	3	10	19	73	26	26	3
Pacific Islands	0.01	14	0.01	14	0.05	71	0.1	0.1	0.1
World	429	11	723	19	2 710	70	3 862	3 856	9
High-income	145	16	392	43	383	42	920	916	10
Middle-income	195	12	287	18	1 136	70	1 618	1 616	6
Low-income	90	7	44	3	1 191	90	1 324	1 324	18
Low-income food deficit	182	8	184	8	1 813	83	2 180	2 179	16
Least-developed	10	5	3	1	190	94	203	203	5

* Includes use of desalinated water

Source: FAO (2010c)
Note: See Annex A1 for the definition of regional and subregional country groupings.

Water resources are very unevenly distributed, with some countries having an abundance of water while many manage conditions of extreme scarcity. In addition, even where water may appear abundant, much of it is not accessible or is very expensive to develop, or is not close to lands that can be developed for agriculture. Water scarcity has three dimensions: physical (when the available supply does not satisfy the demand), infrastructural (when the infrastructure in place does not allow for satisfaction of water demand by all users) and institutional (when institutions and legislations fail to ensure reliable, secure and equitable supply of water to users).

In terms of physical water scarcity, it is estimated that on average a withdrawal rate above 20 percent of renewable water resources represents substantial pressure on water resources – and more than 40 percent is 'critical'. In some regions, particularly in the Middle East, Northern Africa and Central Asia, countries are already withdrawing in excess of critical thresholds. The resultant stresses on the functions of ecosystems are increasingly apparent. It is now estimated that more than 40 percent of the world's rural population lives in river basins that are physically water scarce. Map 1.2 shows the global distribution of water scarcity by major river basin, based on consumptive use of water in irrigation.

Equally, countries have developed their water resources extensively through a combination of policies and investments to increase supply and stimulate demand. As a result, in many countries demand is outstripping supply, and this imbalance is creating new stresses on the agricultural sector. There remain few opportunities for easy and low-cost infrastructure, and thus the marginal cost of new water development projects is high.

At the same time, demand from other sectors, particularly municipal and industrial demand, has been growing faster than agricultural demand. Whereas in less-developed countries agricultural use remains dominant, in Europe 55 percent of water is withdrawn by industry. Water stresses occur locally across the globe, but some entire regions are highly stressed, particularly the Middle East, the Indian subcontinent and northeastern China. Sub-Saharan Africa and the Americas generally experience lower levels of water stress.

When water is used in domestic and productive activities, and discharged again into the environment, water quality is changed. In general, increasing population and economic growth combined with little or no water treatment have led to more negative impacts on water quality. Agriculture, as the largest water user, is a major contributor. Key non-point source pollution includes nutrients and pesticides derived from crop and livestock management. A further problem arises from salinization: many soil and water salinity problems have been reported in large irrigation schemes in Pakistan, China, India, Argentina, Sudan and many countries in Central Asia, where more than 16 Mha of irrigated land are now salinized (FAO, 2010c).

Land and water resources in rainfed agriculture

Rainfed agriculture is the predominant agricultural production system worldwide. As practised in highland areas and in the dry and humid tropics, it is the system in which poorer smallholder farmers predominate and where the risks of resource degradation are highest. Soil nutrient availability in many rainfed lands tends to be

MAP 1.2: GLOBAL DISTRIBUTION OF PHYSICAL WATER SCARCITY BY MAJOR RIVER BASIN

Low

Moderate

High

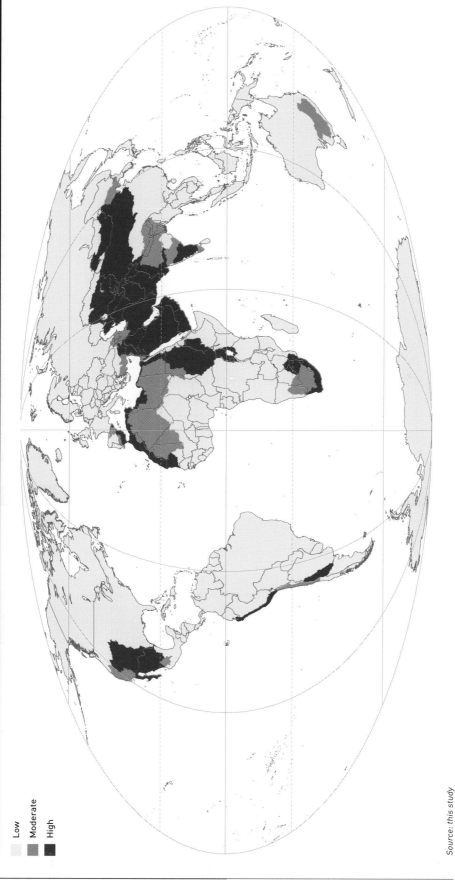

Source: this study

Chapter 1. Status and trends in land and water resources

29

low, and sloping terrain and patterns of rainfall and runoff contribute to erosion. High temperatures and low and erratic precipitation often make soil moisture availability inadequate, and techniques to improve water availability (such as water harvesting) are expensive. Higher levels of input and management can increase productivity, but many farmers cannot afford the costs or risks. All these factors affecting land and water for rainfed agriculture as practised by the poor contribute to their vulnerability and to their food insecurity.

Land and water resources distribution

Rainfed agriculture depends on rainfall for crop production, with no permanent source of irrigation. Of the current world cultivated area of 1 600 Mha, about 1 300 Mha (80 percent) are rainfed. Rainfed agriculture produces about 60 percent of global crop output in a wide variety of production systems (Table 1.5; Map 1.3). The most productive systems are concentrated in temperate zones of Europe, followed by Northern America, and rainfed systems in the subtropics and humid tropics. Rainfed cropping in highland areas and the dry tropics tends to be relatively low-yielding, and is often associated with subsistence farming systems. Evidence from farms worldwide shows that less than 30 percent of rainfall is used by plants in the process of biomass production. The rest evaporates into the atmosphere, percolates to groundwater or contributes to river runoff (Molden, 2007).

Depending on temperature and soil conditions, rainfed cropping of some kind is possible where annual rainfall exceeds 300 mm. The distribution of rainfall during

TABLE 1.5: TYPES OF RAINFED SYSTEMS

System	Characteristics and selected examples
Rainfed agriculture: **highlands**	Low productivity, small-scale subsistence (low-input) agriculture; a variety of crops on small plots plus few animals.
Rainfed agriculture: **dry tropics**	Drought-resistant cereals such as maize, sorghum and millet. Livestock consists often of goats and sheep, especially in the Sudano-Sahelian zone of Africa, and in India. Cattle are more widespread in southern Africa and in Latin America.
Rainfed agriculture: **humid tropics**	Mainly root crops, bananas, sugar cane and notably soybean in Latin America and Asia. Maize is the most important cereal. Sheep and goats are often raised by poorer farmers while cattle are held by wealthier ones.
Rainfed agriculture: **subtropics**	Wheat (the most important cereal), fruits (e.g. grapes and citrus) and oil crops (e.g. olives). Cattle are the most dominant livestock. Goats are also important in the southern Mediterranean, while pigs are dominant in China and sheep in Australia.
Rainfed agriculture: **temperate**	Main crops include wheat, maize, barley, rapeseed, sugar beet and potatoes. In the industrialized countries of Western Europe, the United States and Canada, this agricultural system is highly productive and often combined with intensive, penned livestock (mainly pigs, chickens and cattle).

Source: this study

MAP 1.3: MAJOR AGRICULTURAL SYSTEMS

Rainfed agriculture: humid tropics

Rainfed agriculture: dry tropics

Rainfed agriculture: subtropics

Rainfed agriculture: temperate

Rainfed agriculture: highlands

Rangelands: subtropics

Rangelands: temperate

Rangelands: boreal

Irrigated crops: paddy rice

Irrigated crops: other than paddy rice

Desert

Forest

Other land

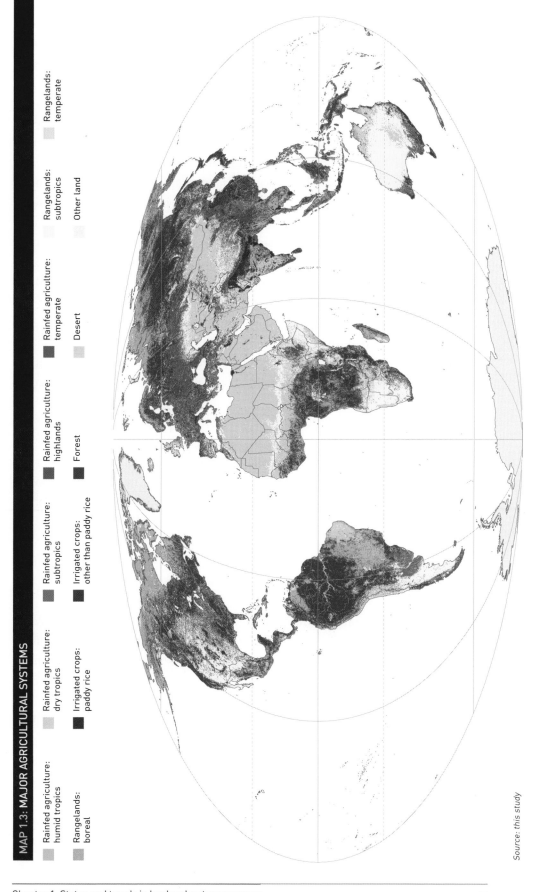

Source: this study

the growing season is also a key factor: ample annual averages may conceal poor spacing in relation to the growing season and, combined with uncertainties such as rainfall variability between years, this increases risks and reduces the chances of rainfed agriculture being highly productive.

The extent of rainfed area has not grown in recent years, but this masks the replacement of some land too degraded for further cropping and consequently abandoned, and their replacement by lands newly converted from forests and grasslands to arable farming. This process of land degradation and abandonment, and the development of new lands in replacement, is particularly characteristic of low-input, low-management farming systems such as 'slash-and-burn' in the humid tropics, or cultivation on steep slopes. Because data on these farming systems are sparse, and because some of these lands may not be permanently degraded but may be brought back into cultivation after long fallow, it is difficult to estimate the areas involved.

Trends in rainfed areas differ by region. Sub-Saharan Africa, where 97 percent of staple production is rainfed, has doubled cultivated cereals area since 1960. In Latin America and the Caribbean, rainfed cultivation has expanded by 25 percent in the last 40 years (FAO, 2010b).

Soil and terrain constraints

Provided that adequate moisture is available in the soil, the broad potential of rainfed lands is determined largely by soil quality (Map 1.4). The most important factor is nutrient availability and related nutrient retention capacity of the soil. In addition, soil depth affects plant rooting, and drainage characteristics affect the availability of oxygen as roots grow. Soil structure is important for ease of cultivation, and is linked to soil chemistry and cultivation practices. Finally, the slope of the land can affect soil quality as sloping terrain erodes as a result of runoff and mass wasting.

Soil nutrient availability is the prevalent soil limitation in current cultivated land in most regions, particularly in tropical developing countries. This is due in part to lower availability of natural nutrients than in temperate lands. Sub-Saharan Africa, Southern America, East Asia, Southeast Asia, and Australia and New Zealand have particularly low levels of natural soil nutrient availability. The share of soils with no or minor nutrient availability constraints is highest in high-income countries (76 percent), compared with 68 percent in low-income countries (Table 1.6). In addition, the natural fertility status of some soils has deteriorated over time through 'nutrient mining'.

In several regions, soil quality constraints affect more than half the cultivated land base, notably in sub-Saharan Africa, Southern America, Southeast Asia and

MAP 1.4: DOMINANT SOIL AND TERRAIN CONSTRAINTS FOR LOW INPUT FARMING

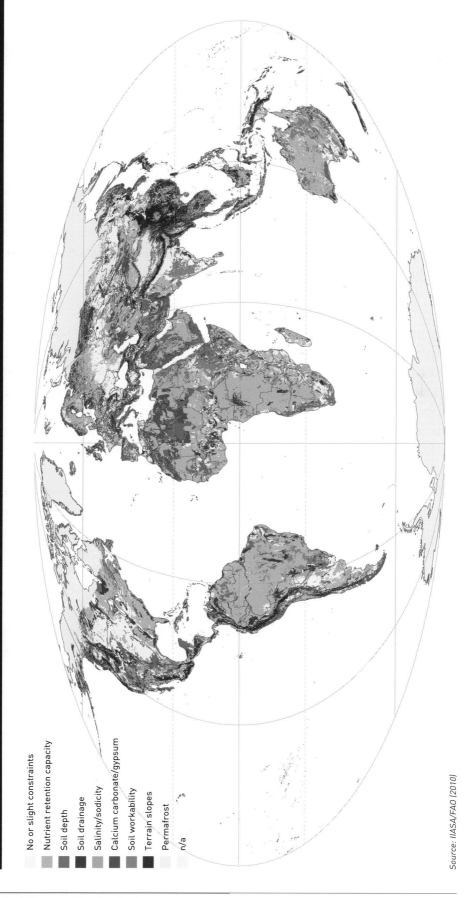

No or slight constraints
Nutrient retention capacity
Soil depth
Soil drainage
Salinity/sodicity
Calcium carbonate/gypsum
Soil workability
Terrain slopes
Permafrost
n/a

Source: IIASA/FAO (2010)

Country category	Cultivated land (Mha)	Area by class of soil nutrient availability rating (%)			
		< 40	40–60	60–80	> 80
Low-income countries	443	0	20	12	68
Middle-income countries	740	1	16	15	67
High-income countries	382	1	9	13	76

Source: adapted from Fischer et al. (2010)

Northern Europe. In low-income countries, only 44 percent of cultivated soils (about 196 Mha), have no or only minor constraints. The main constraint on the remaining 247 Mha is poor nutrient availability, affecting about 24 percent of the soils with varying levels of constraints from light to very severe.

But with good soil management, quality can be improved. Under high-input farming conditions, a low natural nutrient availability can be alleviated by fertilizer application, provided the soil has adequate nutrient retention capacity. However, low nutrient retention capacities are found in Southern Africa, the Amazon area, Central Asia and Northern Europe. In those areas increased use of fertilizers alone may prove ineffective for increasing crop yields, and thus additional forms of soil enhancement are necessary. Another major obstacle to crop cultivation is poor soil structure and 'workability', which is, for example, prevalent in large parts of Ethiopia, Sudan and central India. Such constraints may again be reduced with the use of high input and appropriate soil management. Often these are areas dominated by vertisols, which ideally should be cultivated with zero-tillage techniques.

Rainfed productivity and production gaps

The productivity of rainfed cropping is measured by yields (production per unit of area). Productivity varies enormously, and is highly sensitive to factors other than soil and water – for example, the availability and affordability of technologies and inputs, access to markets, and the local financial returns. At one extreme, dry farming systems produce sorghum or millet yields of a few hundred kilograms per hectare. At the other extreme, farmers in Europe achieve yields as high as 7–10 t/ha for wheat (FAO, 2010b; Molden, 2007).

In sub-Saharan Africa, yields have changed little since the 1960s, and increases in production have come almost entirely from land expansion. Rainfed maize yields, for example, have remained constant at around 1t/ha. In Latin America and the Caribbean, by contrast, yields for rainfed maize tripled over the same period, from little more than 1t/ha to over 3t/ha. Average wheat yields across

Europe more than doubled (2t/ha to over 5t/ha). FAO has calculated a 'yield gap' by comparing current productivity with what is potentially achievable assuming that inputs and management are optimized in relation to local soil and water conditions (Map 1.5; Table 1.7).

These results show that the yield gap is greatest in sub-Saharan Africa (where yields are only 24 percent of what could be produced under higher levels of management). The gap is lowest in East Asia (11 percent). This implies that if all current land and water were managed optimally, output could double in the regions where the yield gap is less than 50 percent: Northern Africa, sub-Saharan Africa, Central America and the Caribbean, Southern America, Western Asia, Central Asia, South Asia, Eastern Europe and Russian Federation, and the Pacific Islands. By contrast, much of Asian farming is already using advanced management, with Eastern Asia in particular rivalling the most productive systems in the developed world, at 89 percent of potential.

Land and water resources in irrigated agriculture

Irrigated systems have expanded in recent years to bring water control, which, together with rapid increases in water productivity, has greatly boosted agricultural production and incomes. However, most irrigated farming systems are performing well below their potential, and there is considerable scope for improving land and water productivity. Groundwater abstraction has provided an invaluable source of ready irrigation water, but has proved almost impossible to regulate. As a result, agriculture withdrawals of groundwater are intensifying and some key aquifers are being depleted. Water quality is deteriorating, with impacts from irrigation on both surface and groundwater, and the salinization of irrigated lands is a growing problem. Competition for water from domestic and industrial users is growing fast, and many countries and basins face water scarcity with reduced quantities available to irrigation. New impoundments and diversions have higher marginal costs and pose increasing environmental challenges. Recycled water can increase supply, but it is a limited and costly resource and it needs careful management.

Extent of land use and water resources control

In 2006, the global area equipped for irrigation stood at 301 Mha (Table 1.8). Irrigation has developed rapidly in recent decades, particularly in developing countries, in response to the need to ensure controlled water sources for optimal crop productivity (Figure 1.4). As the global population grew, the area equipped for irrigation more than doubled – from 139 Mha to 301 Mha – and water withdrawals for irrigation almost doubled – from about 1 540 km³ to 2 710 km³. Over the same period the proportion of total cultivated land that is irrigated grew from 10 to 20 percent.

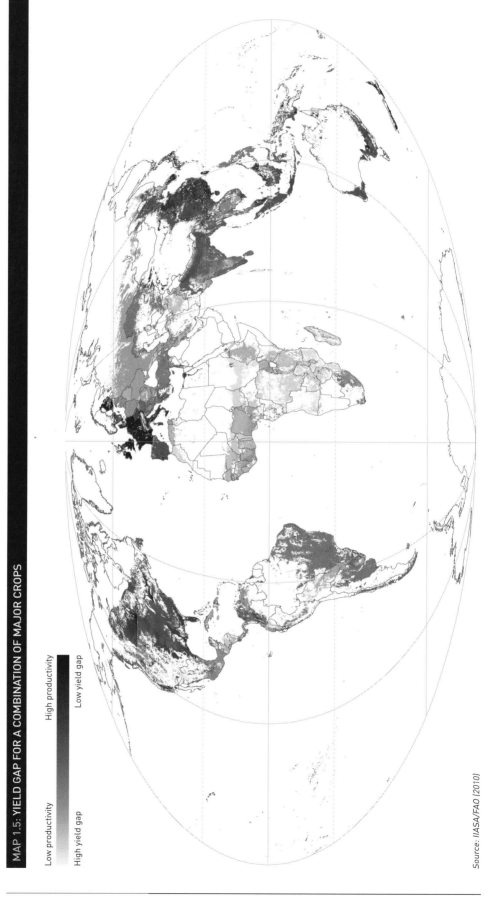

MAP 1.5: YIELD GAP FOR A COMBINATION OF MAJOR CROPS

Low productivity   High productivity

High yield gap   Low yield gap

Source: IIASA/FAO (2010)

TABLE 1.7: ESTIMATED YIELD GAPS (PERCENTAGE OF POTENTIAL) FOR CEREALS, ROOTS AND TUBERS, PULSES, SUGAR CROPS, OIL CROPS AND VEGETABLES COMBINED

Region	Actual yields in 2005 compared with potential yield (%)	Yield gap (%)
	Year 2005	
Northern Africa	40	60
Sub-Saharan Africa	24	76
Northern America	67	33
Central America and Caribbean	35	65
Southern America	48	52
Western Asia	51	49
Central Asia	36	64
South Asia	45	55
East Asia	89	11
Southeast Asia	68	32
Western and Central Europe	64	36
Eastern Europe and Russian Federation	37	63
Australia and New Zealand	60	40
Pacific Islands	43	57

Source: adapted from Fischer et al. (2010)

FIGURE 1.4: AREA EQUIPPED FOR IRRIGATION

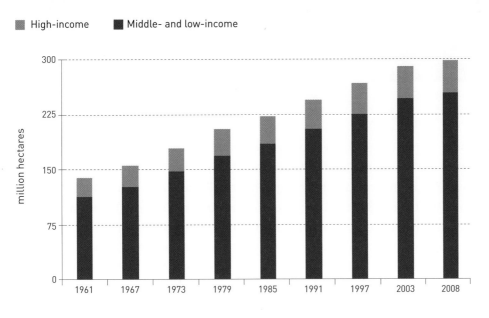

Source: FAO (2010b)

TABLE 1.8: AREA EQUIPPED FOR IRRIGATION
(PERCENTAGE OF CULTIVATED LAND AND PART IRRIGATED GROUNDWATER)

Continent Regions	Equipped area (million ha)		As % of cultivated land		of which groundwater irrigation (2006)	
Year	1961	2006	1961	2006	Area equipped (million ha)	As % of total irrigated area
Africa	**7.4**	**13.6**	**4.4**	**5.4**	**2.5**	**18.5**
Northern Africa	3.9	6.4	17.1	22.7	2.1	32.8
Sub-Saharan Africa	3.5	7.2	2.4	3.2	0.4	5.8
Americas	**22.6**	**48.9**	**6.7**	**12.4**	**21.6**	**44.1**
Northern America	17.4	35.5	6.7	14.0	19.1	54.0
Central America and Caribbean	0.6	1.9	5.5	12.5	0.7	36.3
Southern America	4.7	11.6	6.8	9.1	1.7	14.9
Asia	**95.6**	**211.8**	**19.6**	**39.1**	**80.6**	**38.0**
Western Asia	9.6	23.6	16.2	36.6	10.8	46.0
Central Asia	7.2	14.7	13.4	37.2	1.1	7.8
South Asia	36.3	85.1	19.1	41.7	48.3	56.7
East Asia	34.5	67.6	29.7	51.0	19.3	28.6
Southeast Asia	8.0	20.8	11.7	22.5	1.0	4.7
Europe	**12.3**	**22.7**	**3.6**	**7.7**	**7.3**	**32.4**
Western and Central Europe	8.7	17.8	5.8	14.2	6.9	38.6
Eastern Europe and Russian Federation	3.6	4.9	1.9	2.9	0.5	10.1
Oceania	**1.1**	**4.0**	**3.2**	**8.7**	**0.9**	**23.9**
Australia and New Zealand	1.1	4.0	3.2	8.8	0.9	24.0
Pacific Islands	0.001	0.004	0.2	0.6	0.0	18.7
World	**139.0**	**300.9**	**10.2**	**19.7**	**112.9**	**37.5**
High-income	26.7	54.0	6.9	14.7	26.5	49.1
Middle-income	66.6	137.9	10.5	19.3	36.1	26.1
Low-income	45.8	108.9	13.1	24.5	50.3	46.2
Low-income food deficit	**82.5**	**187.6**	**16.6**	**29.2**	**71.9**	**38.3**
Least-developed	**6.1**	**17.5**	**5.2**	**10.1**	**5.0**	**28.8**

Data sources: FAO (2010b,c)

About 70 percent of the world area equipped for irrigation is in Asia, where it accounts for 39 percent of the cultivated area (Map 1.6). South and East Asia account for over half of the world's area equipped for irrigation, and India and China alone (each with about 62 Mha equipped for irrigation), account for 40 percent. Most of this irrigation is large-scale development within major basins, primarily for paddy rice production. Irrigation is also very important in Western Asia, where it accounts for 37 percent of the cultivated area, and in Northern Africa (23 percent of cultivated area). The region with the least irrigation is sub-Saharan Africa, where only 3 percent is irrigated.

MAP 1.6: AREA EQUIPPED FOR IRRIGATION AS A PERCENTAGE OF LAND AREA

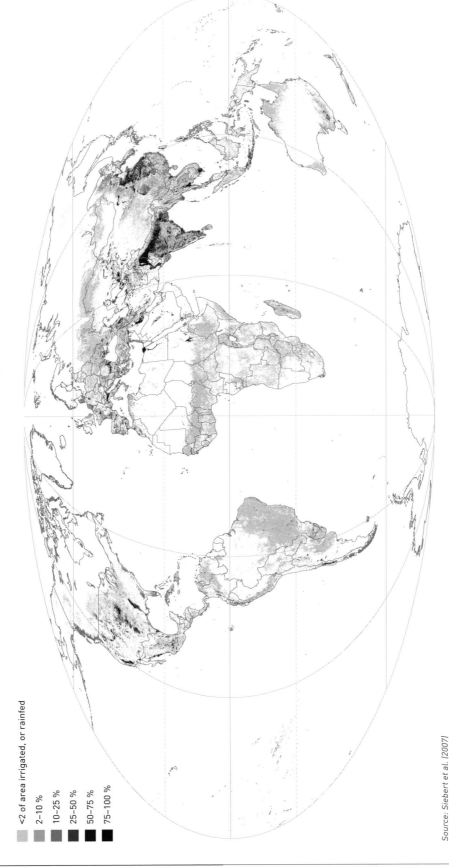

<2 of area irrigated, or rainfed

2–10 %

10–25 %

25–50 %

50–75 %

75–100 %

Source: Siebert et al. (2007)

Chapter 1. Status and trends in land and water resources

39

Rate of expansion

The rate of expansion of irrigation, over 2 percent a year in the 1960s and 1970s, has decreased substantially. The reasons are many, and include a long period of stable food supply and declining food prices (until 2007), declining population growth rate, and the rising importance of investment in other sectors (Faurès *et al.*, 2007). In addition, rising investment and maintenance costs (and associated low economic return of irrigation schemes), and concerns over negative social and environmental impacts, have led to reduction in government and donor interest.

Most irrigation expansion has taken place by conversion from rainfed agriculture. Part of irrigation, however, takes place on arid and hyper-arid (desert) land that is not suitable for rainfed agriculture. It is estimated that of the 219 Mha irrigated at present in developing countries, some 40 Mha are on arid and hyper-arid land, which could increase to 43 Mha in 2050. In some regions and countries, irrigated arid and hyper-arid land forms an important part of the total irrigated land presently in use: 19 out of 28 Mha in the Near East and Northern Africa, and 15 of 85 Mha in South Asia.

Some regionally specific factors also played a part. In Asia, almost all sites had been developed. Eastern Europe and the countries of Central Asia, which developed irrigation rapidly in the 1960s and 1970s, entered a period of economic crisis and reorganization after the break-up of the former Soviet Union. Some parts of Eastern Europe and the Russian Federation have seen large areas equipped for irrigation abandoned in the last two decades.

Sources of irrigation water

Irrigation extracts water from rivers, lakes and aquifers. About 188 million ha (62 percent of the irrigated area), is supplied from surface water, and 113 Mha (38 percent) from groundwater (Map 1.7). Following the introduction of tubewell technology, and driven by low energy prices, groundwater use has grown rapidly in recent years, particularly in Asia, Northern Africa and the Middle East. From agricultural census data for India, the irrigated areas equipped with groundwater structures rose from approximately 10 Mha in 1960 (Mukherji and Shah, 2005) to almost 40 Mha by 2010 (Seibert *et al.* 2010). In South Asia, groundwater now accounts for 57 percent of the total irrigated area, and in the Arabian Peninsula for 88 percent.

Non-conventional sources of water such as treated wastewater and desalinated water provide a minor source of irrigation water (about 1 percent). Use of treated wastewater is on the increase as urban areas invest in treatment, and its use is popular for peri-urban cropping. Desalinated water is used for irrigation where high-value crops are grown and no alternative sources of water are available, but these tend to be exceptional cases.

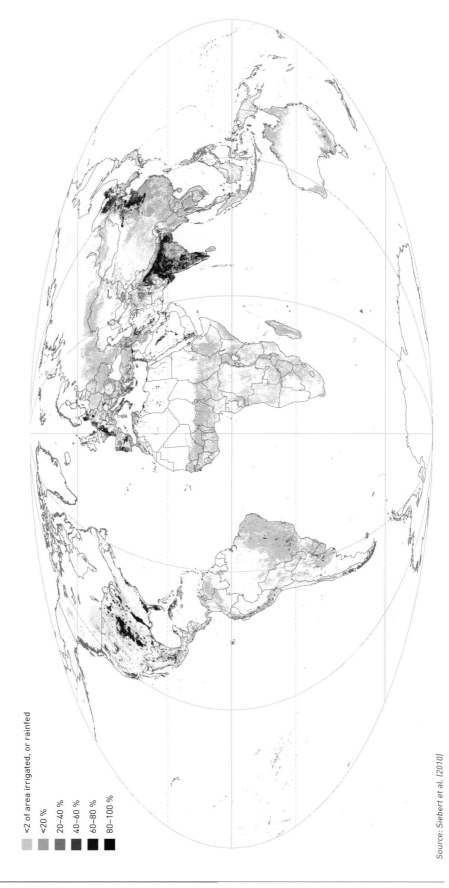

MAP 1.7: PERCENTAGE OF IRRIGATED AREA SERVICED BY GROUNDWATER

<2 of area irrigated, or rainfed

<20 %

20–40 %

40–60 %

60–80 %

80–100 %

Source: Siebert et al. (2010)

CHAPTER 1

Water resources constraints

In some regions, the competition for water and the growing water scarcity are constraining both current availability of water for irrigation and further expansion of the irrigated area. There are already very severe water shortages, in particular in Western, Central and South Asia, which use half or more of their water resources in irrigation (Table 1.9), and in Northern Africa, where withdrawals for irrigation exceed renewable resources due to groundwater overdraft and recycling. By contrast, Southern America barely uses 1 percent of its resources. In many parts of the Middle East, North Africa, China and elsewhere, water tables are declining as farmers abstract over and above rates of replenishment from recharge and aquifer leakage.

TABLE 1.9: ANNUAL LONG-TERM AVERAGE RENEWABLE WATER RESOURCES AND IRRIGATION WATER WITHDRAWAL

Continent Regions	Precipitation (mm)	Renewable water resources* (km³)	Water-use efficiency ratio (%)	Irrigation water withdrawal (km³)	Pressure on water resources due to irrigation (%)
Africa	**678**	**3 931**	**48**	**184**	**5**
Northern Africa	96	47	69	80	170
Sub-Saharan Africa	815	3 884	30	105	3
Americas	**1 091**	**19 238**	**41**	**385**	**2**
Northern America	636	6 077	46	258	4
Central America and Caribbean	2 011	781	30	15	2
Southern America	1 604	12 380	28	112	1
Asia	**827**	**12 413**	**45**	**2 012**	**16**
Western Asia	217	484	47	227	47
Central Asia	273	263	48	150	57
South Asia	1 602	1 766	55	914	52
East Asia	634	3 410	37	434	13
Southeast Asia	2 400	6 490	19	287	4
Europe	**540**	**6 548**	**48**	**109**	**2**
Western and Central Europe	811	2 098	43	75	4
Eastern Europe and Russian Federation	467	4 449	67	35	1
Oceania	**586**	**892**	**41**	**19**	**2**
Australia and New Zealand	574	819	41	19	2.3
Pacific Islands	2 062	73	-	0.05	0.1
World	**809**	**43 022**	**44**	**2 710**	**6**
High-income	622	9 009	45	383	4
Middle-income	872	26 680	39	1 136	4
Low-income	876	7 332	50	1 191	16
Low-income food deficit	**881**	**13 985**	**48**	**1 813**	**13**
Least-developed	**856**	**4 493**	**28**	**190**	**4**

* Refers to internal renewable water resources; it excludes 'incoming flows' at the regional level.

Source: FAO (2010c)

At the country level, variations are even higher. In 2005–7, four countries (Libyan Arab Jamahiriya, Saudi Arabia, Yemen and Egypt) used volumes of water for irrigation that were larger than their annual renewable water resources. Overall, eleven countries used more than 40 percent of their water resources for irrigation, the threshold that is considered critical. An additional eight countries withdrew more than 20 percent of their water resources, indicating substantial pressure and impending water scarcity.

For several countries, relatively low overall figures may give an overly optimistic impression of the level of water stress: China, for instance, is facing severe water shortage in the north while the south still has abundant water resources. Ground-water mining also occurs in certain parts of some other countries of the Near East, and in South and East Asia, Central America and in the Caribbean, even if at the national level the water balance may still be positive.

Irrigation and land productivity

Irrigation has contributed greatly to the improvements in global agricultural productivity and output in recent decades. India and China tripled production in the 25 years from 1964–6 to 1997–9, mainly through investment in irrigation and widespread adoption of measures to enhance land and water productivity. At present in developing countries, irrigated agriculture covers about a fifth of all arable land, but accounts for nearly half (47 percent) of all crop production and almost 60 percent of cereal production. In the least-developed countries, irrigation accounts for less than one-fifth (17 percent) of the harvested cereals area but almost two-fifths (38 percent) of cereal production (Table 1.10).

Irrigated agriculture is highly diverse. The irrigation unit may range from an individual farm up to massive integrated schemes such as the Rohri canal system in Pakistan, which covers 1.04 Mha.

The predominant models are: large-scale public systems (either paddy fields for rice production in humid areas or for staples and cash crops in dry areas); small- and medium-scale community-managed systems; commercial private systems for cash crops; and farm-scale individually managed systems producing for the local market (Molden, 2007: 359). Water conveyance and distribution may be by gravity or under pressure, and management and institutional set-up public, user-run, private, community-based, or a combination.

Water productivity and productivity gaps

In water-scarce countries such as Mexico, the challenge is to optimize water productivity in the face of competition from municipal and industrial demand. In much of China and India, the very high agricultural use of water is prompting improvements

TABLE 1.10: SHARES OF IRRIGATED LAND AND SHARE OF IRRIGATED CEREAL PRODUCTION IN TOTAL CEREAL PRODUCTION (2006)

Continent Regions	All irrigated crops		Irrigated cereals		
	Actually irrigated land as % of cultivated land	Harvested irrigated land as % of total harvested land	Harvested irrigated cereal land as % of total harvested irrigated land	Harvested irrigated cereal land as % of total harvested cereal land	Harvested irrigated cereal production as % of total cereal production
Africa	**5**	**7**	**48**	**7**	**24**
Northern Africa	21	43	48	33	75
Sub-Saharan Africa	2	3	48	3	9
Americas	**10**	**15**	**44**	**14**	**22**
Northern America	11	20	43	15	22
Central America and Caribbean	7	18	32	17	32
Southern America	8	8	47	13	22
Asia	**34**	**43**	**68**	**51**	**67**
Western Asia	28	49	52	32	48
Central Asia	30	43	45	27	45
South Asia	38	41	70	52	70
East Asia	44	58	69	68	78
Southeast Asia	19	21	84	35	49
Europe	**5**	**9**	**28**	**4**	**8**
Western and Central Europe	9	12	30	5	10
Eastern Europe and Russian Federation	1	5	23	2	4
Oceania	**7**	**12**	**14**	**2**	**7**
Australia and New Zealand	7	12	14	2	7
Pacific Islands	1				
World	**17**	**25**	**62**	**29**	**42**
High-income	11	19	39	13	20
Middle-income	26	28	63	32	49
Low-income	14	26	69	33	55
Low-income food deficit	**26**	**34**	**68**	**42**	**64**
Least-developed	**8**	**10**	**83**	**17**	**38**

Sources: FAO (2010b,c)

in water productivity, but environmental issues of pollution and groundwater over-draft are threatening the resource base. In Pakistan, drainage problems and resultant salinization dominate the irrigation agenda, while flood control is a preoccupation in the coastal deltas of Bangladesh and Vietnam.

Irrigation systems typically have yields at least twice those of nearby rainfed crops. Globally, rainfed cereals yields in the developing world average 1.5t/ha, but irrigated yields are 3.3t/ha. Irrigated cropping intensities are typically higher too, with two crops per year in most of Asia (Faurès *et al.*, 2007). Water productivity has also been increasing: over the last 40 years, both rice and wheat have more than doubled their yield per unit of water. But as demand grows, more production will be needed from these same equipped areas.

Over the last 50 years, the rate of increase in production for globally important crop groups exceeds the rate of increase of the extent of arable land and permanent crops. Cereals are by far the most important crop group (on the basis of total harvested area) and have registered relatively large average increases in yields (Figure 1.5). More than two-thirds of the increase in production has come from yield increases, especially under irrigated conditions. Bruinsma (2003) estimated that 77 percent of production increases in developing countries came from 'intensification' arising from increases in both yield and cropping intensities. South and East Asia, where the share of irrigation in the cultivated area is highest, produced the most rapid growth in productivity, with 94 percent of increased production attributable to intensification.

Two main factors have driven up irrigated yields: the widespread adoption of new varieties, inputs and husbandry practices; and breakthroughs in irrigation technology, such as tubewell and pressurized irrigation.

Forests, rangelands, inland fisheries and aquaculture

Forests

FAO's *Global forest resources assessment* provides regular estimates of the state of the world's forests, their extent and health, and the status of their socio-economic and environmental functions (FAO, 2010d). In 2010, forests covered approximately 4 billion ha. Deforestation arising mainly from the conversion of tropical forests to agricultural land has recently shown signs of decreasing, but still continues at an alarming rate. Around 13 Mha of forest were converted to other uses or lost through natural causes each year in the last decade, compared with 16 Mha per year in the 1990s. However, during the last decade, the net reduction in forest areas has been significantly limited by large-scale planting of trees, estimated at 5.2 Mha per year during the first decade of the 21st century. Net losses of forested land were concentrated in South America, sub-Saharan Africa, Southeast Asia and Oceania, while the US, India, China, Russia and several European countries showed net gains in forested land. Primary forests account for 36 percent of forest area, but have decreased by more than 40 Mha since 2000. Reduction in primary forests may have important impacts on forest biodiversity.

Forests play a crucial role in the hydrological cycle, which is why they must be taken into consideration when analysing water issues at landscape level. They capture and store water, prevent soil erosion, and serve as natural water purifica-

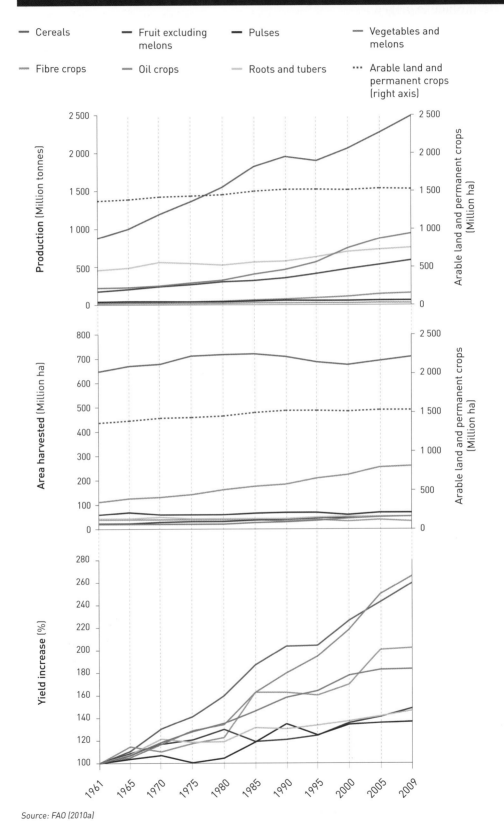

FIGURE 1.5: INCREASES IN WORLD PRODUCTION, AREA HARVESTED AND CROPLAND EXTENT, 1961–2009

— Cereals
— Fruit excluding melons
— Pulses
— Vegetables and melons
— Fibre crops
— Oil crops
— Roots and tubers
··· Arable land and permanent crops (right axis)

Source: FAO (2010a)

tion systems. Forests influence the amount of water available, regulate surface and groundwater flows, and ensure high water quality. Moreover, forests and trees contribute to the reduction of water-related risks such as landslides, local floods and droughts, and help prevent desertification and salinization. Forested watersheds and wetlands supply three-quarters of the world's accessible fresh water to satisfy domestic, agricultural, industrial and ecological needs (FAO, 2008c).

Rangelands

Rangelands extend over all latitudes, and are usually characterized by low biomass production due to constraints related to soil, temperature and water availability. They cover some 25 percent of the global land area, and include the drylands of Africa (66 percent of the total continental land area) and the Arabian Peninsula, the steppes of Central Asia and the highlands of Latin America (Nori and Neely, 2009). Vegetation is mostly dominated by natural plant communities of perennial and annual species, including grasses, shrubs and trees. By their nature, rangelands are fragile ecosystems and when mismanaged readily result in degradation, loss of biodiversity and water retention capacity, carbon emissions and reduced productivity.

The extent and trends in rangelands are hard to assess. Global statistics indicate that the total area of rangelands was 3.43 billion ha in 2000, and decreased slightly to 3.36 billion ha by 2008. The reasons for these minor changes cannot be easily identified, though may include poor data, desertification and encroachment of agriculture. Large-scale conversion of drier grasslands to crops and inappropriate management has had unfortunate consequences, such as the 'dust bowl' of the Great Plains of the USA in the 1920s and 1930s. In the mid 20th century, drylands were widely cultivated in the USSR, but crop production was also unsustainable in that region (Boonman and Mikhalev, 2005) and these lands are now reverting to rangelands.

The contribution that rangelands make to the maintenance of ecosystem functions and biodiversity is important. In addition to providing feed for livestock, they play an important role as a habitat for wildlife, for water retention and for the conservation of plant genetic resources. The flora of rangelands is rich: about 750 genera and 12 000 grass species. These ecosystems are also important for the maintenance of fauna; for example, grasslands contain 11 percent of the world's endemic bird areas (White *et al.*, 2000: 40), and contribute to the maintenance of pollinators and other insects that have important regulating functions. Ecosystem benefits, especially regulating services such as water infiltration and purification, climate regulation (e.g. carbon sequestration) and pollination, have begun to be assigned an economic value, and systematic data-gathering in rangelands of both developed and developing countries should be a global priority.

Over 600 million people depend on rangelands for their livelihoods. Pastoral societies have developed strategies that continuously adapt to limited, highly variable and unpredictable resource endowments (e.g. by migratory livestock rearing), but both the rangelands and their users are also vulnerable to the changes brought by demographic pressure, conversion of cropland (Box 1.2) and climate change. Fluctuations in rainfall and drought are recurring problems in rangelands – for example, 70 million people in the Horn of Africa, many of whom are pastoralists, suffer from long-term chronic food insecurity (FAO, 2000). Table 1.11 lists major pastoral systems and illustrates how they evolve with time.

Significant amounts of carbon are lost from drylands due to poor management, driven largely by increasing human and livestock pressures. Due to degradation, dryland soils are now far from being saturated in carbon and their potential to sequester carbon may be very high. It has been estimated that improved range-

BOX 1.2: CONVERSION OF PASTURE TO CULTIVATION IN NORTH AFRICA, THE NEAR EAST AND THE MEDITERRANEAN

Degraded pastureland in Morocco

Escalating human and livestock populations combined with loss of traditional grazing rights have led to serious overstocking and degradation of pastures around the Mediterranean littoral. Much semi-arid land has been ploughed for annual cropping, which is unsustainable under current practices. Livestock production systems are changing through intensification, the gradual control of animal diseases and commercialization of livestock products, particularly in peri-urban areas. Drought and desertification processes are being exacerbated by climate change.

Photo: G. Schwilch

TABLE 1.11: REGIONAL ZONATION OF PASTORAL SYSTEMS

Zone	Main Species	Current Status
Sub-Saharan Africa	Cattle, camel, sheep, goats	Declining due to advancing agriculture
Mediterranean	Small ruminants	Declining due to enclosure and advancing agriculture
Near East and South-Central Asia	Small ruminants	Declining in some areas due to enclosure and advancing agriculture
India	Camel, cattle, sheep, goats	Declining due to advancing agriculture but peri-urban livestock production expanding
Central Asia	Yak, camel, horse, sheep, goats	Expanding following de-collectivization
Circumpolar	Reindeer	Expanding following de-collectivization in Siberia, but under pressure in Scandinavia
North America	Sheep, cattle	Declining with increased enclosure of land and alternative economic opportunities
Andes	Llama, alpaca	Contracting llama production due to expansion of road systems and European-model livestock production but expansion of alpaca wool production

Source: Bleach (1999)

land management has the biophysical potential to sequester 1 300–2 000 Mt CO_2eq worldwide to 2030 (Tennigkeit and Wilkes, 2008). Strategies to increase the stock of carbon in rangelands include restoring soil organic matter and root biomass, thereby enhancing soil biota (e.g. rehabilitation with improved legumes and grasses; manure cycling and agroforestry; erosion control; afforestation and forest restoration; optimal livestock densities; water conservation and harvesting; land-use change, such as from crops to grass/trees; set-aside). However, there are still significant gaps in knowledge about dryland carbon sequestration potential, acceptable methodologies and cost–benefit analysis of carbon-sequestering practices for small-scale rural farmers and pastoralists.

Fodder and grasslands

Grasslands (including rangelands, shrubland, pasture land, and cropland sown with pasture trees and fodder crops) occupy almost 30 percent of the emerged ice-free land areas. Fodders and pastures cover over 60 percent of the world's agricultural land (FAO, 2010b). Fodder and grasslands are multipurpose: they provide essential ecosystem services and support livelihoods in a number of ways (e.g. as a genetic resource for food production and sustainable production intensification; as a resource for energy production; as a raw material in industrial production; and for carbon sequestration). Many permanent fodder and grassland areas are used for watershed protection, polluted-land rehabilitation and bio-energy production. The sustainable intensification of crop–livestock systems based on improved management of fodders, grasslands and rangelands could therefore contribute significantly to the enhancement of sustainable development on a wide scale (Box 1.3). Globally, grassland soils have the potential to sequester 0.2–0.8 Gt CO_2 per year by 2030, depending on grazing and other management practices applied. Grassland cover can capture 50–80 percent more water, reducing risks of droughts and floods. These attributes taken together are critical for climate change mitigation and adaptation.

The crop–livestock sector provides livelihoods to the majority of smallholders around the world, and rapidly increasing demand for livestock products implies that means must be found to decrease the production footprint of livestock systems. This is an urgent rationale for integrated crop–livestock systems, for which crop residues provide feed for livestock, which in turn produce manure to fertilize crops, in on-site or within-landscape nutrient cycling. Although they have been a feature of traditional agriculture for centuries, integrated crop–livestock systems are now benefiting from synergistic components provided by the modern crop, livestock and agroforestry sectors.

Grasslands are important to the livelihoods of almost a billion people, including some 200 million pastoralist households. Improving crop intensification and diversification practices through the introduction of fodders, forage legumes and mixed grass–forage species, efficient use of manure and nutrient management, and diversification of crop and livestock production at farm level, will assist these people to increase the stability of their incomes and the efficient use of their soil and water resources, and to improve the mitigation and adaptation potential of their agricultural practice.

Inland fisheries and aquaculture
Globally, lakes, reservoirs and wetlands important for inland fisheries cover an area of about 7.8 million km^2. Relatively high proportions of land are covered with surface

---

BOX 1.3: FODDER GRASSES FOR FEED AND FUEL FOR ENERGY

Today we utilize large amount of plant produce for animal feed, and we need to rethink our systems by improving the use of flexible fodders that can provide feed, fuel, carbon sequestration, increase biodiversity of the ecosystem and improved soil fertility, according to the economic and sustainability priorities of the farmer. Among such fodders are *Pennisetum purpureum* (elephant grass), *Miscanthus giganteus* (switchgrass) and *Setaria* spp. They produce high biomass yields, can be converted to biofuels in biorefineries and leave a surplus of fodder for livestock production. They also contain material that can be utilized as raw material in industry.

---

waters in Southeast Asia, North America, east and central West Africa, the northern part of Asia, Europe and South America (FAO 2010a). Inland fisheries represent an extremely diverse activity that includes large-scale industrial fishing, as well as small-scale and subsistence fishing that require little or no financial investment in order to participate. As such, inland fisheries provide quality nutrition, livelihood opportunities and a safety net for the poor when other food production sectors may fail.

About 90 percent of inland fish is caught in developing countries and 65 percent is caught in low-income, food-deficit countries. Asia and Africa regularly account for about 90 percent of reported landings. The reported harvest from the world's inland fisheries has grown from 2 million tonnes in 1950 to over 10 million tonnes in 2008. However, the production is believed to be much higher, as much of the small-scale and subsistence fishing is not registered. Large-scale and industrial inland fisheries, for example on the Great Lakes of Africa, can produce hundreds of millions of US dollars' worth of fish, which are often exported (FAO, 2010a).

Globally, aquaculture has increased from less than 1 million tonnes of annual production in 1950 to 52.5 million tonnes in 2008, and accounts for 45.7 percent of the world's food fish production for human consumption (FAO, 2010a). Integrated approaches to land and water use have been successfully applied in many parts of the world (FAO/ICLARM/IIRR, 2001; Halwart and Van Dam, 2006). Rice–fish culture, often operating at family scale with renovated paddy fields, has expanded rapidly among rice farmers in China in recent decades, and the total area of rice fields used for aquaculture was 1.47 Mha in 2008. Cage aquaculture in both freshwater lakes and rivers has flourished in many countries, as a very efficient non-consumptive use of freshwaters.

Asia (and especially China) has the greatest freshwater aquaculture production in relation to land area and water surface area, although some European and African countries are also significant, while the Americas have relatively low freshwater aquaculture production per unit area of land or water, although the potential is there (Bostock *et al.*, 2010; Aguilar-Manjarrez *et al.*, 2010). While in Africa and Latin America there is still important room for freshwater aquaculture growth, the use of freshwaters for this sector will become more restricted due to urban development and high competition for land, and especially freshwater resources in countries and regions with high population density, such as in Asia. Fish production in the coastal and offshore marine environment offers alternative and new opportunities for aquaculture and for the supply of world food fish when freshwater and land become more scarce (FAO, 2010a).

Agricultural demand towards to 2050

Demand for food and fibre towards 2050

It is expected that world population will grow from the current about 6.9 billion to about 9 billion in 2050. Demand for food and fibre will grow more quickly as incomes and standards of nutrition rise and populations move towards more land- and water-intensive diets, in particular the consumption of more meat and dairy products. Current trends and model simulations indicate that global cereal demand will grow from roughly 2.1 billion tonnes today to about 3 billion tonnes in 2050 (FAO, 2006b). Thus, by 2050, the world will be demanding the production of almost an extra billion tonnes of cereal grain annually, and 200 million additional tonnes of livestock products.

Production response

Estimates of growth in crop production (Bruinsma, 2009) are that world agricultural production could rise by about 1.3 percent annually to 2030 and by 0.8 percent annually over the period 2030–50. To keep pace with population growth, food production is expected to rise slightly faster in developing countries than in developed countries: 1.5 percent a year from 2005–2030, and 0.9 percent a year over 2030–50. These estimates are based on an assessment of production capacity to respond to effective demand. Globally, the result would be a 43 percent increase in output by 2030, and 70 percent by 2050 over 2005–7 levels. Regionally, the fastest rates of growth of cereals production are anticipated in sub-Saharan Africa, where demographic pressure remains strong, and in Latin America and Australasia, where there is scope for expansion of commercial food production (Table 1.12).

These rates are lower than those over the last half-century (Table 1.12). Estimates of future growth are based on projections that about four-fifths of the growth in developing countries could come from intensification in the form of yield increases (71 percent) and higher cropping intensities (8 percent). The share of intensification would be even higher in land-scarce regions such as South Asia (95 percent), and Near East and North Africa (100 percent). By contrast, arable land expansion is expected to remain a factor in crop production growth in some areas of sub-Saharan Africa and Latin America, although less so than in the past (Bruinsma, 2009). However, this is likely to lead to losses in important ecosystem and cultural services. Furthermore, even with a doubling of production in developing countries by 2050, 5 percent of their population would remain undernourished (Table 1.13).

TABLE 1.12: HISTORICAL AND PROJECTED GROWTH IN CEREAL PRODUCTION

Continent Regions	Annual growth in cereal production (%)	
	1961–2006	2006–2050
Africa	**2.4**	**1.9**
Northern Africa	3.0	1.6
Sub-Saharan Africa	2.3	2.0
Americas	**2.0**	**1.2**
Northern America	1.8	1.0
Central America and Caribbean	1.7	1.8
Southern America	2.6	1.7
Asia	**2.5**	**0.7**
Western Asia	2.4	1.0
Central Asia	1.1	0.8
South Asia	2.3	1.1
East Asia	2.5	0.3
Southeast Asia	2.9	0.8
Europe	**1.1**	**0.3**
Western and Central Europe	1.5	0.2
Eastern Europe and Russian Federation	0.3	0.5
Oceania	**2.3**	**2.0**
Australia and New Zealand	2.3	2.0
Pacific Islands	-	-
World	**2.0**	**0.9**
High-income	1.6	0.8
Middle-income	2.1	0.8
Low-income	2.4	1.2
Low-income food deficit	**2.7**	**0.9**
Least-developed	**1.9**	**1.9**

Source: FAO (2010a)

TABLE 1.13: PROJECTED GROWTH IN AGRICULTURAL PRODUCTION: MOST LIKELY OUTCOMES

	Agricultural production index			Remaining undernourished	
	2005–7	2030	2050	%	Millions
World	100	143	170	n.a.	n.a.
Developing countries	100	158	197	4.8	370

Source: Alexandratos (2009)

Implications for irrigated agriculture

Potential for intensification in irrigation

The area equipped for irrigation is projected to increase by about 6 percent by 2050. Water withdrawals for irrigation are projected to increase by about 10 percent by 2050. Irrigated food production is projected to increase by 38 percent, due to projected increases in cropping intensities and increases in productivity (Tubiello and van der Velde, 2010). Overall, the scope to improve both land and water productivity on irrigation schemes is considerable, as illustrated by the large discrepancies observed between schemes and within schemes.

It is projected that cropping intensities on irrigated land actually in use will increase worldwide from 127 percent to 129 percent by 2050. In developing countries, higher intensities are expected, rising from 143 percent in 2005–7 to 147 percent by 2050 (Bruinsma, 2009; Frenken, 2010). These increases are technically feasible, and the best-managed systems already have cropping intensities of 200 percent or more. Key factors in achieving higher intensities will be modernization of infrastructure and institutional change to improve water service, together with the development of profitable agricultural markets (Nachtergaele *et al.*, 2010b).

Scope for expanding irrigated area

The potential for expansion of irrigated areas is difficult to establish. Past efforts by countries to assess their irrigation potential have resulted in estimates that combine land and water resources, economic and environmental considerations. Yet irrigation potential should be calculated on the basis of river basins, the logical geographical unit for water resources. When countries share common rivers, the risk is that the same water is double-counted in assessing irrigation potential in several countries. Furthermore, many irrigation potential estimates date from when environmental concerns were less acute and other sectors of water use were less demanding than today.

While potential for irrigation development is still abundant in several water-rich regions, it is in water-scarce regions where limits have already been reached. Sub-Saharan Africa and Latin America are the two regions that have exploited the least of their evaluated irrigation potential. In sub-Saharan Africa there is technically ample scope for expansion of irrigation. Highland areas such as the Fouta-Djallon and the Ethiopian highlands, for example, produce high volumes of runoff, but have low levels of water infrastructure. Subject to the availability of suitable sites and favourable economics, areas such as these could see diversion and development of irrigated agriculture. At the other extreme, the countries of Northern Africa, West Asia, Central Asia, and large parts of South Asia and East Asia have reached or are reaching their potential. Among these countries, FAO estimates that eight countries have expanded their irrigation beyond its potential, while 20 countries (including China) are above 75 percent of their potential.

The rate of expansion of land under irrigation is slowing substantially. Based on a comparison between supply (irrigation potential) and demand (for agricultural products), FAO has projected that the global area equipped for irrigation may increase at a relatively modest rate to reach 318 Mha in 2050, compared with around 301 Mha in 2006 (Table 1.14). This would represent an increase of around 6 percent (0.12 percent per year). Most of this expansion is projected to take place in developing countries. This rate of increase is much slower than in recent years; between 1961 and 2009, irrigated area worldwide grew at 1.6 percent a year, and at over 2 percent in the least-developed countries.

TABLE 1.14: AREA EQUIPPED FOR IRRIGATION PROJECTED TO 2050

Continent Regions	Area equipped for irrigation				
	Area (million hectares)			Annual growth (%)	
Year	1961	2006	2050	1961–2006	2006–2050
Africa	7.4	13.6	17.0	1.3	0.5
Northern Africa	3.9	6.4	7.6	1.0	0.4
Sub-Saharan Africa	3.5	7.2	9.4	1.5	0.6
Americas	22.6	48.9	46.5	1.6	−0.1
Northern America	17.4	35.5	30.0	1.5	−0.4
Central America and Caribbean	0.6	1.9	2.4	2.5	0.5
Southern America	4.7	11.6	14.1	1.9	0.5
Asia	95.6	211.8	227.6	1.7	0.2
Western Asia	9.6	23.6	26.9	1.9	0.3
Central Asia	7.2	14.7	15.0	1.5	0.0
South Asia	36.3	85.1	85.6	1.8	0.0
East Asia	34.5	67.6	76.2	1.4	0.3
Southeast Asia	8.0	20.8	23.9	2.0	0.3
Europe	12.3	22.7	24.6	1.3	0.2
Western and Central Europe	8.7	17.8	17.4	1.5	0.0
Eastern Europe and Russian Federation	3.6	4.9	7.2	0.6	0.9
Oceania	1.1	4.0	2.8	2.7	−0.8
Australia and New Zealand	1.1	4.0	2.8	2.7	−0.8
Pacific Islands	0.001	0.004	–	2.9	–
World	139.0	300.9	318.4	1.6	0.1
High-income	26.7	54.0	45.1	1.5	−0.4
Middle-income	66.6	137.9	159.4	1.5	0.4
Low-income	45.8	108.9	113.8	1.8	0.1
Low-income food-deficit	82.5	187.6	201.9	1.7	0.2
Least-developed	6.1	17.5	18.4	2.2	0.1

Sources: FAO (2006b, 2010b,c)

The expansion of the area equipped for irrigation is projected to be strongest (in absolute terms) in the more land-scarce regions hard-pressed to raise crop production through more intensive cultivation practices. Middle-income countries are projected to add 21 Mha, and the low-income food-deficit countries about 14 Mha. By contrast, high-income countries in North America, Western Europe and Australasia are expected to reduce their irrigated area. Irrigated areas in Eastern Europe, the Russian Federation and Central Asia are expected to return towards the levels prior to the break-up of the Soviet Union. Although the overall arable area in China is expected to decrease further, the irrigated area is projected to continue to expand through conversion of rainfed land. Most of the expansion of irrigated land will be achieved by converting land in use in rainfed agriculture into irrigated land. The pressure on water resources will continue to increase everywhere, even in places where water resources are already stretched, like Northern Africa and large parts of Asia (Table 1.15).

Non-conventional sources of water

Use of non-conventional sources of water as an alternative to freshwater, although currently a minor source, is increasing in certain regions and countries. Globally, only 1 percent of the water used in agriculture consists of treated wastewater or desalinated water. However, in regions such as the Arabian Peninsula, the rate of use is around 10 percent, and in countries such as Kuwait, Malta or Qatar, non-conventional sources of water constitute more than 50 percent of the water used, of which around 40 percent is desalinated water and 10 percent wastewater. The top five countries reporting the highest annual per capita volume of treated waste water used for irrigation (cubic metres per year per capita) are Kuwait (82.3), United Arab Emirates (71.1), Qatar (51.7), Israel (46.4) and Cyprus (31.9) (Mateo-Sagasta and Burke, 2010). While desalinated water is still rarely used for irrigated agriculture, mainly because of the high cost of desalination, peri-urban agriculture often relies on urban wastewater to satisfy water needs.

Implications for rainfed agriculture

Although irrigated agriculture is expected to produce most of the increased production needed in coming years, rainfed agriculture, which currently accounts for 60 percent of all agricultural output in developing countries, will remain an important contributor to the world's food production. Bruinsma (2003) projected that 43 percent of the production increment over 1997-2030 would come from rainfed agriculture. If considerable expansion of rainfed cultivated area is to be avoided, the productivity of rainfed cultivation would need to rise.

TABLE 1.15: ANNUAL LONG-TERM AVERAGE RENEWABLE WATER RESOURCES AND IRRIGATION WATER WITHDRAWAL, 2006, 2050

Continent Regions	Precipitation (mm)	Renewable water resources * (km³)	Water use ratio ** (%)		Irrigation water withdrawal (km³)		Pressure on water resources due to irrigation (%)	
			2006	2050	2006	2050	2009	2050
Africa	**678**	**3 931**	**48**	**53**	**184**	**222**	**5**	**6**
Northern Africa	96	47	69	81	80	95	170	204
Sub-Saharan Africa	815	3 884	30	32	105	127	3	3
Americas	**1 091**	**19 238**	**41**	**41**	**385**	**438**	**2**	**2**
Northern America	636	6 077	46	46	258	244	4	4
Central America and Caribbean	2 011	781	30	33	15	23	2	3
Southern America	1 604	12 380	28	29	112	171	1	1
Asia	**827**	**12 413**	**45**	**48**	**2 012**	**2 073**	**16**	**17**
Western Asia	217	484	47	56	227	251	47	52
Central Asia	273	263	48	50	150	133	57	50
South Asia	1 602	1 766	55	58	914	889	52	50
East Asia	634	3 410	37	42	434	458	13	13
Southeast Asia	2 400	6 490	19	21	287	342	4	5
Europe	**540**	**6 548**	**48**	**48**	**109**	**100**	**2**	**2**
Western and Central Europe	811	2 098	43	43	75	81	4	4
Eastern Europe and Russian Federation	467	4 449	67	67	35	19	1	0
Oceania	**586**	**892**	**41**	**41**	**19**	**25**	**2**	**3**
Australia and New Zealand	574	819	41	41	19	25	2	3
Pacific Islands	2 062	73	–	–	0.05	–	–	–
World	**809**	**43 022**	**44**	**47**	**2 710**	**2 858**	**6**	**7**
High-income	622	9 009	45	45	383	317	4	4
Middle-income	872	26 680	39	42	1 136	1 330	4	5
Low-income	876	7 332	50	52	1 191	1 212	16	17
Low-income food-deficit	**881**	**13 985**	**48**	**51**	**1 813**	**1 992**	**13**	**14**
Least-developed	**856**	**4 493**	**28**	**31**	**190**	**263**	**4**	**6**

* Refers to internal renewable water resources; excludes 'incoming flows' at the regional level.
** The water use ratio is the ratio of the irrigation water requirement to the amount of water withdrawn for irrigation

Source: FAO (2010c)

Opportunities for expansion of rainfed agriculture

In some areas, cultivated land is already very limited in relation to population. Overall, developing countries are more constrained by land shortages than developed countries. Availability of cultivated land per capita in the developed world (0.5 ha) is twice that of developing countries (0.2 ha). The per capita availability of cultivated land is less than 0.1 ha in East Asia, compared to more than 2 ha in Australia. Apart

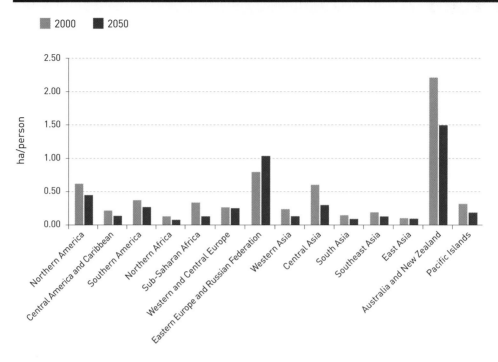

Source: adapted from Fischer et al. (2010)

from Central Asia, no region of the developing world has as much land per capita as the developed world average (Figure 1.6), and the situation is deteriorating.

Under strong demographic pressure in the coming decades, the per capita availability of land in developing countries is expected to halve (to 0.12 ha) by 2050, resulting in increasing pressures for expanding the cultivated area (Fischer *et al.*, 2010).

Suitability of further land for cultivation

Worldwide, land suitable for cropping (prime and good categories combined) is about 4.4 billion ha (4.0 billion ha if areas with protected status are excluded). This is considerably more than the 1.6 billion ha currently cultivated (Table 1.16). There is thus a large area of currently uncultivated land that could theoretically be brought into production. However, much of this land is effectively not available for crop production. In addition, it is generally of lower food potential than existing cultivated land: much of the presently agriculturally unused land suffers from constraints such as ecological fragility, low fertility, toxicity, high incidence of disease or lack of infrastructure. These constraints reduce productivity, require high input use and management skills to permit its sustainable use, or require prohibitively high investments to be made accessible or disease-free. Fischer *et al.* (2002) show that over 70 percent of the land with rainfed crop production potential in sub-Saharan Africa and Latin America suffers from one or more of these constraints.

TABLE 1.16: GLOBAL AVAILABILITY AND QUALITY OF LAND RESOURCES SUITABLE FOR CROP PRODUCTION (VALUE IN BRACKETS EXCLUDES LAND WITH PROTECTION STATUS)

Land quality	Cultivated land (billion ha)	Grassland and woodland ecosystems (billion ha)	Forest land (billion ha)	Other land (billion ha)	Total (billion ha)
Prime land	0.4	0.4 (0.3)	0.5 (0.4)	0.0	1.3 (1.2)
Good land	0.8	1.1 (1.0)	1.1 (1.0)	0.0	3.1 (2.8)
Marginal land	0.3	0.5 (0.5)	0.3 (0.3)	0.0	1.1 (0.9)
Not suitable	0.0	2.6 (2.3)	1.8 (1.5)	3.4 (3.0)	7.8 (6.9)
Total	1.6 (1.5)	4.6 (4.1)	3.7 /(3.2)	3.4 (3.0)	13.3 (11.8)

Source: Fischer et al. (2010)

Thus, much of the land would be capable of producing only at low to medium average yields. Typical medium average yields for winter wheat are in the range 3–5 t/ha, or for wetland rice 3–6 t/ha. Only with very intensive management and high levels of inputs could most of these lands produce maximum attainable yields of up to 10t/ha for winter wheat and 9t/ha for wetland rice. In addition, there would be a high opportunity cost to conversion from existing land use. All of this land currently forms part of existing ecosystems with high economic, social and environmental value, which would be lost by change of use. A large fraction may not available for crop production due to its protected status, its carbon sequestration and biodiversity value (including forests), and its current use for feeding the world's 3.5 billion ruminant livestock (Fischer *et al.*, 2010).

Finally, land with crop production potential not in agricultural use is unevenly distributed between regions and countries, and does not always correspond to where the market and economic opportunities for expanded production exist. In the developing world, the regions with the largest apparent potential for agricultural expansion are sub-Saharan Africa and Southern America. In the developed world, Europe, Russia, Northen America and Australia have large areas of suitable land. Half of the total balance is concentrated in just seven countries: Brazil, Democratic Republic of the Congo, Angola, Sudan, Argentina, Colombia and Bolivia. At the other extreme, there is virtually no spare land available for agricultural expansion in the agricultural areas of South Asia, East Asia, the Near East and Northern Africa.

Conclusions

This chapter has shown how global land and water resources have been exploited to respond to large increase in demand. Most of the additional agricultural production has been derived from intensification, particularly on prime agricultural land with the application of irrigation. Rainfed systems in the tropics and mountain regions, by contrast, have exhibited slower increases in productivity and have proved more vulnerable to food insecurity and poverty. Many uses of land and water systems are continuing to impose negative impacts on ecosystem services, both on- and off-site.

Yet world food production could increase by 70 percent over the next 40 years (and could double in developing countries). While it is likely that production will respond to rising demand, it is the way it will achieve it that will be important. Success will therefore be measured not just in terms of a stable and reliable supply of quality food for the world's population. The environmental sustainability of the main land and water systems, and their capacity to satisfy the livelihood requirements of both urban and rural populations, will be important criteria as well.

Policy-makers will need to take decisions on trade-offs between production and environment. It is only in the light of full information on the consequences for socio-economic outcomes and environmental impacts that decisions can be make. Decisions will need to be accompanied by measures to reduce negative impacts of policy decisions, and risks will require management if production is to meet rising demand without further degradation of land and water resources, or without compromising food security and poverty targets.

Photos: FAO Mediabase, J. Morgan

Chapter 2
SOCIO-ECONOMIC PRESSURES AND INSTITUTIONAL SET-UP

Population increase and changed consumption patterns are the major drivers of the pressures on land and water systems that have been described in Chapter 1. Social and cultural dependency on land and water has changed as agricultural transitions and urbanization have accelerated in a more interconnected world. Many inter-related policies (including trade, rural subsidy regimes and production incentives) have promoted land and water use. But land and water management tends to lag behind macro-economic policy and sector development plans. In many cases active management has occurred only after environmental degradation has occurred.

This lack of natural resource perspective continues even where a limited natural resource base and high population growth rates are placing extreme pressure on resources. In short, macro-economic planners tend to be more concerned with supply and demand for agricultural products than with the supply of natural resource inputs and whether these are constrained or are reaching limits.

The large-scale spatial management of land and water systems started with the rise of river valley civilizations and associated agrarian development. More recently, land and water institutions have evolved to facilitate the success of intensive crop production associated with the breakthrough in genetic research – the so-called 'green revolution'. But in practice, few successful institutions have been developed specifically for integrated land and water management. Recent research has found that land and water institutions have not kept pace with patterns of use and competition, and have rarely succeeded in regulating environmental and economic impacts. In this respect, policy alignment and institutional integration have remained an aspiration rather than an operational reality. Land-use and agriculture planning, for example, is often decoupled from river basin planning and operational management for hydropower or navigation purposes. As a result, it can be argued that economic opportunities have been forgone and that a return to a much better-informed, more knowledge-rich integration of land and water is warranted.

This chapter examines the current state of institutions for land and water, and how they have both driven ever higher levels of output, as well as providing too little for social, economic and environmental sustainability. This has been to the detriment of the land and water resource base and related ecosystems, and has had severe implications for poverty and food insecurity.

Socio-economic dependency on land and water

As agriculture becomes more productive, output per unit of land and per capita grows, incomes can be expected to rise, poverty reduces and food security improves, leading to reinvestment in the rural economy. In general, more intensive agriculture through irrigation has often arisen where the variability of rainfed production has proved intolerable. However, intensive agriculture has not always resulted in more rural employment and in many cases public agencies with limited budgets have had to make choices about the most desirable styles of agriculture. For instance, public investment in promoting rainfed agriculture may generate high distributional impacts but lower total growth when compared with investment in irrigated agriculture, where growth can be high but beneficiaries fewer. These considerations notwithstanding, the worldwide distribution of undernourished and food-insecure people, including those in countries in protracted crises, remains varied (FAO and WFP, 2010) and cannot always be linked to levels of agricultural productivity. Population pressure in resource-poor countries remains a key driver (Alexandratos, 2005, 2009).

The links between poverty, access to land and water, and land degradation

Worldwide, the poorest either have no land or have the lowest access to land and water (Figure 2.1), and low access to land is a predictor of poverty. In addition, poor resource management and type of farming system are also linked to poverty. The poorest often have the least-diversified farming systems. However, not all the poor live in lands considered degraded (Figure 2.2). Worldwide, only 16 percent of the poor live in degraded areas. Small changes in ecosystem health, in poor and populous areas have a significant effect, irrespective of the current ecosystem status, as the poor are heavily dependent on ecosystem health and the small surpluses they obtain can be wiped out by small negative changes in system health.

A wide variety of monetary and non-monetary indicators have been used to assess poverty levels (Coudouel *et al.*, 2002). FAO uses stunting among young children as a poverty-related chronic undernourishment measure (Gross *et al.*, 1996; FAO and FIVIMS, 2003). Indeed, where a single indicator of poverty is sought, 'stunting prevalence is one of the most reliable and most suitable indicators for monitoring and assessing poverty' (Simondon, 2010). Map 2.1 shows the prevalence of stunting among children under five years of age. It shows that high concentrations of poverty are found in Africa and Asia, particularly in sub-Saharan Africa and India. In sub-Saharan Africa as a whole, nearly half (45 percent) of the rural population are classified as poor. Map 2.2 shows the distribution of the number of poor people (based on density distribution of stunted children): in absolute terms, most of the world's poor people live in Asia.

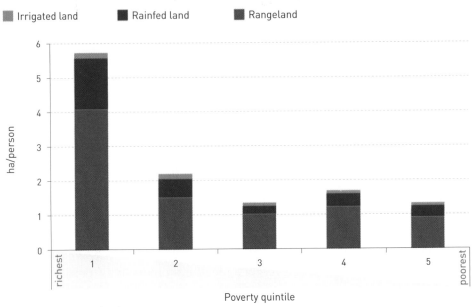

Source: Geodata Institute (2010)

FIGURE 2.2: RELATION BETWEEN LAND DEGRADATION AND POVERTY

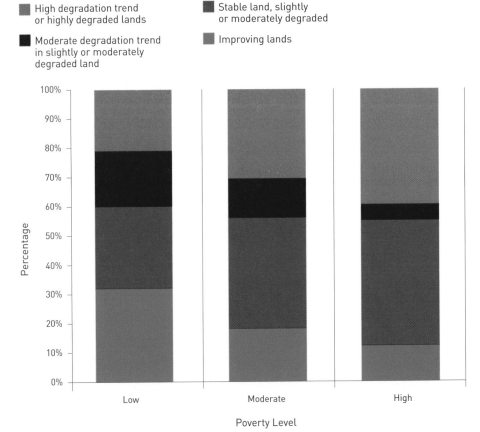

Data sources: FAO (2007a); LADA (2010a)

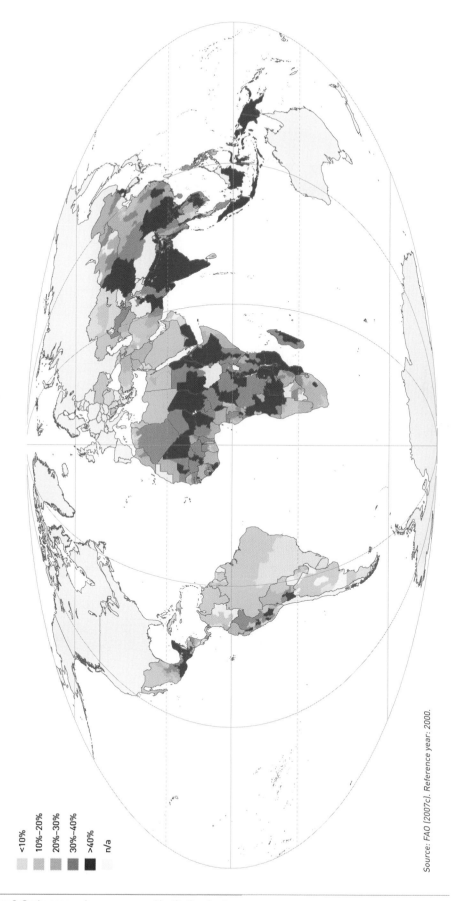

<10%
10%–20%
20%–30%
30%–40%
>40%
n/a

Source: FAO (2007c). Reference year: 2000.

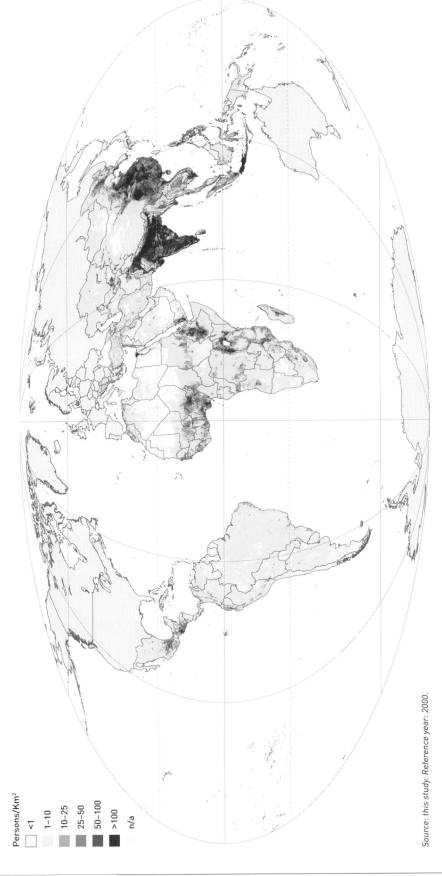

MAP 2.2: DENSITY DISTRIBUTION OF POOR PEOPLE, BASED ON STUNTING AMONG CHILDREN

Persons/Km²

- <1
- 1–10
- 10–25
- 25–50
- 50–100
- >100
- n/a

Source: this study. Reference year: 2000.

The concentrations of rural poverty can be linked to marginal lands where access to land and water is uncertain. Commonly, poor farmers are locked in a poverty trap of small, remote plots with no secure tenure, poor-quality soils and high vulnerability to land degradation and climatic uncertainty. At the same time, technologies and farming systems within their reach are typically low-management, low-input systems that often contribute to resource degradation. However, improved farming systems can modify the relationship between land and water resources and poverty: the likelihood of being poor is much lower (less than half) when improved farming systems are employed (Hussain and Hanjra, 2004). Thus, improving land and water tenure arrangements and management practices in these areas is likely to have a direct positive impact on food insecurity and poverty (Lipton, 2007).

Intensification and poverty reduction

The rapid productivity gains of the green revolution in Asia during the second half of the 20th century was achieved through technologies of nitrogen-responsive, short season cultivars and application of irrigation. It helped create a 'springboard' out of poverty in Asia, and provided the foundation for the broader economic and industrial development that has occurred in the last 20 years (World Bank, 2005; Huang *et al.*, 2006). Empirical evidence for a sample of 40 countries shows that for each 1 percent improvement in crop productivity, poverty fell by 1 percent and the human development index rose by 0.1 percent (Irz *et al.*, 2001). However, it is important to emphasize that distribution of the benefits derived from increased production are not always equitable. In many cases it is the poorest losing both land and employment as a result of production intensification strategies, which could lower commodity prices locally and reduce incomes for poorer producers not engaged with farm intensification.

Irrigation and poverty reduction

A recent study of 26 irrigation schemes across six countries in Asia (Hussain, 2007) has furnished evidence that development of large-scale irrigated agriculture reduces poverty. The proportion of poor in such irrigated areas is much lower than in rainfed ones, especially in Southeast Asia and parts of India. Access to agricultural water reduces the incidence and severity of poverty. Agricultural water enables households to improve and stabilize crop productivity, grow high-value crops, generate high incomes and employment, and earn a higher implicit wage rate. Income inequality and poverty rates are consistently lower for irrigated areas, and households with access to agricultural water and other inputs are less likely to be poor.

A key criticism of irrigation development is that it provides benefits to a relatively small proportion of the population, giving them considerable value in terms of infrastructure and share of water resources (Smith, 2004). This inequity is partially offset by the multiplier effect of irrigation in generating additional welfare through market activity (inputs, labour, contracting, transport, processing and packaging).

Multiplier effects of greater than three have been found by various authors in Asia (Bhattarai and Narayanamoorthy, 2003; Hussain and Hanjra, 2004), although Smith (2004) assessed the range of multipliers to be from 1.3 to 2. The broader benefits of private and communal groundwater development in India have been demonstrated to be 'pro-poor' (Shah and Singh, 2004).

Irrigation reduces poverty in three ways: increased food output, greater demand for employment and higher real incomes. Irrigation also has longer-run effects on the poor through the multiplier effect that drives an increase in non-farm rural output and employment as the level of rural spending rises. Risk reduction is also an important impact of irrigation: reduced variability of output, employment and income reduces the vulnerability to risk of the poor. Improved opportunities for crop diversification also reduce risk. In turn, reduction in risk allows more productive investments to be made, and lessens the need for periodic liquidation of capital (e.g. livestock) in times of crisis. Other benefits may also accrue, such as reduced seasonal rural out-migration and improved girls' attendance at school.

However, despite these poverty-reducing benefits, many irrigated systems are still home to large numbers of poor. Irrigation can also have direct negative impacts on the poor in situations where adverse social, health and environmental costs of irrigation are so high that they outweigh the benefits received by the poor. Poverty incidence is also generally correlated with position within a scheme (tail-enders are typically poor) and with inequitable land distribution: irrigation's impact on poverty is highest where landholdings (and thus water) are equitably distributed (World Bank, 2008). It is also the case that the introduction of irrigated production in food staples can undermine the seasonal progression of producer prices enjoyed by rainfed producers who compete in the same local markets (FAO, 2006c).

Multiple uses of water

Beyond agricultural production, irrigation systems and infrastructure can provide further services, such as provision of potable water supply (formal and informal), stock watering, washing and laundry facilities, fishing (in ponds, rice paddies, irrigation and drainage channels), and fluvial transport. In some cases, well-designed systems provide electricity supply and bulk water (e.g. for cities and towns of the Fergana Valley in Central Asia). Despite these many potential uses of irrigation water and infrastructure, it is only recently that development projects have systematically incorporated these multiple functions and taken their benefits into account in the economic evaluation of irrigation development (Smits et al., 2008; FAO, 2011e).

Fish capture and production is also an important source of livelihood in rural areas. While most rural people, particularly in Africa and Asia, identify themselves as 'farmers', their households are usually engaged in a range of activities. People move and alter their activities in response to seasonal and annual variations, in particular the flood cycle. Each piece of land may seasonally serve as farmed field, grazing area and fishing ground. The importance of each activity depends on the socio-economic status of the people involved and the cultural settings, and is highly dynamic, changing as a response to environmental conditions. Such a strategy therefore not only ensures a diversified food base, but equally reduces the dependency on any single resource, and thus adds resilience to their livelihoods. Access rights change during the hydrologic cycle as ownership usually only applies to the land during the dry phase; when fields are flooded, everybody, including landless people, have rights to use the resources.

A sectoral approach to improve food security would therefore be counterproductive, as many rural people are involved in a variety of livelihood activities, inland fisheries often being one activity much overlooked.

Finding the balance between distribution and growth

As agriculture becomes more productive, output increases and food security improves. As agricultural productivity has doubled over the last 40 years, global levels of poverty and food insecurity have declined, even though malnourishment has persisted. Intensification of rainfed and irrigated production, combined with reduction of post-harvest losses and more reliable storage and transport, have been instrumental. However, these gains have not come without exerting pressure on natural capital to the extent that some land and water systems are exploited to their limits or degraded beyond economic remediation. The process of agricultural intensification has typically also been accompanied by a demographic transition out of agriculture as land consolidation, intensification and mechanization of agriculture proceed, even though labour intensity per hectare is higher in irrigated production.

By contrast, investment in rainfed agriculture generally results in higher distributional impacts but lower income growth outcomes for farmers. A policy choice between investing in rainfed agriculture as an instrument of poverty reduction with well-distributed impacts and in intensive, irrigated agriculture as an engine of growth (World Bank, 2007a) may become apparent when public budgets are limited. But generally, where rainfed agriculture is possible, a well-structured agriculture sector will have elements of both, with policies ensuring that investments in rainfed agriculture optimize growth as well as distribution, and that investments in irrigation maximize distributional impacts through a pro-poor strategy. The minimization of negative environmental impacts is critical for both.

Basic systems of allocation

Land and water management is underpinned by systems of allocation and tenure that provide access, security and incentives for profitable and sustainable use. Traditional land tenure systems may include protected rights, but often they are communally held. However, the pace of demographic and economic growth has created stresses over allocation and security of tenure, resulting in disputes over land and water, sometimes spilling over into conflict. In many cases this has led to widespread appropriation of communal rights by the powerful. At the same time, a variety of modern land tenure institutions have emerged. Formal and informal land tenure systems now overlap, although incorporating traditional institutions into modern ones remains a challenge. Such institutional adaptation has tended to lag behind the economic and social changes it was intended to accommodate. Arguably, the lack of secure tenure combined with rigid land markets has resulted in under-investment and inefficiency in the use of resources.

Irrigation water use rights have always been protected, but rapid economic and technological change has overwhelmed many traditional rights systems. Attempts are being made to recreate local communal institutions through water user associations (WUAs). At the basin level, competition between irrigation, municipal and industrial use, and increasingly hydropower is being addressed, but often there is a mosaic of tenure and use rules, so that there are few examples of well-ordered and regulated rights in use. At transboundary level, principles of equitable benefit-sharing and no uncompensated harm are accepted by many countries in regional and basin level protocols, but, again, are only applied sporadically.

Land tenure

Formal and informal land tenure systems now overlap. Through historic processes of competition and dispute resolution, land tenure institutions have been adapted to local socio-economic conditions (FAO, 2002a). The predominant form of traditional tenure was communal, with well-negotiated rules and norms for individual access. The resulting tenure usually provided security and incentives for farmers to invest in land and water development. Modern systems of legislation have then tended to overlay individual property rights systems on these traditional institutions. As a result, modern laws have rarely defined or protected communal rights. In some situations, this has led to progressive dispossession and inequity in land distribution.

Institutional adaptation has been slow. When population densities were low and farming systems at subsistence level, the tensions implicit in this legal asymmetry were largely latent. However, demographic pressures on resources have put stress on both resources and traditional institutions. At the same time, rapid technological and economic changes have taken place but have not been accompanied by adaptation of institutions.

Competition and disputes over land and water in rainfed cultivation areas have intensified. As competition has increased, institutions have not adapted to address emergent conflict over land and water. Such conflict has arisen from inequitable distribution, with concentration of resources in the hands of a few, and from the appropriation of traditional rights, often by former traditional leaders who converted communal tenure into private property. Clashes between traditional and modern systems have also resulted from changes in land and water use, for example between forest dwellers and agriculturalists, or when settlement agriculture has interrupted traditional pastoral practices. Conflicts have also arisen when land-use changes have caused separation of land and water rights previously managed jointly, for example when local watersheds that used to provide runoff to fields below have been converted to cultivation.

Conflict has also arisen between cultural groups within the production system. For example, conflict between landowners and landless labourers has long existed in Latin America, and has emerged in Africa between pastoralists and cultivators as population pressures on limited land and water resources have increased. In some countries, such as Brazil, landlessness has become a major political issue. Tensions between large landlords and tenants or share-croppers are also widespread in the Indian subcontinent and the Philippines.

Communal rights are often poorly defined and protected by law and regulations, resulting in widespread appropriation by the powerful in many places. Systems of communal tenure coexist in many countries with individual tenure. Communal systems are found in Africa, India, Brazil and Mexico. Historically, the introduction of modern individual tenure into predominantly communal tenure systems resulted in tensions, for example between indigenous populations and colonial settlers. More recently, similar tensions have arisen between farmers settling in new irrigation schemes and pastoralists (Hardin, 1968; McCay and Acheson, 1987). These kinds of conflicts tend to diminish incentives to adopt or maintain sustainable land and water management.

Communal systems are, nonetheless, capable of adapting. They give tenure security by providing individual and inheritable use rights, and have often adapted to rising scarcity by allowing for the emergence of rental markets for land and for sales within the community. Communal systems can thus provide some of the security of tenure that underpins sustainable land and water management. However, there are drawbacks: investment in land is often constrained because communal rights cannot be used as collateral for loans. The lack of secure status for traditional land tenure has resulted in underinvestment and inefficiency in the use of resources. Rainfed farmers with insecure tenure will either not invest or will opt for technologies with short-term returns, preferring, for example, vegetative contour strips rather than stone bunds to slow runoff and erosion, because the contour strips have a shorter pay-off period and therefore offer a quicker return with lower risk.

There has been no easily identifiable trend in land tenure reform. Land tenure reforms have been initiated on a periodic basis in response to population pressures and associated impacts on land quality, but such national initiatives as the enclosure or sale of public land are typically sporadic. However, these pressures are promoting more progressive examination of regional approaches and generic problems in land tenure (FAO, 2011b), and links between reliable land tenure systems and poverty reduction have been recognized.

Two broad lessons of experience have emerged. First, the nature of land tenure arrangements determines scope and quality of land management, and without stable and transparent arrangements, underinvestment and less sustainable farming practices result. Second, the incorporation of traditional or customary institutions into modern legal regimes remains a challenge.

Water-use rights

Water rights traditionally evolved to share irrigation water, but these have been overtaken by economic and technological change. Historically, the evolution of water-use rights systems has been driven more by irrigation development agendas than any other sectoral interest (Caponera, 1992; FAO, 2006e). For irrigation systems, land and water are inseparable components of the production system, and management institutions have dealt with them jointly in the form of irrigation districts, command area authorities and WUAs.

The development of water control technologies and energized pumping has enabled the expansion and intensification of irrigated areas. These have, however, been largely outside of communal institutions and regulation, and have altered previous patterns of use within irrigation schemes and across river basins. Traditional institutions have proved unable to cope with many of these alterations, and disputes over entitlements to water are now common (Box 2.1).

There has been a marked expansion of groundwater use in irrigated agriculture. Aquifer depletion and the accompanying deterioration of groundwater quality have been driven by demand for precision irrigation and economic incentives, such as rural energy tariffs that encourage a 'race to the pumphouse'. As shown by Shah (2009) in the case of India, formal attempts by states to regulate groundwater rights and extraction have had little or no impact. The challenge of intervening at the local

BOX 2.1: CONFLICT, ADAPTIVE CAPACITY AND A SHIFTING EQUILIBRIUM IN YEMEN'S WADI DAHR

Yemen has a long history of water conflict and of subsequent accommodation of change. Yet Wadi Dahr (close to Sana'a) had a long, well-documented history of managing its water resources well. Rules had been agreed over centuries through an evolving process of conflict, contentious judgements, and ultimate development and acceptance of new rules that progressively crystallized into an 'established tradition'.

In 1970, tubewell technology burst into the finely balanced water economy. A downstream community in the wadi complained to the court of the sheikh that upstream motor pumps had reduced the stream flow and disturbed 'laws and customs ... by which we have been guided for thousands of years'. This new conflict was resolved, but not by the courts. The rich and influential downstream farmers simply invested in the new pump technology themselves. 'The stream dwindled and died, but no one with influence any longer cared.' A new equilibrium emerged: assets were rebalanced and concentrated more in the hands of the richer. The conflict was resolved, and a new 'established tradition' had emerged.

Sources: Mundy (1995); World Bank (2010b)

level in the regulation of hundreds of thousands of groundwater users can exceed the capacity of many water pressure administrations, but this is not to say that local autonomous solutions are impossible (Blomquist, 1992).

If the institutional and incentives framework remains unchanged, the current patterns of agricultural groundwater use (Siebert *et al.*, 2010) will continue to result in permanent damage to both the quantity and quality of strategic groundwater reserves. Important sources of freshwater for growing rural, municipal and industrial demands are also affected. For groundwater, local 'point of abstraction' regulation is required, and better-informed management by water user groups may offer a way to moderate the demand for groundwater, or at least bring local agreement on the maximum admissible drawdown in shared aquifers (World Bank, 2010a).

Institutions also have to arbitrate between agriculture, municipal and industrial needs (and increasingly hydropower). Governments generally give priority to abstractions for municipal and industrial supplies. Although the volumes are often relatively small in comparison with uses in agriculture or the in-stream requirements for maintaining hydropower generation, rising allocations to municipal and industrial uses are raising levels of water stress. In water-scarce regions such as the Middle East and Northen Africa, there is strong competition among sectors, and water allocations to agriculture are diminishing, such as in Jordan. The institutional rules to govern surrender of water entitlements are highly contested, and reallocation of water out of agriculture can lead to social unrest. In many developed river basins, competition for releases between irrigation and hydropower can both constrain optimal allocation between the productive sectors and compromise the reliability and quality of flows for municipal water supply.

At the transboundary level, cooperative principles rather than water rights have been adopted as the best approach. The high political and economic cost of development by individual states, and the loss of the extra value if investment were planned at the basin scale, have led to a number of cooperative agreements and the development of principles of 'equitable use' and 'no significant harm', which are codified in the (as yet unratified) Convention on the Law of Non-Navigational Uses of International Watercourses. In practice, though, nations have largely given priority to their own internal water agendas over those that require cooperation and benefit-sharing (Bingham *et al.*, 1994; Yetim, 2002).

Under conditions of intensifying competition, the need to manage land and water jointly becomes even more pressing (FAO, 2004b). However, the relationship between land tenure and water-use rights is highly variable, with a mosaic of regimes even within countries. For example, some states in the USA and in India adopt prior appropriation rules while others give precedence to upstream claims. At the same time, the use of land has major impacts on both the quality and quantity of water resources, so that decisions regarding the use and allocation of one resource impact directly or indirectly on the use and allocation of the other. There is thus strong advocacy in many countries for integrated approaches to the use and management of land, water and other natural resources. In rare cases, such as the Andhra Pradesh Water, Land and Trees Act of 2002, these approaches have been translated into law.

Policy responses to date

Policies and their incentive frameworks are the mechanisms by which governments seek to align development with societal objectives. Land and water use in agriculture is at the crossroads between several suites of policies, which can easily lack alignment or work at cross-purposes. As a result, policies and incentives have often driven unsustainable use and the proliferation of negative environmental externalities.

Agricultural policies typically aim at growth with equity, but sometimes result in damage to the environmental services on which growth depends – for example, fertilizer subsidies contribute to nutrient pollution, or energy subsidies to groundwater depletion. The typical objective of land policy is to ensure equitable, secure access. Yet institutions for defining, negotiating and managing access problems are often under-resourced. Past supply-driven water policies have created excess demand for water in many basins. In recent years, integrated water resource management policies have been adopted, applying intersectoral, often decentralized approaches. As a result, better options have emerged for efficient allocation and management of scarce water resources, but these are only slowly being applied.

By contrast, environmental policy has emerged as an active force in diagnosing problems, but it is often catching up rather than intervening with foresight, and is generally weak in regulatory capacity. Environmental policy faces particular challenges in low-income countries in influencing the development agenda, where it may be seen as anti-development, or even anti-poor. Some joint land and water management approaches have arisen, both for specific environmental problems and from introduction of basin planning, and land and water master-planning. However, these have had little impact on macro-economic planning or on development, although basin planning has improved water resource management practices and accountability.

Agriculture and related policies

The policies and institutions related to land and water management are generally designed in line with national objectives, typically principles of efficiency, equity and sustainability. But choices and decisions at lower levels (provincial, local, individual farmers) also shape policies and institutions. Policy objectives aimed at efficiency in the allocation of resources to create the highest economic value are tempered by an equity objective that may aim to alleviate poverty in rural economies. The third objective of sustainability reflects the long-run interest in protecting natural capital to maintain a flow of environmental services upon which growth and livelihoods depend.

Objectives have tended to be translated into a policy and institutional framework through a range of instruments. These include price and trade policy, fiscal policy and budget allocations, legislation and institutional set-ups for land and water administration, and agricultural services. A dominant feature of agricultural policy has been the influence of the incentive framework transmitted through the tax regime, subsidy policies and the pricing of inputs, particularly for fertilizers and energy. Policies that affect the costs of production, such as trade policy, tariff barriers and export bans, have also proved powerful incentives. Some of these policies have led to unintended negative impacts on the environment.

Land policy

The typical objective of land policy is to ensure equitable, secure access (Molden, 2007). Land policies set the framework for how land is allocated and how land use is planned. Land policies may also set rules for investment in land, including commercial and sovereign investment. Land policies also define and regulate land tenure rules, administration and dispute resolution, and manage the information base for land-based taxation (FAO, 2004a). A land policy may also provide for specific land tenure measures, such as: management, development and privatization of public lands; consolidation of fragmented land (FAO, 2003); and land reform and distribution of former collective lands (as in the former Soviet Union). Particular problems are:

- **Under-resourced institutions for defining, negotiating and managing access** – poorly functioning land registration, weak defence of rights, and poorly performing markets for both ownership and rental.

- **Common property regimes that adapt poorly to changing socio-economic conditions.** Well-functioning common property regimes are governed by agreed rules with no free riders, with low competition and high cooperation. As discussed above, where traditional institutions become weak or do not adapt, individuals may exploit common resources outside the rules, with resulting overexploitation and degradation.

- **Gender and land access.** In many societies women perform most of the agricultural work, and may be sole operators of a family farm, yet tenure rules often exclude them, so that they have no access to land title, and hence have no security of tenure or access to bank credit (FAO, 2002c; Ellis, 2000).

- **Inward commercial and sovereign investment.** Inward investment in land for production is on the rise. Lands may be allocated by governments under modern land tenure statutes when the lands are already owned and in use under traditional tenure arrangements. Unless policies and institutional mechanisms are in place to ensure the interest of local people, growth of this phenomenon could lead to impoverishment, food insecurity, and social and political tensions (Cotula *et al.*, 2009).

Water policy

Many water policies and sector strategies have been dominated by a focus on supply. The development of water resources to supply irrigation, hydropower, and municipal and industrial demands has characterized the activities of river basin agencies for most of the 20th century. Massive investments have been made in large public irrigation schemes, and during the 1960s to the 1980s more than half the public agriculture budget in many countries and more than half of World Bank agricultural lending was directed to irrigation (Rosegrant and Svendsen, 1993). Arguably, this supply-driven approach has led to excess demand in many countries. In countries where water is short, resources may have been over-allocated to one sector (typically agriculture), creating rigid entitlements. Water charging policies that have depressed the real cost of supply may have encouraged overuse (FAO, 2004c). Water entitlements locked into these uses have proved hard to negotiate downward even as farmers have increased their water productivity. However, the pressure to account for water use in agriculture in social, economic and environmental terms is building (OECD, 2010a).

As many nations came to the end of the period of 'easy' expansion of irrigation, problems of rising costs, excess demand and fiscal over-commitment have become apparent. At the same time, negative environmental and socio-economic impacts emerged. Adjusting supply and demand while also taking into account sets of environmental externalities requires institutional change. Responses typically include demand management measures, such as pricing measures, rationing and reduced allocations. However, poverty reduction and food security goals also had to be taken into account and a rationale for integrated water resource management set.

Integrating land and water into macro-economic planning processes

The need for more integrated land and water planning and management to address intensifying competition for resources has been identified, and some joint land and water approaches have emerged. What began as the aspiration of geographers to combine hydrology with earth and social sciences (Chorley, 1969) was integrated into global initiatives such as the 1992 Rio Conference on Environment and Development and the related conventions on biodiversity, desertification and climate change. To date, two types of approach have emerged: (1) as a remediation of the negative side-effects of intensive agriculture (the clean-up of the Rhine and Danube systems in Europe and the adoption of the European Union Water Framework Directive are cases in point; see Box 2.2); and (2) as a means of planning development at the basin or regional scale, which forced consideration of land management and the circulation of water through and across it.

Generally, it is in the highly developed river basins in post-industrial economies, such as the Danube and the Rhine (with correspondingly high levels of infrastructural development and intensive use), where the management of land and water have been tightly linked and regulated to protect rights in use and to reduce environmental impacts. Elsewhere, land and water management have been decoupled by default, as different institutions have responded to specific demands from their respective sectors, or by design in order to free up natural resource transfers among users and sectors. The evolution of the Murray-Darling basin, Australia is a case in point.

Despite these advances, few natural resource management criteria are used in macro-economic and sector planning. It is only where land and water constraints impact economic growth that more explicit forms of land and water planning and management appear on the political agenda, as for example with integrated landscape planning ('*gestion du terroir*') in Burkina Faso.

The EU Water Framework Directive (WFD) was adopted in October 2000 in response to increasing demand by EU citizens and environmental organizations for cleaner rivers, lakes, groundwater and coastal beaches. Early European water legislation began with standards for rivers and lakes used for drinking water abstraction in 1975, followed in the 1980s by quality targets for drinking water, and legislation on fish and shellfish waters, bathing waters and groundwater. In 1991, the Urban Waste Water Directive imposed secondary wastewater treatment, and the Nitrates Directive addressed water pollution by nitrogen from agriculture. Later, the Drinking Water Directive reviewed and tightened drinking water quality standards, and in 1996 an Integrated Pollution Prevention and Control Directive (IPPC) addressed pollution from large industrial installations.

Pressure for a fundamental rethink of EU water policies came to a head in mid-1995, when the EU was requested to address in a more coherent fashion the increasing awareness of citizens and other involved parties for the quality and the management of their water resources. The main purpose of the new European Water Policy was to reduce pollution and ensure clean waters are kept clean. It had the following aims:

- expanding the scope of water protection to all waters, surface waters and groundwater;
- achieving 'good status' for all waters by a set deadline;
- water management based on river basins;
- 'combined approach' of emission limit values and quality standards;
- getting the prices right;
- getting the citizen involved more closely; and
- streamlining legislation.

Citizens were put at the centre of the reform process: the policy was thus developed through an inclusive and open consultation process involving representatives of Member States, regional and local authorities, enforcement agencies, water providers, industry, agriculture and, not least, consumers and environmentalists.

Source: European Commission (2010)

Integrated spatial 'master plans' today have little influence on development. In the 1970s and 1980s, detailed land-use planning was carried out for agricultural purposes (e.g. classification of soils and land-use suitability) and incorporated in area development 'master plans'. However, these plans were generally used as information repositories rather than as spatial planning instruments. District or county structure plans today in industrial countries give broad zoning demarcations, including 'green space' and environmental reserves, but they are not generally used for detailed agricultural planning or environmental management of land use.

Basin planning has, however, improved water resource management and accountability. The emphasis on district or river basin water master plans in the 1970s and 1980s has not continued, although their legacy has formed a variety of river basin-based water allocation and management institutions (e.g. River Basin Offices in Tanzania), and continues to provide a strong information baseline for national inventories of water use. These master plans also helped in the first compilation of FAO AQUASTAT data in the late 1980s. Overall, although land policy and management may not have always been coupled with basin planning, the 'sentiment' of integrated water resource management has prompted adoption of more progressive water accounting and environmental regulation. The degree to which these basin planning approaches have succeded in mitigating negative socio-economic and environmental impacts remains open to question (Molle and Wester, 2009).

Institutional approaches and performance

The institutional responses to rising demands on land and water include the policies, incentives, norms laws and rules that allocate resources and regulate their use. These land and water institutions are taken to include:

- land and water development policies, plans and organizations, and systems of allocation and protection of land and water rights;

- related agricultural policies, plans and organizations, together with broader policies affecting incentives such as fiscal policy and trade policy; and

- environmental policy and organizations dealing with regulations and incentives for natural resource protection, and the consequences of the 'externalities' of land and water use.

For land and water, the challenge is that, while governments may make policies, management is largely the responsibility of farmers. Ministries of agriculture or rural development usually have primary responsibility for guiding land and water management, but it has become increasingly common for services such as extension to decline precisely where they are most needed. Some attempts at joint approaches to land and water have been effective at the watershed level, but much more attention is needed to integrate approaches for land and water. Few programmes are yet to persist long enough to achieve significant results.

Nonetheless, land-use planning has improved, with more accessible tools, and it has been effective in land resource allocation in some developed countries. But such land-use planning has had little impact on development programmes in developing countries, and there has been limited compliance with plans in countries with little or no institutional capacity. Some decentralized and participatory land-use planning has been successful, but generally only at local levels.

Agriculture agencies

The primary institutional responsibility for land and water management has rested with ministries of agriculture or rural development. The role of these agencies in delivering technical and support services to rural communities or to individual farmers has been to encourage the uptake of inputs and the adoption of improved agronomic practice. In some cases, the role of the private sector and equipment suppliers has been important, particularly in the application of precision irrigation. It has been rare for traditional extension services deploying under-resourced government officers in the field to have more than limited impact on improving productivity in land and water management. In a recent global review of extension practice (FAO, 2008b) the case has been made for transforming national advisory services into decentralized, farmer-led, market-driven extension systems.

Watershed management approaches

An example of an institutional approach is the watershed management approach, which seeks to manage both land and water and the wider ecosystem of the watershed in an integrated way. Successes have been limited so far, partly because of the asymmetry of interests between upstream and downstream stakeholders, and partly because of the sheer complexity of the perceptions of natural and anthropogenic functions at the scale of a watershed (see Box 2.3).

The first generation of watershed management projects in developing countries in the 1970s and 1980s applied a soil and water planning approach that emphasized engineering works for specific on-site and downstream physical outcomes. In general, too little attention was paid to the needs of upstream populations or to their ownership of programme actions. As a result, investments were high-cost and not always well justified, and the assets created often had a limited life. By the end of the 1980s, the comparative failure of this 'engineering-led' approach was clear, and a major rethinking of watershed management approaches was undertaken by national and international agencies.

The 1990s represented a departure for watershed management programmes supported by the international community in developing countries. While engineering solutions were not excluded, the emphasis was placed more on farming systems and on participatory approaches implemented in a decentralized fashion. Support was given by the renewed emphasis on rural poverty reduction in development programmes. The move away from planned investments towards participatory approaches was designed to seek synergies between both local land and water

BOX 2.3: WATERSHED MANAGEMENT EFFECTS ON THE WATER CYCLE

Experience from SE Zimbabwe exposes the myth that 'poor agricultural practices in the headwaters lead to increased siltation in reservoirs'. The large sugar estates of the lowlands are major agribusiness users of water, and rely on an extensive series of mid-catchment storage dams that now face problems of sedimentation. This increased sediment is blamed on poor farming practices, including deforestation and overgrazing by the 'indigenous', 'subsistence' farmers of the headwaters.

Following the devastating drought of the early 1990s, some of the sugar estates started outreach programmes to work with farmers in the headwaters to 'improve' their land management. By the late 1990s, those involved in the outreach programme were reporting positive results: the suspended solids entering their dams were decreasing dramatically. Yet, there appeared a contradiction: the outreach programme was tiny, and the catchment area large. Research also revealed a ten-year cyclical pattern of above and below 'average' rainfall, possibly related to the El Niño southern oscillation (ENSO). The 1980s had been the driest on record.

The combination of research and local farmers' perspectives resulted in an alternative narrative to that of the sugar cane farmers. During the long dry years, water levels drop, shrubs and grass die, and livestock (before dying) exacerbate the situation by eating everything available. During this period, sediment levels generally increase, as erosion occurs when rain does come. In particular, large storm events at the end of the dry period move huge quantities of 'stored' soil. However, once a wetter period is entered, browse and crop cover quickly returns, aided by low livestock numbers, and erosion more or less ceases. Photographs of the study site in the 1990s show bare red earth; yet since then, vegetation has been lush. Sediment measured leaving a small headwater catchment where there had been no outreach programme and where subsistence agriculture was being practised never exceeded 5 t/ha – far below the 70-100 t/ha reported from many plot-based experiments.

Source: FAO (2002b)

management benefits and downstream impacts. However, the timeframe for implementation is generally long, and few programmes have persisted for long enough to achieve significant results, and even then the long-term impacts on the water resource base can be questionable (Batchelor *et al.*, 2003).

Land-use planning

Land-use planning has formed a part of area development planning since the 1970s, such as through soil surveys and land capability or evaluation mapping exercises (FAO, 1976, 2007b). With the advent of cheaper computing systems, more sophisticated geographical information system (GIS) approaches have been deployed, for example in Kenya, Swaziland and Bangladesh (all supported by FAO). However, while national capacities in land-use decision-making have been strengthened, these have not translated into agricultural plans or investment strategies, mainly because they were attempting to be too deterministic (deciding which crops should be grown based on soil and terrain conditions) at a time when economic liberalization and market penetration was advancing. Where plans have been developed, compliance has been limited as there is little or no institutional capacity to regulate land-use. By contrast, land use planning in Europe has tended to play a more structural role in allocating land to different uses: urban, forests, farming or protected areas.

In general, land-use planning has been more successful at the local scale and generally has had only weak links to the larger scale. When tied to decentralization and agriculture sector support programmes, there is more evidence of localized investment and support for land-use planning. The adoption of participatory rural appraisals (PRAs) as a primary planning tool in the 1990s has improved local-level ownership. However, the decentralized and demand-driven focus has contributed to fragmentation. This remains one of the main issues in watershed management, for example, where participatory and demand-driven planning at local level is not matched with the needs of those downstream or with integrated plans for basin-wide land and water management.

Irrigation management agencies

Given the scale of public funding to medium- and large-scale irrigation, the role of government agencies in developing, operating and maintaining irrigation systems has been dominant. But few publicly managed large irrigation schemes have achieved fiscal efficiency or demand-responsive water service (Molden, 2007). The major causes of poor service delivery are bureaucratic institutions and rigid techni-cal design, both of which generally originate in a top-down, planning-led approach to irrigation. There has been a vicious circle of insufficient funding, inadequate operation, and maintenance and system deterioration, often leading to the need for successive rehabilitations.

Nonetheless, governments have been transferring some responsibility for large-scale irrigation management to user groups. But the experience with partici-patory irrigation management (PIM) and irrigation management transfer (IMT) has been mixed (FAO, 2007a; Molden, 2007, Ch. 5). In the evolution from public to collective and market-oriented institutions, irrigation management is going to have to be more contextualized and pluralistic (Meinzen-Dick, 2007). However, the issue of covering operation and maintenance costs and turning transferred assets into profitable, viable operations remains considerable (Box 2.4).

In Romania, irrigation systems depend heavily on pumping. Out of a total of 3.1 Mha of developed land in the late 1980s, about 2.85 Mha were under sprinkler irrigation, with heavy energy costs: in some places, the static lift of irrigation systems exceeds 270 m. After the dissolution of state and collective farms in 1990, there was no clearly designated authority for the operation and maintenance of irrigation infrastructure, and national organizations had neither the staff nor the budgetary resources to take such responsibility. As a result of ageing of the irrigation infrastructure, complicated by an inability of both the government and farmers to pay for energy costs, the earlier annual irrigation use of 2 500–3 000 m³/ha dropped to about 1 000 m³/ha, and the revenues from fee collection became insufficient to cover the cost of maintenance of the infrastructure. In addition, on-farm equipment and pumps had been destroyed or stolen, or were too old to operate properly.

The Land Reclamation Law of 1999 formalized the creation of WUAs and completely restructured the National Land Reclamation Society (SNIF) into a land reclamation agency, which included significant staff reduction, transfer of authority to regional offices, as well as a stronger WUA role in systems management. Now canals and secondary pressure pump stations are operated by WUA staff who are also responsible for fee collection. The law was further modified in 2004 and 2005 to allow WUAs to control management from the primary pumps to the river. At present only about 700 000 ha are being irrigated, owing to lack of maintenance of the irrigation systems and the age of the large pumping units, as well as the costs of energy. The Land Reclamation Law established that an irrigation system can only be operated if there is a demand for water of at least 20 percent of its command area, both at the distributary canal and overall system levels. The challenge for the WUAs remains that of being able to maintain enough area under irrigation to be able to properly maintain the existing infrastructure.

Source: FAO (2007a)

In some cases, the private sector has been effective in introducing modern irrigation by helping to introduce more advanced farming practices, such as downstream control, surge irrigation, subsoil drip and fertigation. These have been led by privately financed initiatives where market conditions have exerted a strong pull for precision irrigation. The efficiency of some private initiatives sometimes stands in stark contrast to publicly run schemes: for example, the productivity of the privately run Kenana sugar estate in central Sudan compared with the vast public Gezira scheme only 100 km to the north, where the full operation of the sugar estate compares with only partial cropping within the Gezira. Another example is the advent of shallow groundwater access in many gravity irrigation commands across India, which has triggered what Shah (2009) terms 'atomistic irrigation' – a private response to the institutional and hydraulic failure of the command area authorities.

Overall, there is a need for more flexibility and responsiveness in irrigation management, which requires well-thought-out capacity-building programmes as much as modernized infrastructure (FAO, 2007e).

As these private operators have demonstrated they can manage commercial schemes, so public–private partnership (PPP) models might be adaptable to private management of smallholder schemes. Large-scale commercial operators in premium crops such as sugar, tea and citrus fruits have been efficient irrigation managers, even under difficult circumstances. It is possible that private operators could run public schemes; however, experience is limited to date. A review of emerging PPPs in irrigation (World Bank, 2007b) recommends that bringing in a third-party service provider to improve service efficiency makes sense, but that in doing so careful attention has to be paid to mitigating risks for third-party service providers.

The emergence of flexibility outside the public sector

Overall, the liberalization of irrigated agriculture, away from centralized planning and production quotas or the dominance of price support schemes, has seen irrigated production respond to changing market demands with a more diverse set of crops. Traditional surface irrigation schemes have not been able to match the on-demand, just-in-time requirements for irrigation, but flexibility has been provided by a deepening reliance on groundwater (Shah, 2009), with all the consequent externalities generated by more intensive aquifer use (Llamas and Custodio, 2003).

As a result of growing water scarcity, both informal and formal water markets have developed for surface water and groundwater. Water markets have strong theoretical advantages and can be efficient, particularly local markets which can increase water-use efficiency with little infrastructure and minimal governance structures. Informal water markets have proven effective in distributing benefits derived from groundwater (Shah, 1993). Yet such formal markets exist only in Chile, Australia and the western USA. They have demanding requirements: clear, defensible water rights, an institutional and legal framework for trade, and infrastructure to transfer water between users.

Environmental consequences of past policy choices

Past policy and institutional approaches have raised land and water productivity and output, but have also led to environmental externalities in some regions. Agricultural policy has promoted mechanization, fertilization and pesticide use, all of which have created environmental risks and costs. In some cases, land policy has promoted expansion into marginal lands, along with forest and wetland clearance, while tenure insecurity has led to underinvestment and short-horizon production strategies. Water policy has promoted large-scale irrigation schemes, groundwater development and wholesale water abstractions. While most of these policies contributed to the rapid rise of productivity, they also contributed to widespread degradation of land and water resources. In recent years, environmental policy and organizations have been active in diagnosing these problems, but have been reactive rather than predictive, and have often been weak in regulatory capacity.

Environmental institutions have emerged in response to these environmental impacts of intensified farming, but face challenges in developing countries in influencing the development agenda. Following the 1992 Rio Conference, awareness of environmental problems rose, and most nations established an institutional framework of laws, policies and organizations to influence growth and natural resource management towards paths of environmental sustainability, and to limit and mitigate environmental degradation. These institutions have been effective in 'greening' the agenda, particularly in developed countries. For example, the US Environmental Protection Agency has established major programmes to reduce non-point sources of fertilizers and pesticides from agricultural land. However, environmental institutions have to cope with weak compliance, and tend to be reactive rather than proactive. A further problem is the ownership of the environmental agenda: although the environment has a voice in developed countries, in developing countries concern for the environment can be seen as anti-development, or even anti-poor, and environmental policy faces challenges in influencing the development agenda.

Unintended perverse incentives have also been a powerful driver of negative externalities. The incentives with which countries have promoted agricultural growth have frequently produced negative externalities, for example macro-economic and trade policies favouring food production and natural resource extraction in areas without comparative advantage. In some countries, distorted incentives have contributed to degradation of land and water (Box 2.5). Subsidized energy prices, for example, have driven the depletion of groundwater reserves in many countries.

The problem is not just the application of poorly adapted policies, but also the absence of good ones. Examples from Kenya and Ethiopia (Box 2.6) show the powerful effect on land and water of getting policies right, and the negative impacts of getting them wrong or leaving a policy vacuum.

A central problem is that costs and benefits of externalities are asymmetrical. On-site intensification may produce both on-site and downstream risks to land and water. For example, higher stocking rates for animals can exacerbate soil loss on-site, causing loss of fertility as well as downstream siltation. Intensified use of fertilizers may contaminate on-site groundwater and also cause downstream water pollution. On-site costs can be internalized; that is, if the incentive and enabling

BOX 2.5: THE IMPACT OF DISTORTED INCENTIVES ON LAND AND WATER MANAGEMENT

In some countries, a distorting incentive framework encourages degradation of land and water resources. Where fertilizer is heavily subsidized (e.g. Bangladesh, China), application rates tend to be beyond recommended levels, resulting in overuse. In 2008, Chinese farmers received US$84 per ha in fertilizer subsidy. In 2008–9, Bangladesh spent US$758 million on urea support. In both countries, large adverse impacts on groundwater quality resulted.

In Brazil, until the economic crisis of the early 1990s, credit subsidies and tax exemptions favoured the clearing of land in the Amazon region for often unsustainable production. The distorted incentive framework contributed to the permanent loss of forest ecosystems, but failed to encourage an efficient, equitable or sustainable agriculture.

Sources: Huang et al. (2011); Binswanger (1991)

BOX 2.6: HOW OVERALL POLICIES CAN INFLUENCE SUSTAINABLE LAND MANAGEMENT

In the former Machakos district of Kenya, population increased sixfold from the 1930s to 1990s, while agricultural output increased tenfold. Recent years have witnessed widespread adoption of erosion control measures and a significant increase in tree coverage. The conditions that favoured these developments were relatively favourable price policies, access to international markets for export crops, the development of infrastructure, the proximity to the market in Nairobi, the remittances sent by temporary migrants, secure individual rights to land, and local extension services helping with soil conservation practices.

In Ethiopia during the time of Haile Selassie and the Derg, farmers were heavily taxed through a variety of methods. Infrastructure and market development was minimal, and agricultural services largely absent. Access to domestic and international markets was often disrupted. Employment opportunities in the rural non-farm sector and the urban economy were limited. Land rights were highly insecure. Widespread deterioration of land resources resulted from the insecure rights, combined with poor infrastructure, market access and incentives, and from the policy distortions.

Sources: Tiffen et al. (1994); Grepperud (1994); Heath and Binswanger (1996)

framework encourages natural resource conservation, the farmer will correct practices that impair the productive capacity of his farm. But farmers rarely have incentives to correct externalities. Usually some adjustment to the incentive framework is needed. There is thus now a challenge of how to adjust the actual incentive structure so that upstream farmers (who bear most of the costs of acting on externalities but receive a smaller part of the benefits) are motivated to practise land and water conservation in their part of the watershed. There are some good examples of reconciliation of such conservation and intensification objectives (Box 2.7), but other programmes have had difficulty in establishing incentive structures that work.

As competition for land and water has increased, the lack of clear and stable use rights has reduced private incentives to invest and manage, and policies have too often driven unsustainable use and the proliferation of negative externalities. Despite the functional systemic integration of land and water, modern law and institutions now tend to deal with land and water separately. Even institutions dedicated to integrated resource management (such as basin agencies) deal primarily with a single resource in multiple uses, rather than with land and water jointly. This institutional gap has widened as natural resource planning has become increasing micro-focused, with decentralization and demand-driven approaches.

In addition to impacts on natural resources, there have been socio-economic costs such as competition and conflict where land and water resources have become scarcer and competition from other sectors has grown. Poverty and food insecurity have resulted from changes in the allocation of land and water resources, insecurity of tenure, or deterioration of land and water assets. In most basins and countries, the rate of socio-economic change and the accumulation of environmental impacts has outpaced institutional responses. The growing intensity of river basin development

---

BOX 2.7: WATERSHED REHABILITATION IN THE LOESS PLATEAU OF CHINA'S YELLOW RIVER BASIN

Unsustainable farming practices on the Loess Plateau of China's Yellow River Basin, including deforestation, overgrazing and poor land reclamation practices, together with growing population pressure over the last hundred years, has resulted in the reduction of protective vegetative cover to only 20 percent of the total area (Brismar, 1999). A successful watershed rehabilitation programme was implemented, including terracing, strip farming, sediment retention dams, and the large-scale planting of trees and grasses. About 2 100 small sediment control structures were built, capturing an estimated 25 million tonnes of sediment per year.

These measures improved both land and water quality through reduction of soil erosion and river sedimentation. Grazing bans, particularly on sloping lands, generated dense natural vegetation cover at low cost. Artificial grasses and herbs (mainly astragalus and alfalfa) were planted on flat or gently sloping wasteland as fodder for pen-fed animals and to reduce unsustainable grazing on slopes. The sustainable production systems established are now profitable for farmers. They now have the incentive to maintain these investments. This outcome has been obtained after high initial levels of public investment.

Sources: World Bank (2003, 2007d)

---

and the degree of interdependence and competition over land and water resources require more adaptable and authoritative institutions (Molle and Berkoff, 2006).

Investments in land and water

Investment in land and water management is essential for attaining sustainable increases in agricultural productivity. Overall investment in land and water has increased slightly in the last five years, but levels remain below those necessary to intensify production while minimizing negative impacts on the ecosystem. A particular concern is the low level of investment in the more vulnerable rainfed systems where poverty and food insecurity are prevalent and risks of land and water resource degradation are high.

Public investment in agriculture

Global public expenditure in agriculture doubled in real terms between 1980 and 2002, although declining from 11 percent to 7 percent of total public expenditures (Table 2.1). The increase in real expenditure is particularly evident in Asia, where it almost tripled to US$192 billion in 2002. Levels of public investment in agriculture across sub-Saharan Africa have remained low.

Private capital and foreign direct investments

In recent years, private capital and trade flows have concentrated more on the industrial nations which account for much of the surge in global foreign direct investment (FDI) flows, which reached US$1.1 trillion in 2000. Within developing countries, the overall flow of FDI has been heavily concentrated in East Asia and the Pacific, and in Latin America and the Caribbean, with scant investment in sub-Saharan Africa. The long-term trend, however, suggests a larger share for sub-Saharan Africa (Winpenny, 2010).

TABLE 2.1: PUBLIC EXPENDITURE IN AGRICULTURE IN SELECTED DEVELOPING COUNTRIES 1980–2002

Regions*	Constant 2000 US$ (billion)				Percentage of agricultural GDP				Agricultural share of total government expenditure (%)		
	1980	1990	2000	2002	1980	1990	2000	2002	1980	1990	2002
Africa (17)	7.3	7.9	9.9	12.6	7.4	5.4	5.7	6.7	6.4	5.2	4.5
Asia (11)	74	106.5	162.8	191.8	9.4	8.5	9.5	10.6	14.8	12.2	8.6
Latin America and Caribbean (16)	30.5	11.5	18.2	21.2	19.5	6.8	11.1	11.6	8.0	2.0	2.5
Total	111.8	125.9	190.9	225.6	10.8	8	9.3	10.3	11.3	7.9	6.7

* Number of developing countries examined in each region.

Source: Akroyd and Smith (2007)

Although agriculture attracts less than 1 percent of overall FDI in developing economies (US$14.3 billion from a total US$2 trillion stock in 2004), investment in the sector has been growing, tripling between 1990 and 2004 (Table 2.2). Part of these capital inflows have been commercial and sovereign investment in land and water under deals to produce food and biofuel feedstock. Concerns have been raised about the possible impact on equity and food security in host countries from this kind of investment (Box 2.8).

Future investment needs

Based on long-term estimates for food demand, FAO projects that gross investment requirements 2007–50 for primary agriculture and its related industries in developing countries could amount to US$9.2 trillion, with 18 percent of the total (US$960 billion) allocated to water management and irrigation, and about 3 percent (US$161 million) for land development, soil conservation and flood control (Table 2.3).

The bulk of the investment (58 percent) is expected to be in Asia, reflecting the region's large agricultural base, its high overall output and its relatively capital-intensive forms of agricultural production (Table 2.4). Rates of growth in agricultural production in Asia are more modest. The opposite is true for sub-Saharan Africa, where the overall level of investment requirements is expected to be relatively low as a consequence of the region's generally labour-intensive and capital-saving forms of production (9 percent of the total). Growth rates, however, are projected to be higher, reflecting a very gradual shift to a more capital-intensive form of agriculture and moderately rising per capita production levels, driven by a doubling of its population and consumer base.

TABLE 2.2: ESTIMATED INWARD FDI STOCK, BY SECTOR AND INDUSTRY, 1990 AND 2004 (MILLION US$)

Sector	1990			2004			
	Developed countries	Developing economies	World	Developed countries	Developing economies	Southeast Europe and CIS	World
Primary	139 563	23 715	163 278	268 171	151 632	20 725	440 529
• Agriculture	3 193	4 063	7 256	7 739	14 339	483	22 561
• Mining, quarrying and petroleum	136 371	17 601	153 972	256 642	137 294	20 242	414 177
• Unspecified Primary	–	2 051	2 051	3 791	–	–	3 791
Manufacturing	586 379	144 372	730 750	2 406 127	613 559	20 448	3 040 135
Services	716 544	151 589	868 133	4 624 699	1 224 356	34 286	5 883 341

Source: UNCTAD (2006)

Investments in fertile land in developing countries have significantly increased. Typically, land deals are for substantial blocks of land (over 10 000 ha) and have a lease period of between 50 and 99 years. The main actors involved are national governments, agricultural investment funds and the private sector, including investment banks, agribusinesses, commodity traders and mining companies (Smaller and Mann, 2009). These land acquisitions can be categorized into four types (Bickel and Breuer, 2009):

• Countries with large populations and sustained growth (China, India, Japan, South Korea) undertake investments to satisfy the increasing internal demand for agricultural products.
• Countries with negative food balances and limited land and water resources but rich in capital (Gulf states, Libya).
• Industrialized countries target land investments for biofuel production.
• Domestic land speculation in developing countries (e.g. for touristic purposes).

Land acquisition can be seen as a win–win strategy. The investor country acquires land and guaranteed access to the food produced, while reaping high financial returns. The recipient country

Number of land acquisition operations

Investor Countries

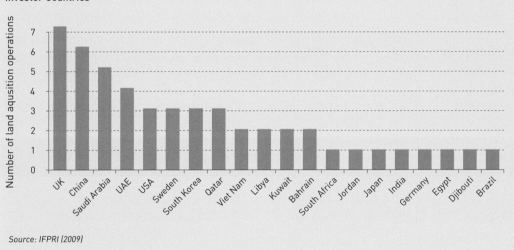

Source: IFPRI (2009)

International cooperation on land and water

International cooperation on land and water originated in the 1940s with concerns about food security, linked to the need for rural development in the newly emerging nations. From the 1980s, negative environmental impacts from unregulated use of natural resources became increasingly apparent at local, regional and global scales. The evaluation of the causes of these impacts brought land and water issues such as soil erosion, salinization of irrigated lands, spread of waterborne diseases, obtains an infusion of capital into its agricultural sector, leading to economic development. Yet these arrangements do contain risk for the investor (e.g. political risk in the host country) and for the citizens of the host country, who may face expropriation of land, labour abuses and loss of their own food security (Cotula et al., 2009).

As is the case for other international trade and foreign direct investment, 'rules of engagement' are advisable to ensure that foreign investments are beneficial to both host countries and land users who lose their land permanently or temporarily. These rules could include transparency in negotiation and trade deals, protection of investors, compensation of land users, respect for existing land rights, focus on investments with benefits for local communities, and assessment of potential positive or negative environmental impacts (Von Braun and Meinzen-Dick, 2009; Cotula et al., 2009). No single institutional mechanism will ensure favourable outcomes for all parties involved: rather, cooperation through international law, government policies, and the involvement of civil society, the media and local communities is needed to ensure that the land transactions follow the rules of engagement.

Target Countries

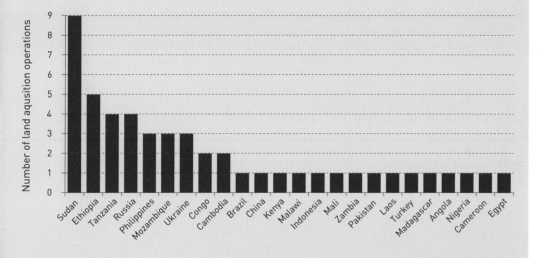

water resource depletion and pollution to international attention. Since the 1990s, further land and water issues in relation to reduction of biodiversity, climate variability and climate change have joined earlier environmental concerns. From these origins, sustainable land and water management issues have become an integral component of global focus on the food security, environment and climate change nexus of challenges.

TABLE 2.3: PROJECTED INVESTMENT NEEDS OVER THE PERIOD 2005–7 TO 2050 IN BILLION 2009 US$

	Net	Depreciation	Gross
Total for 93 developing countries	3 636	5 538	9 174
Total investment in primary production	2 378	2 809	5 187
of which crop production	*864*	*2 641*	*3 505*
Land development, soil conservation and flood control	139	22	161
Expansion and improvement of irrigation	158	803	960
Permanent crops establishment	84	411	495
Mechanization	356	956	1 312
Other power sources and equipment	33	449	482
Working capital	94	0	94
of which livestock production	*1 514*	*168*	*1 683*
Total investment in downstream support services	1 257	2 729	3 986

Source: Schmidhuber et al. (2009)

TABLE 2.4: REGIONAL DISTRIBUTION OF PROJECTED INVESTMENTS IN CROP PRODUCTION 2005–7 TO 2050

	Net	Depreciation	Gross	Share in total
	Billion 2009 US$			%
93 developing countries	3 636	5 538	3 505	100
Sub-Saharan Africa	478	462	319	9.1
Latin America and Caribbean	842	962	528	15.1
Near East and North Africa	451	742	619	17.7
South Asia	843	1 444	1 024	29.2
East Asia	1 022	1 928	1 015	29.0

Source: Schmidhuber et al. (2009)

Milestones and achievements

From the 1980s, the UN emerged as the forum where global values and principles for sustainable development were negotiated. Milestone conferences, including the Rio Summit (1992), the Millennium Summit (2000), and the Johannesburg Summit on Sustainable Development (2002), helped shape the global development agenda that was summarized in the 2002 Millennium Development Goals (MDGs). The Convention to Combat Desertification (UNCCD, Box 2.9), the Convention on Biological Diversity (CBD) and the Framework Convention on Climate Change (UNFCCC), all have important linkages to land and water management. In addition, the UN has sponsored global research and synthesis efforts like the Millennium Ecosystem Assessment (MEA), the Global Environmental Outlook, and the Intergovernmental Panel on Climate Change (IPCC).

The remarkable mobilization of the global community around sustainable development over the past 30 years has seen a consensus emerge on development pathways and benchmarks. Principles of economic, social and environmental sustainability have been adopted. From the successive conferences and resulting actions, there are clearer principles for important parts of the land and water management agenda, particularly for sustainable management of forests, for integrated water resource management and for combating desertification.

BOX 2.9: DESERTIFICATION: THE CHALLENGES OF LAND AND WATER IN DRYLANDS AND THE UNCCD RESPONSE

The world's drylands include desert, grassland, savannah and woodland, in climates ranging from the hottest deserts to the coldest arctic regions. Most of the dryland ecosystems are fragile, and suffer from water scarcity and low productivity. Dryland resources are increasingly threatened, as results of inappropriate management practices and overpopulation. The fight against desertification is also a fight against rural poverty and food insecurity, which are all strongly inter-related.

The United Nations Convention to Combat Desertification (UNCCD) is the centrepiece in the international community's efforts to combat desertification in the drylands. It was adopted in 1994, entered into force in 1996 and currently has 194 parties. The UNCCD recognizes the physical, biological and socio-economic aspects of desertification, the importance of redirecting technology transfer so that it is demand-driven, and the involvement of local communities in combating desertification and land degradation. The core of the UNCCD is the development of action programmes by national governments in cooperation with development partners. A strategic plan of action and framework was devised in 2008 to promote the mainstreaming and upscaling of sustainable land management (SLM) practices and enabling policies, in synergy with the food security, climate change and biodiversity agendas. These programmes aim to build collaboration among the concerned line agencies, and strengthen farmer and pastoralist organizations, along with decentralized capacities. They promote secured land tenure arrangements, new market opportunities (including green products), as well as participatory land use planning, research and extension programmes.

Action on the ground to combat desertification includes the upscaling of a number of practices based on sustainable intensification, such as conservation agriculture and no-tillage techniques, crop rotations and intercropping, integrated pest management, agro-forestry and reforestation schemes, and pasture improvement with planned grazing processes. Improved water management is promoted through the implementation of water harvesting and small-scale irrigation investments, at watershed and village levels.

International cooperation has also allowed countries to share knowledge and develop principles and approaches that can be applied at regional, national and local levels. The process has enabled countries to agree on actions where each nation and individual can contribute to sustainable management of 'global commons'. International cooperation has also given countries access to financial and technical resources, and innovative financing mechanisms such as PES, the Clean Development Mechanism (CDM) and carbon trading have begun to test ways to improve incentives.

However, there have been disappointments on the sustainable development agenda both at the international level and at the national level. At the international level, progress on increasing levels of aid and improving its effectiveness has been slower than expected, and a further slowdown may be anticipated from the global economic crisis. In addition, there has been lack of unanimity on important parts of the agenda, including stalemate in the World Trade Organization (WTO) Doha round, particularly on the key issue of trade in agricultural products. Divergent donor agendas have further complicated the prioritization of key development requirements.

On land issues, countries have recently developed and implemented biofuel policies without international consultation, and international land leases and purchases have been concluded by several countries without broader consultation or consideration of the ramifications for local and global communities. On water issues, where transboundary resources are concerned, nations have not ratified the UN Convention on International Watercourses, and have often given priority to their own internal agendas over those that require cooperation and benefit-sharing. Major water impoundment and diversion investments have been made without consideration of the possibility of optimizing benefits at the basin scale, or of negative impacts of unilateral development on other riparians.

Overall, the principles and programmes agreed at the international level have made a substantial contribution to changing policies and approaches, but their impact on changing behaviour on the ground has been limited. Only in a few places has the challenge of intensifying land and water use while limiting negative impacts on the resource base and on the broader environment been successfully met. The challenges of the vulnerability of the major food-producing systems of the developing world remain outstanding, while little progress has been made with pro-poor and ecologically sustainable intensification in the rainfed systems of the tropics and mountain areas. Agreements on sustainable groundwater management have been followed by increasing levels of overdraft. The elaborate and well-thought-out integrated water resource management framework agreed at the Dublin International Conference on Water and the Environment in 1992 has been widely incorporated into policy and institutions, but results on the ground have been limited.

Is there an agreed framework for sustainable land and water management?

Despite agreement on important component principles, there is no consolidated and agreed set of principles for the joint management of land and water within a sustainable ecosystems context, joining up the principles and practices that have been discussed throughout this report. There is thus no agreed international integrated framework around which major initiatives for sustainable land and water management can be formulated. Nonetheless, in response to land and water degradation and increasing levels of risk, several programmes, supported by the GEF and the UNCCD in particular, have developed visions and strategies, and recent conceptual and empirical work has defined ecosystem services, and placed agricultural production and land and water management within an ecosystems framework. Advantage should be taken of these advances to work towards an agreed set of principles for the management of land and water resources.

Trends in official development assistance

Total donor assistance to developing countries in 9 broad sectors of relevance to land and water[1] shows an upward overall trend, increasing from US$57 billion annually in 1995 to US$158 billion in 2008 (in constant 2008 US$ terms). However, overall support to specific land and water sectors in agriculture (namely, Sector 3 – Agricultural land resources, and Sector 4 – Agricultural water resources) dropped in the 1990s and stagnated until some recovery, largely attributed to commitments to environmental policy and research (Sector 8), was apparent starting in 2005. The share of land and water in overall official development assistance (ODA) for rural, water and environmental investment has also been declining (Figure 2.3). In recent years, most of the ODA for land and water (54 percent) went to Asia, and almost a quarter (21 percent) was invested in sub-Saharan Africa (Figure 2.4) (OECD, 2010b).

The gap between commitments and actual investments

In the framework of commitments made at the FAO High-Level Conference on World Food Security (Rome, 2008), the G8 summits in Japan (2008) and in Italy (2009) agreed that US$30 billion should be invested each year in agriculture in developing countries (equivalent to just 8 percent of the subsidies paid by OECD countries to their farmers). The G8 L'Aquila summit pledged US$20 billion to be mobilized over three years specifically for investment in food production in order to move from emergency food relief to reliable and sustainable domestic production.

These commitments were paralleled on a regional scale by the governments of sub-Saharan Africa. In Maputo in 2003, African Union governments committed

---

[1] Major 'land and water' sectors defined by OECD: (1) Water resources protection, (2) River development, (3) Agricultural land resources, (4) Agricultural water resources, (5) Forestry development, (6) Environmental policy and administrative management, (7) Flood prevention/control, (8) Environmental research and (9) Rural development.

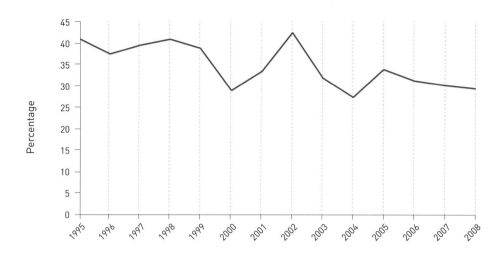

Sources: CRS Database of OECD (accessed June 2010); OECD (2010b)

FIGURE 2.4: DISTRIBUTION OF AID FOR LAND AND WATER BY REGION (MEAN 1995–2008)

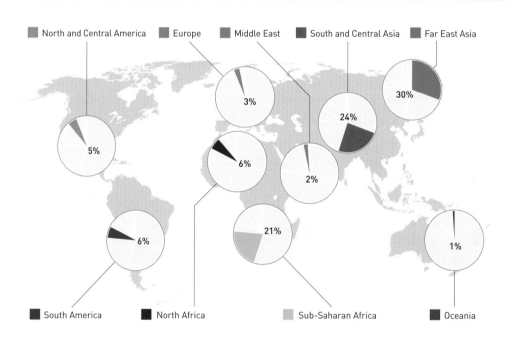

Sources: ODA data; CRS Database of OECD (accessed June 2010); OECD (2010b)

to allocating at least 10 percent of their national budgets to agriculture and rural development. However, actual transfers and investments have fallen short of these targets. Governments, authorities and development practitioners are thus facing the paradox of having agreed to development goals requiring increased production with diminishing per capita natural resources, but without the accompanying investment to do this.

Conclusions

Maintaining the integrity of linked land and water systems to meet an increasingly sophisticated set of competing demands has become a well-accepted global priority. Integrated river basin development has been embraced as an ideal tool for reconciling these demands since the mid-20th century. But the practice has been overrun by the sheer pace of economic development, and the subsequent expansion of urban, industrial and agricultural land use in river basins. A decade into the 21st century, a return to integration should be much better informed. Advanced knowledge on the hydrological cycle, improved agricultural practices and new tools for mitigating the impacts of chemical pollutants and managing wastewater now offer a set of knowledge-rich solutions to reduce environmental impact. When combined with stakeholder-centred institutional approaches to resource management, the scope for effecting positive change across the key land and water systems that furnish the global food supply is expanded. Conservation of forests and wetlands will be particularly important in this context, as they play a crucial role as natural regulators of the hydrological cycle. Addressing systems at risk will require land and water management institutions to become much more resourceful in the way they engage with stakeholders and deploy solutions.

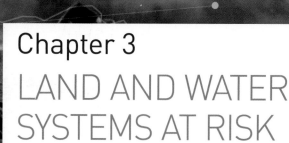

Chapter 3
LAND AND WATER SYSTEMS AT RISK

The previous chapters have highlighted the current and future threats to agricultural systems across the world. It is clear that current practices and models of agricultural development that have been followed during the last 50 years are far from satisfactorily addressing the challenges of poverty reduction, food security and environmental sustainability. A total of 975 million people, most living in rural areas, do not have the food security they deserve. Under pressure from agriculture, both soil and water are being harmed, erosion accelerated, salinization and seawater intrusion progressed, and groundwater depleted. In addition, the current model of intensive agriculture is associated with a high carbon and greenhouse gas footprint, while at the same time many agricultural systems are highly vulnerable to the predicted impacts of climate change.

The situation, however, varies substantially from one region to another in response to a combination of biophysical and socio-economic factors: climate, soil, water, population and economic development, as well as national policies and global changes. In the framework of this global study, it is thus necessary to describe and analyse the world's main agriculture production systems and the particular challenges they face. The problems discussed in this chapter include the growing competition for land and water, land and water degradation, and the expected impacts of climate change. They occur with varying incidence and severity in the different agricultural land- and water-use systems across the world, and the main systems at risk are discussed at the end of this chapter.

Map 1.3 in Chapter 1 shows a global overview of major agricultural production systems. Both rainfed and irrigated areas are experiencing degradation or risk due to limitations in land and water resources, to current land and water use and management practices, and to institutional and socio-economic factors.

Growing competition for land and water

With increased pressure on land and water resources, a problem is that some of the countries experiencing the fastest population growth are those where land and water resources are least abundant. Land and water for crop production, already constrained in some locations, will experience rising competition, particularly from fast-growing urban settlements. Increasing respect for conserving broader ecosystem services will further limit access to land and water. Competition within agriculture will increase too.

Patterns of increasing water stress due to irrigation withdrawals

Globally, the expected increases in water withdrawals for irrigation from 6 to 7 percent, or in developing countries from 8 to 9 percent, may not seem to be very alarming, but this is without accounting for the fact that a large part of irrigation is practised in water-scarce regions. There are wide regional and country-level variations in water resource availability, with a number of countries already experiencing water stress.

In industrial and transition countries, water withdrawals for irrigation are expected to stabilize or even to reduce. Overall, withdrawals in the high-income countries are expected to decline by 17 percent. By contrast, withdrawals in the low-income, food-deficit countries are expected to increase by 10 percent. The largest increases in absolute terms are expected in Southeast Asia (where irrigation is already very important – an increase of 55 km^3 annually, or 19 percent of current withdrawal levels) and in Southern America (an increase of 59 km^3, or 53 percent over present withdrawal levels). In relative terms, the increase in water withdrawals for irrigation is also expected to be high in sub-Saharan Africa (21 percent), although there is currently relatively little land irrigated, so in absolute terms the growth in water withdrawals remains modest (22 km^3). In all three of these regions, the share of water resources withdrawn for irrigation will remain low (less than 5 percent), and water availability will not generally be a constraint.

The regions that cause most concern are the Near East and Northern Africa, where water withdrawals are already near or above total renewable resources and where precipitation is low. In Northern Africa, pressure on water resources due to irrigation is extremely high, resulting in extensive water recycling and groundwater overdraft.

Just as global averages mask regional differences, variations at the country level can be hidden. In at least three countries (Libya, Saudi Arabia and Yemen) evaporation rates due to irrigation in 2005–7 were higher than each of their annual renewable water resources (FAO, 2010c). In China, for example, regional stresses are greater in the north of the country, and this will intensify. Areas dependent on non-renewable groundwater, such as parts of the Arabian peninsula, face a particular challenge: the potential depletion of their entire resource (Nachtergaele *et al.*, 2010b).

Urbanization

Crop production will have to compete with growing needs for land and water from other users. Urbanization will continue, and the expansion of urban areas and land required for infrastructure and other non-agricultural purposes is expected to at least keep pace with population growth. Growing cities, industries and tourism will have priority for water supply, and this is likely to reduce the water available locally to agriculture and thus lead to further loss of cultivated land, particularly in dry areas. This phenomenon is already under way in the Sana'a Basin in Yemen and in the Oum er Rbia River in Morocco, where water is being transferred to municipal and industrial uses, and the area under irrigation is progressively dwindling.

Competition for land with growing cities will be strongest in developing countries, which will account for more than 90 percent of the additional urban and built-up land required. At the same time, rapid urbanization will create markets for high-value agriculture, and intensive peri-urban market gardening is likely to be a growth sector. A useful synergy will be the safe re-use of wastewater in peri-urban agriculture. Treated wastewater provides a year-round supply of low-cost water rich in nutrients and organic matter, and its re-use lessens the pollution load on downstream watercourses. It needs, however, clear guidelines for safe re-use and an effective regulatory framework (Mateo-Sagasta and Burke, 2010; Fischer *et al.*, 2010).

Increasing attention to environmental requirements

Changes from other land and water uses to cultivation have important impacts on ecosystem services, and poor management may diminish the ability of ecosystems to support the functions or services required to ensure their sustainability (Molden, 2007). As awareness grows about the interdependence of parts of ecosystems, pressures will grow for agriculture to reduce negative impacts on ecosystems (for example, by reducing erosion or maximizing carbon storage). At the limit, land- and water-use planning will increasingly constrain the release of resources for cultivation purposes. Already cultivation is partially to totally restricted on 1.5 billion ha (11 percent of global land area) that have been declared protected areas (Fischer *et al.*, 2010).

Livestock production

Competition for water is expected to grow as result of changing patterns of livestock production and the demand for fodder. Dietary preferences for animal protein are changing consumption patterns across the world (FAO, 2006b,c) and this is expected to increase demand for fodder significantly. The fodder–animal protein conversion involves a loss – it takes five times more fodder to produce the equivalent calories for human consumption (Fischer *et al.*, 2010). The expansion of land for livestock grazing has led to deforestation in many countries. Intensive livestock production is also a major source of pollution. Livestock farming also contributes less than 2 percent of global GDP, and yet it is said to produce some 18 percent of GHGs (FAO, 2006b).

Up to 2030 and beyond, growth in consumption of livestock products is expected to continue, but the rate will vary. In high-income countries, where population growth is slow, the scope for growth will be limited as the consumption of livestock (meat and dairy) products is already very high (around 305 kg per person per year). This against 60 kg per person per year in low- and middle-income countries and a world average of 115 kg per person per year. In 2050, these figures are projected to be 330, 110 and 150 kg per person per year, respectively. At the same time, health and food safety concerns focused on animal fats and the emergence of new diseases may hold back demand for meat (FAO, 2006c).

Inland fisheries and aquaculture

Disputes over uses of water for irrigation and fisheries are often difficult to resolve due to the different spatial and temporal water needs of crops and fish. Expansion and intensification of crop production through draining of wetlands, extension of irrigation systems, flood protection, and increased use of fertilizer and pesticides will affect fisheries negatively. Any water development project should therefore take into consideration the needs of fish and fisheries in terms of water quantity and quality. In most developed countries and in some developing countries, strict regulations for environmental flow and water quality criteria are now in place, which is helpful in sustaining fish and fisheries while competing with other users for water resources. Some problems can be mitigated, and with proper planning and a holistic approach to development, farming and fisheries are not incompatible practices. The rice field fisheries in Asia are excellent examples of how the two activities coexist. There are, for instance, many examples that demonstrate that fish have a positive impact on the rice crop, and where fish are present there is less need for applying pesticides.

Large-scale acquisition of cropland

In recent years, two new areas of investment in commercial agriculture have emerged. One is where countries with high dependence on food imports seek to assure food supplies through agricultural investment in developing countries. The other is investment in liquid biofuel feedstock production (see below). Several drivers underpin inward investment in agriculture: commodity prices, land values, policy shifts in investing and recipient countries, and concerns about food and energy security. The shock of global food price rises experienced in 2007 and the persistent high levels of energy prices have sharpened interest. Key investor countries are in Europe and Africa, as well as the Gulf, and South and East Asia. Land acquisitions by domestic investors are also significant. Sub-Saharan Africa, South-east Asia and Latin America are the main target areas (Cotula, 2010).

The scale of the phenomenon is considerable, and competition with existing agricultural uses is heightened because investor interest tends to focus on higher-value lands in terms of higher fertility, greater irrigation potential, better infrastructure or greater proximity to markets. These lands are usually keenly sought after by local people for smallholder cultivation, and there is a risk to local livelihoods and food security if they are assigned to estate cultivation without proper consultation and safeguard (Cotula, 2010).

IBRD (2011) examines the issue by distinguishing countries on the basis of land that may be suitable for cropland expansion and yield gap, with the implication that different development pathways to deal with the associated risks and opportunities may be appropriate, depending on local context. The significant interest in countries with weak governance (notably, those pertaining to local rights) is cited as a major factor contributing to several risks (e.g. inadequate compensation, delays in implementation, low job creation, etc.). While opportunities may exist through these investments to remove existing constraints to agricultural production (e.g. access to technology, capital, infrastructure), this would require, among others, a strategic approach that proactively engages investors, changes in land governance and policy, and greater institutional capacity.

Liquid biofuel feedstock production

Currently, bioenergy represents about 10 percent of global energy use, and is used mainly for traditional cooking and heating in developing countries. Approximately 2.5 billion people in developing countries depend on traditional biomass as their main cooking fuel. But among these traditional bioenergy products it is the increasing production of liquid biofuels (bioethanol and biodiesel) that is expected to have the greatest impact on land and water use. Bioenergy has begun to compete with food production for land and water resources, and this competition is likely to increase as food crops, ethanol and biodiesel feedstock production have virtually the same land suitability requirements. The rises in recent world prices of food have been partly attributed to diversions for liquid biofuels.

Liquid biofuel has been forecast to account for 5 percent of total road transport energy use by 2030, and pressures for carbon savings may increase this. To produce this volume, land use for liquid biofuel feedstocks would need to more than double between 2007 and 2030 to 3–4.5 percent of cultivated land. Implementing all current national liquid biofuel policies and plans worldwide could already take 30 Mha of cropland (2 percent of the current cultivated land), displacing current food crop production and driving further conversion of current forest and grassland (Fischer *et al.*, 2010).

Liquid biofuel production also places pressure on water resources – the water required to produce one litre of liquid biofuel is approximately the amount needed to produce food for one person for one day. Currently, global irrigation water used for liquid biofuel production is estimated to be 1–2 percent of world total irrigation water use. If all current national liquid biofuel plans were implemented, liquid biofuel production could require 5–10 percent of worldwide irrigation water (Hoogeveen *et al.*, 2009).

However, these ambitious expansion plans may be scaled back, as there are concerns about competition of bioenergy and food over resources, related impacts on food security, and questions over the environmental sustainability of production (Tilman *et al.*, 2009). In addition, there are questions about the extent of net greenhouse gas emissions savings, particularly where forest or grassland has been converted for liquid biofuel production.

These considerations have led many countries to reassess their near-term production targets (Box 3.1) and to evaluate the potential of second-generation liquid biofuels derived largely from biomass waste, which does not compete directly with food crops.

BOX 3.1: TRENDS IN LIQUID BIOFUEL DEMAND AND PRODUCTION

Global liquid biofuel supply reached 0.7 million barrels (Mb) daily in 2007, an increase of 37 percent on 2006, equivalent to 1.5 percent of road transport fuel. Trends indicate worldwide demand will rise significantly to 1.6 Mb/d by 2015 and to 2.7 Mb/d in 2030, thus meeting 5 percent of total world road transport energy demand. A coordinated global commitment to stabilize the concentration of greenhouse gases at 450 ppm of CO_2 equivalent would require a further doubling of global liquid biofuel demand in 2030, with increased use of liquid biofuels in the transport sector accounting for 3 percent of CO_2 savings.

But concerns about competition of bioenergy and food over scarce land and water resources, impacts on food security, actual GHG emission savings, and environmental sustainability of production, have had many countries reassessing their near-term production targets for liquid biofuels. This is particularly true for 'first generation' liquid biofuels (i.e. those obtained largely from dedicated energy crops such as maize and sugar cane). Potential negative impacts on cropland and food security may be reduced by the introduction of second-generation liquid biofuels (i.e. fuels derived largely from biomass waste). By 2030 a quarter of liquid biofuel production could be of this origin.

Sources: Tubiello and van der Velde (2010); IEA (2009)

Degradation of land and water: impacts and causes

Past achievements in terms of agricultural production growth have been accompanied by negative side-effects or externalities on land and water resources, both on-farm and downstream. Part of this degradation has been caused by poorly adapted production systems, and part by deliberate choices or trade-offs to increase agricultural output at the expense of ecosystem services.

Land and water use and the ecosystem: definition of land degradation

Recent studies (Nachtergaele *et al.*, 2011) have broadened the definition of 'land degradation' beyond simply soil erosion or loss of soil fertility, extending it to the deterioration of a balanced ecosystem and the loss of the services that ecosystem provides. Land degradation thus needs to be considered in an integrated way, taking into account all ecosystem goods and services – biophysical as well as socio-economic.

Ecosystems in which cultivation, forest management or grazing are dominant activities are at present often negatively affected by human-induced causes, most importantly by land use and land-use changes (Box 3.2) that affect the biophysical characteristics of the land (e.g. pollution, salinization, nutrient depletion). Where management practices are poorly adapted to local ecological conditions, degradation can occur. Even a number of causes that are seemingly natural can have wholly or partly indirect human causes (bush invasion, forest fires, floods, landslides and droughts).

LADA: FAO's framework for assessing land degradation

A new, scalable and 'integrative' framework for assessing land degradation has been recently developed by FAO in close collaboration with the World Overview of Conservation Approaches and Technologies (WOCAT), as part of the Land Degradation Assessment in Drylands (LADA, 2010a). This programme was originally initiated at the request, and in support, of the UNCCD. It builds on the concept of ecosystem services developed by the Millennium Ecosystem Assessment (MEA, 2005), and reflects a methodological shift in evaluating the occurrence, severity, driving forces and impacts of land degradation, and extent and effectiveness of good management practices. This approach to assessment is different from earlier methods such as Global Assessment of Soil Degradation (GLASOD; Oldeman *et al.*, 1990), which focused primarily on soils (Box 3.3). 'Land degradation' is thus a broader concept than just soil degradation or water pollution. It also allows assessment of the inter-related components of the ecosystem and of the trade-offs that may exist between them: loss of biodiversity, for example, matched against improvements in economic services under intensive farming.

BOX 3.2: LOSS OF NATURAL FORESTS IN LATIN AMERICA AND THE CARIBBEAN

Logs felled to open new fields with traditional slash-and-burn practices in Santa Cruz, Bolivia

Between 1990 and 2010, the net forest area in the Latin America and Caribbean region decreased by about 87 Mha, or almost 9 percent (FAO, 2011c). In particular, the Amazon Basin, which contains the world's most extensive tropical rainforest, encompassing unique biodiversity, has one of the world's highest rates of deforestation. Commercial farmers have cleared large areas for soybean exports in Brazil, Bolivia and Paraguay, for coffee in Brazil, and for bananas in Central America, Colombia, Ecuador and the Caribbean. Small-scale farmers also cause forest degradation by employing slash-and-burn practices in migrating their agricultural practices around forests.

Source: CDE (2010) Photo: Wocat

The FAO-LADA framework for land degradation assessment has recently been applied at national level in several countries of the LADA project (Argentina, China, Cuba, Senegal, South Africa, Tunisia), for which the total area of selected types of biophysical degradation, land management practices and ecosystem impacts have been estimated. Results from the LADA national- and local-level land degradation assessments are used in support of policy formulation and interventions for natural resources management, as well as in countries reporting to the UNCCD (Box 3.4).

An operational methodology for applying the FAO-LADA framework to the integrative analysis of global datasets (GLADIS: Global Land Degradation Information System) is in final stages of development by FAO (LADA, 2010a). GLADIS assesses the status, trends and impacts of land degradation on local populations using a set of indicators spanning the social, economic and environmental dimensions of

- The key role of **stakeholder evaluation** of the status and trends of **multiple ecosystem benefits** spanning three dimensions – social, economic and environmental – widely recognized as the three pillars of 'sustainability'.
- Degradation is deemed to be occurring whenever pressures exerted upon an ecosystem trigger a continual declining trend (over a period of approximately ten years or more) in the value of one or more benefits to levels **below that which is considered acceptable by the community of stakeholders** that, directly or indirectly, is responsible for the 'management' of the ecosystems. The underlying rationale is that stakeholders will continually make trade-offs among various benefits in order to 'manage' the ecosystem towards the attainment of acceptable levels on all three 'sustainability' criteria.
- Degradation can be considered to be permanent when the cost of rehabilitating degraded land using currently available technologies would be judged unacceptable by stakeholders, from economic and or social standpoints.
- The 'state of land degradation' (equated to the condition of ecosystem benefits at a point in time) as well as 'trends' in land degradation can only be evaluated against a reference year. Both 'state' and 'trend' are important considerations in evaluating the urgency for remedial actions. Critical situations occur when low 'state' occurs simultaneously with a rapidly declining 'trend' in ecosystem services. Areas with low to moderate 'state' and declining 'trend' should be highlighted for preventative actions, for greater cost-effectiveness.
- Data collection methodologies used to measure various aspects of degradation evolve over time. The FAO-LADA framework can be applied independently of specific methodologies and at various scales. Either measured variables or related indicators can be used.
- Drivers and impacts of land degradation are assessed at different scales. This allows comprehensive understanding of the behaviours and strategies of various land users, and facilitates coherent actions at different levels of decision-making.

ecosystem services. In GLADIS, the condition of multiple ecosystem benefits is represented in the form of radar diagrams that allow rapid assessment of the status and trends in six main dimensions of land- and water-related ecosystem services: biomass, soil, water, biodiversity, economic and social (Figure 3.1).

The GLADIS assessment shows that land use and management are the most important causes of degradation. For example, conversion of forest to cropland causes loss of a range of ecosystem services, and the resulting cultivated lands – often as a result of soil tillage – are more susceptible to degradation. Forests have high capacity to produce biomass, soil health and biodiversity. When forests are converted to cultivation, many of these services are lost and the subsequently cultivated lands are more likely to degrade.

Trends are an important element in the assessment of ecosystem services. GLADIS assesses changes in ecosystems services over 1990–2005 in order to monitor

Following the LADA national assessment methodology, expert estimates were made on the spatial extents of selected types, degree and rate of biophysical degradation, as well as their causes and impacts on ecosystem services, within all major land-use systems. Types of degradation include soil erosion (wind, water) and soil deterioration (chemical, physical, water, biological). Their causes include soil management, crop management, deforestation, over-exploitation of vegetation for domestic use and overgrazing (LADA, 2010b).

Extent of degradation (percentage area of land-use system)

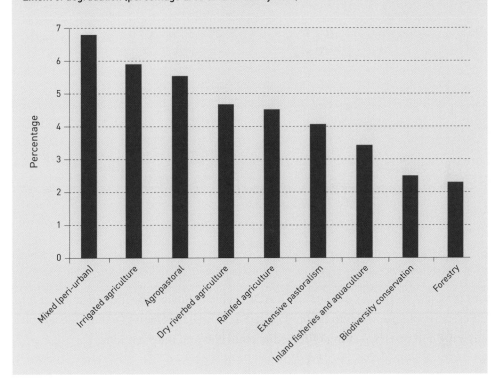

improvement or further deterioration. Large parts of all continents are experiencing degradation, with particularly high incidence of degradation down the west coast of the Americas, across Southern Europe and North Africa, across the Sahel and the Horn of Africa, and throughout Asia. The greatest threat is the loss of soil quality, followed by biodiversity loss and water depletion (Molden, 2007).

Global extent of degraded area – preliminary results from GLADIS

In GLADIS (LADA, 2010a), global datasets covering environmental, economic and social dimensions were input to models, which produced indices that are indicative of the current status (i.e. the 'baseline' condition) of ecosystem benefits as well as trends (i.e. the overall long-term tendency of changes in the flow of such benefits, whether improving or not). Status and trends were determined for eleven globally impor-

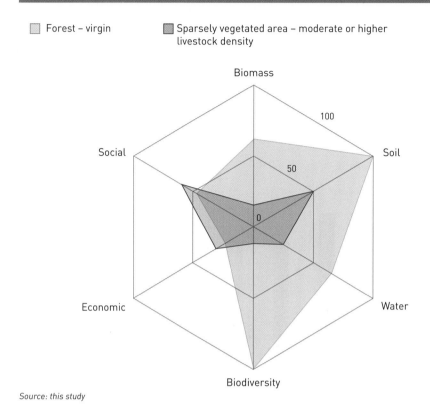

Source: this study

tant land-use classes, as defined in GLADIS, which allowed the identification of four different typologies of degradation (Figure 3.2) . These typologies facilitate geographic targeting and priority-setting of remedial strategies and interventions.

The relative extents of the different typologies of degradation vary depending on land use. Highest values for Type 1 were associated with *sparsely vegetated areas with moderate or high livestock density* (68 percent of the global extent of this land use class). The highest shares of improving lands (i.e. Type 4) are mostly associated with *cropping with little to no livestock* (24 percent). Globally, approximately 25 percent of all land is of the critical Type 1 category, while about 46 percent are stable (neither significantly increasing nor decreasing trends) and are slightly to moderately degraded (Type 3). Only 10 percent is associated with improving conditions (Figure 3.2).

Negative on-farm impacts of agriculture

The current 1600 Mha of cultivated land represent the better and more productive part of global land resources. However, parts of this land are degrading through farming practices that result in water and wind erosion, nutrient mining, topsoil

Typology of degradation of ecosystem benefits	Intervention options
■ Type 1 – High degradation trend or highly degraded lands	Rehabilitate if economically feasible; mitigate where degrading trends are high
■ Type 2 – Moderate degradation trend in slightly or moderately degraded land	Introduce measure to mitigate degradation
■ Type 3 – Stable land, slightly or moderately degraded	Preventive interventions
■ Type 4 – Improving lands	Reinforcement of enabling conditions which foster SLM

Source: this study

compaction, salinization and soil pollution. As a result, the productivity of the land resource base has declined. Land degradation also leads to off-site problems, such as sedimentation of reservoirs, reduced watershed system functioning and carbon dioxide emissions.

Deterioration of land productivity can occur in several ways. First, there may be loss of organic matter and physical degradation of the soil, such as when forests are cleared and soil structure declines rapidly. Second, nutrient depletion and chemical degradation of the soil may occur. Globally, only half the nutrients that crops take from the soil are replaced, with nutrient depletion in many Asian countries equivalent to 50 kg/ha annually. In some Eastern and Southern African countries, annual depletion is estimated at 47 kg/ha of nitrogen, 6 kg/ha of phosphorus, and 37 kg/ha of potassium. When farming systems do not include fertilization or nitrogen fixation, losses from nutrient mining and related erosion are even higher (Sheldrick *et al.*, 2002).

A third aspect of deterioration is on-site soil erosion caused by poor land management. Many studies have demonstrated the effect on yields of loss of nutrients and organic matter and the related deterioration of the water-holding capacity of the soil. Loss of soil quality and its protective cover also affects broader ecosystem services by causing hydrological disturbance, loss of above- and below-ground biological diversity, and reduced soil carbon stocks and associated increases in carbon dioxide emissions.

Soil health is declining in many cropping systems both in developed and developing countries. The worst situations occur in highland rainfed cropping systems in the Himalayas, Andes, Rockies and the Alps, in low-input, low-husbandry systems such as the rainfed cropping systems in the sub-Saharan Africa savannahs (Box 3.5) and agro-pastoral systems in the Sahel, Horn of Africa and Western India, and in intensive systems where nutrients and pesticides can lead to soil and water pollution if not properly managed.

Irrigation development has played a vital function in raising agricultural production worldwide, but the negative side-effects of intensive irrigated farming on soil and water have also been substantial. On-farm, salinization and waterlogging are the main problems. Few plants can tolerate much salt, as it prevents the uptake of moisture, with a consequent rapid decline in yields. Salinization may come about when irrigation releases salts already in the soil, or when irrigation water or mineral fertilization brings new salts to the land. Waterlogging is a related problem. It curtails plant growth by eliminating air from the soil, effectively stifling the plant. Waterlogging also often leads to salinization of soils. Worldwide, FAO estimates that 34 Mha (11 percent of the irrigated area) are affected by some level of salinity (Map 3.1); Pakistan, China, the United States and India represent more than 60 percent of the total (21 Mha). An additional 60–80 Mha are affected to some extent by waterlogging and related salinity.

Off-farm impacts and externalities

In addition to the on-site impacts of land and water management, there are also extensive off-site and downstream impacts, including changes in river hydrology and groundwater recharge rates, the pollution of downstream water bodies and of groundwater, downstream effects of siltation due to runoff from farms, and the overall impact on water-related ecosystems.

Traditionally cultivated, unfertilized fields with high spatial variability in plant growth, Senegal

Only 7 percent of sub-Saharan Africa is under cropland. Crop productivity is low. Soil fertility depletion is reaching a critical level in the region, especially under small-scale land use. It results from a negative nutrient balance, with at least four times more nutrients removed in harvested products compared with nutrients returned in the form of manure and mineral fertilizer.

Source: CDE (2010) Photo: USGS

Impacts on the hydrological regime due to irrigation water withdrawals

Irrigated agriculture has had a profound impact on water-related ecosystems. The flow regimes of rivers have changed, sometimes with substantial negative effects on water availability downstream and on downstream aquatic ecosystems, and with substantial reduction in discharge to the ocean. Many rivers heavily used for irrigation no longer have sufficient levels of flow to keep river systems 'open'. In some heavily populated basins in China and India, rivers no longer discharge to the sea, with resulting saline advance upstream, and loss of coastal habitat and economic activity. But there may be positive impacts through improved flood control and aquifer recharge (Charalambous and Garratt, 2009), although this may also reduce the transportation of beneficial sediments (Molden, 2007). Irrigation withdrawals have also contributed to the shrinkage of vast lakes: Lake Chapala in Mexico lost 80 percent of its volume between 1979 and 2001, and the Aral Sea all but disappeared at the end of the 20th century as irrigation withdrawals for cotton reduced inflows.

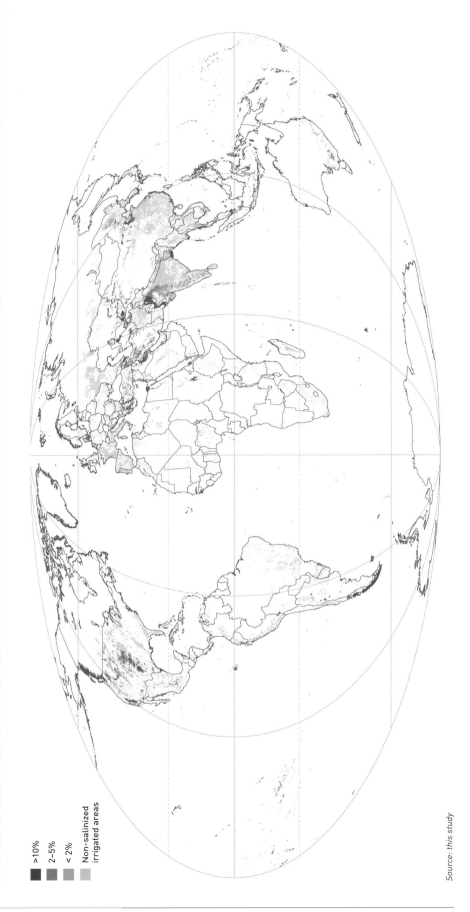

>10%

2–5%

< 2%

Non-salinized
irrigated areas

Source: this study

Wetlands have also been drained. In Europe and North America, more than half of wetlands have been drained for agriculture, leading to loss of biodiversity, risk of flooding and downstream eutrophication (FAO, 2008c; Molden, 2007: 249).

Water pollution from agriculture

The most important water pollution problems related to agriculture are excess nutrients accumulating in surface and coastal waters, nitrate accumulating in groundwater, and pesticides accumulating in groundwater and surface-water bodies.

Water pollution by excessive application of nutrients (particularly nitrate and phosphate) has increased with the intensification of agriculture together with significant inputs from urban sewage. Increased use of mineral fertilizers (Figure 3.3) and higher concentrations of livestock are the main causes. The increase in the load of

FIGURE 3.3: TRENDS IN MINERAL FERTILIZER USE (NPK)

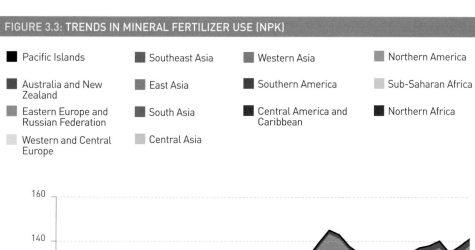

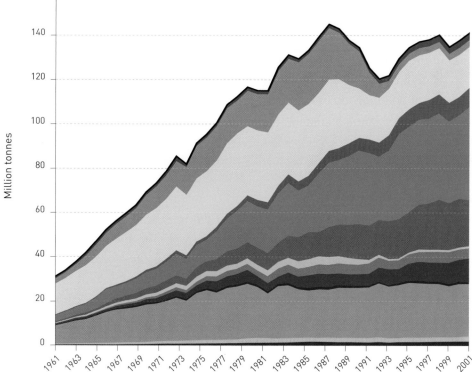

Data source: FAO (2010b)

nutrients in croplands has increased the transport and accumulation of nitrates in water systems through run-off and drainage. Agrochemical pollution is currently a serious and widespread problem, including much of East and Southeast Asia, Europe, parts of the USA and Central Asian countries, as well as on some plantations in Central and Latin America.

Nutrients in surface waters can cause eutrophication, hypoxia (depletion of dissolved oxygen supporting aquatic life), and algal blooms and other infestations, such as of water hyacinth. Coastal areas of Australia, Europe and the USA, and many inland waters, are affected (Mateo-Sagasta and Burke, 2010). Life in some seas, including parts of the Baltic and Adriatic, is often stifled. Wetlands and lakes receiving influxes of nutrients may cross eutrophication thresholds. It has been suggested that the planetary boundary, or upper tolerable limit, for changes to the global nitrogen cycle (Rockström *et al.*, 2011) and for freshwater eutrophication, has already been crossed (Carpenter and Bennet, 2011). It is estimated that there are 12 000 km^3 of polluted freshwater in the world, equivalent to six years of irrigation use.

A further problem is related to the use of some pesticides (Turral and Burke, 2010). Pest management has been a recurrent issue in irrigated agriculture since the emergence of modern large-scale rice and wheat farming. In monocultures, pests and diseases can spread rapidly and result in epidemics when conditions are favourable to a particular pathogen or pest. Some high-yielding varieties of rice have proved to be susceptible to particular pests (e.g. IR64 to brown plant hopper). Early pesticides, such as organochlorines, proved to be persistent, and accumulated in food chains. Although many were banned in the 1970s, their use continued in some parts of the world. They were replaced by more apparently benign formulations, such as organophosphates, which then also became largely banned or restricted. The risks of pollution are linked to the solubility and mobility of different chemical compounds. For example, the herbicide atrazine, widely used in maize production in the USA, has been held responsible for considerable groundwater contamination. Agricultural run-off and drainage readily transport these pollutants to water bodies.

Greenhouse gases

Agriculture also contributes substantially to the release of greenhouse gases. Its emissions amount to about 5–6 billion t CO_2eq per year. Together with deforestation activities, it is responsible for a third of total anthropogenic greenhouse gas emissions, or about 13–15 billion t CO_2eq per year (Table 3.1). It emits about 25 percent of total carbon dioxide (largely from deforestation), 50 percent of methane (rice, enteric fermentation, animal waste) and 75 percent of N_2O (fertilizer application, animal waste) emitted annually by anthropogenic activities. Although much of these emissions may be an unavoidable part of intensified agriculture, a number of mitigation strategies in the agriculture and forestry sectors have been identified as useful in

TABLE 3.1: ANNUAL ANTHROPOGENIC GREENHOUSE GAS EMISSIONS (2005)

	Billion tCO$_2$eq	Share %
Global	50	100 %
Agriculture	5–6	10–12 %
Methane	(3.3)	
N$_2$O	(2.8)	
Forestry	8–10	15–20 %
Deforestation	(5–6)	
Decay and peat	(3–4)	
Total agriculture and forestry	13–15	25–32 %

Source: FAO (2008a)

achieving the goal of stabilization of atmospheric concentrations. These options are discussed in Chapter 5.

Depletion of groundwater

The quantity of water available to agriculture is likely to be affected by dwindling of the groundwater resource in many areas. As discussed earlier, the boom in groundwater use fuelled by tubewell technology, cheap energy and profitable markets has led to widespread depletion of groundwater reserves, including irreversible mining of some aquifers (Shah, 2009; Llamas and Custodio, 2003; Morris *et al.*, 2003). But while depletion has been a dominant impact, in some circumstances pumping can increase recharge (Shamsudduha *et al.*, 2011).

Widespread and largely unregulated groundwater withdrawals by agriculture have resulted in depletion and degradation of some of the world's most accessible and high-quality aquifers. The depletion in the Central Valley of California or the Ogallala aquifer in the US Great Plains are well known. But other examples from key agriculture areas include the Punjab, North China Plain and the Souss basin in Morocco, where annual declines of up to 2 metres since 1980 have been recorded (Garduno & Foster, 2011). Pumping costs to individual farmers and public groundwater supply schemes rise as the water table drops. But in some cases the demand for groundwater to service high-value crops appears inelastic (Hellegers *et al.*, 2011): in Yemen some pumping is from depths of over 1 km.

Groundwater depletion has also contributed to subsidence as aquifer structures collapse. The most notable example to date is the Central Valley of California, due to the continued exploitation of deeper groundwater for irrigation. In Iran, intensive withdrawal of groundwater is contributing to drying up of traditional *qanat* (springs and shallow wells) and has also led to subsidence of productive agricultural land due to compression of underlying aquifers as groundwater is withdrawn.

A further risk is salinization of groundwater resources. This may occur when saline irrigation drainage water percolates to an aquifer. But in many coastal zones and small islands, intensive pumping of groundwater for agricultural use has induced saline intrusion, rendering many economically important aquifers unfit for water supply. Some aquifers are already permanently salinized (for example, the coastal aquifers of Gaza, Gujarat (India), west Java and Mexico).

A global inventory of groundwater use in agriculture conducted by FAO (Siebert *et al.*, 2010) indicates that almost 40 percent of the global irrigated area is now reliant on groundwater (Table 3.2). Key food-producing regions are dependent on groundwater. Regions affected include some of the world's major grain-producing areas, such as the Punjab and the North China Plain. Four of the world's largest food producers depend on groundwater for a third or more of their irrigated area, and India (64 percent) and the USA (59 percent) for up to two-thirds of the irrigated area. Consequently, risks to global food supply from depletion and deterioration of aquifers are high.

Anticipated impacts of climate change

Worldwide, agricultural systems are also considered at risk from climate change (FAO, 2011d). Climate change and variability affect thermal and hydrological regimes, and this in turn influences the structure and functionality of ecosystems and human livelihoods. Expected changes in the mean and variability of temperature and precipitation, elevated CO_2, plus complex interactions among these, will

TABLE 3.2: MAJOR FOOD-PRODUCING COUNTRIES DEPENDENT ON GROUNDWATER

Country	Area equipped for irrigation (ha)	Groundwater (ha)	Surface Water (ha)	Dependence on groundwater (% of area equipped for irrigation)
Brazil	3 149 217	591 439	2 557 778	19%
China	62 392 392	18 794 951	43 597 440	30%
Egypt	3 422 178	331 927	3 090 251	10%
India	61 907 846	39 425 869	22 481 977	64%
Pakistan	16 725 843	5 172 552	11 553 291	31%
Thailand	5 279 860	481 063	4 798 797	9%
USA	27 913 872	16 576 243	11 337 629	59%

Source: Siebert et al. (2010)

have impacts on land and water resources, affecting crop productivity and the agricultural sector in the coming decades (Tubiello and van der Velde, 2010).

These impacts will vary by region and over time. It is expected that up to 2050, moderate warming may benefit crop and pasture yields in temperate regions, while it will decrease yields in semi-arid and tropical regions. Global warming thus has the potential to boost food production in some parts of the world (e.g. Canada, Russia), and to limit it in others (e.g. Southern Africa). Changes in precipitation regimes are also expected. The associated changes in evapotranspiration to precipitation ratios will modify ecosystem productivity and function, particularly in marginal areas. There is likely to be an increased frequency of extreme events – such as heatwaves, hailstorms, excessive cold, heavy and prolonged precipitation, and droughts – with negative impacts on crop yields. Climate change will need to be taken into account in all considerations of future land and water management strategies (FAO, 2010c).

Possible climate change impacts at the global level

Climate change impacts are expected to combine to depress yields and increase production risks in many areas, with increasing aridity, more unpredictable weather patterns and more pronounced rainfall events. Increases in precipitation and temperature may lead to increased pest and disease pressure on crops and livestock. Impacts are expected to grow more negative and pronounced with time, especially in developing regions. There may be some benefits in certain parts of the world from warmer temperatures, more water and a longer growing season. Even increasing atmospheric CO_2 could have a beneficial effect on productivity, although this is uncertain.

The impacts of climate change on world aggregate cereal production, depending on the scenario considered, may vary between –5 percent and +3 percent (Box 3.6). If risks materialize, climate change may have serious consequences in developing countries, due to the vulnerability and food insecurity of the poorer parts of the population, scarcity of capital for adaptation measures, their warmer baseline climates and their heightened exposure to extreme events. It is estimated that climate change could increase the number of undernourished by between 10 and 150 million people.

Anticipated climate change impacts by zone

Although all climate change projections are subject to a wide range of uncertainty, projections indicate an increase in the percentage of current cultivated land falling into arid and semi-arid climatic zones in Africa, particularly in Northern Africa and Southern Africa. By 2080, arid and dry semi-arid areas in Africa may increase by 5–8 percent (60–90 Mha). Drier areas may become less productive, or go out of production altogether. In Asia, by contrast, aridity would decline in all subregions. In temperate zones, impacts may be more favourable, although offset by the likelihood of more extreme weather events. The expected changes in temperature and precipitation regimes, and associated soil moisture conditions, will modify the suitability of crop species and cultivars. This will lead to changing management require-

If impacts are unmitigated, scenario results show an overall decline in the production potential of rainfed cereals of about 5 percent (see table below). If adapted crop types are used or if increased CO_2 associated with climate change has a fertilization effect, then the decline in production potential would be lessened. If both adapted crop types and the CO_2 fertilization effect are assumed, then climate change could result in an overall global increase in production potential of 3 percent. Increases would be largest in East and Central Asia. Production would still decline in some regions, particularly in Western Africa. Within these projections, it is likely that poor rainfed areas and farmers will have the least access to adaptation, and so will suffer the most.

Impacts of climate change on the production potential of rain-fed cereals in current cultivated land

Region	Cultivated land	Percentage changes with respect to potential under current climate*			
		Without CO_2 fertilization; current crop types	Without CO_2 fertilization; adapted crop types	With CO_2 fertilization; current crop types	With CO_2 fertilization; adapted crop types
Northern Africa	19	−15	−13	−10	−8
Sub-Saharan Africa	225	−7	−3	−3	1
Northern America	258	−7	−6	−1	0
Central America and Caribbean	16	−15	−11	−11	−7
Southern America	129	−8	−3	−4	1
Western Asia	61	−6	−6	−1	−1
Central Asia	46	19	19	24	24
South Asia	201	−6	−2	−2	2
East Asia	151	2	6	7	10
Southeast Asia	99	−5	−2	−1	4
Western and Central Europe	132	−4	−4	2	3
Eastern Europe and Russian Federation	173	1	1	7	7
Australia and New Zealand	51	2	4	7	9
Pacific Islands	0	−7	−3	−2	2

* Using Hadley A2 scenario for year 2050 versus reference climate.

Source: adapted from Fischer et al. (2010)

ments, such as increased need for irrigation in many regions, new cropping calendars, and altered planting and harvesting operations (Fischer *et al.*, 2010).

Effects of climate change on irrigation

Although there are many uncertainties about climate change, impacts on water resources are expected to be significant, with projected increases in water stress already pronounced by 2050 (FAO, 2011a). Regional water availability may change through shifts in snow-melt and river flows. Major precipitation changes may impact river flow in key irrigated regions, especially the Indian subcontinent (FAO, 2011a; De Fraiture *et al.*, 2008). Although these impacts are difficult to quantify, a combination of reduced river base flows, increased flooding and rising sea levels is expected to impact highly productive irrigated systems that help maintain the stability of cereals production. The production risks will be amplified in alluvial plains dependent on glacier melt (e.g. Colorado, Punjab) and in lowland deltas (e.g. Ganges, Nile) (Frenken, 2010).

On the demand side, impacts of climate change on irrigation requirements will be felt through net changes in precipitation and evapotranspiration (Bates *et al.*, 2008). Net crop irrigation requirements may increase 5 to 20 percent globally by 2080, with larger changes in some regions; Southeast Asia, for example, may see requirements rise by 15 percent. Larger impacts are foreseen in temperate regions, as a result of both increased evaporative demands and longer growing seasons under climate change (Fischer *et al.*, 2007). The ratio of irrigation withdrawals to available renewable water resources may increase as a result of climate change, especially in the Middle East and Southeast Asia. Irrigation requirements may also increase in North Africa, but decrease in China (Bates *et al.*, 2008). Increased frequency of droughts is expected to stress water reservoirs, as more water will be necessary to offset increased crop demand.

Systems at risk

SOLAW has identified nine major categories of systems at risk for which special attention is needed (further breakdown has led to a total of 14 subsystems presenting specific patterns of risk and development options). All these systems are expected to experience some negative impacts, as well as to impose negative externalities on other systems, unless corrective actions are taken. Key characteristics (status and trends) and options for addressing land and water issues in these systems are shown in Table 3.3. The incidence and severity of negative impacts anticipated are described, together with the main options needed to address risk, restore sustainability, and improve contribution to local and global food needs.

TABLE 3.3: MAJOR LAND AND WATER SYSTEMS AT RISK (A BROAD TYPOLOGY)

Global production systems	Cases or locations where systems are at risk	Risks
RAINFED CROPPING Highlands	Densely populated highlands in poor areas: Himalayas, Andes, Central American highlands, Rift Valley, Ethiopian plateau, Southern Africa.	Erosion, land degradation, reduced productivity of soil and water, increased intensity of flood events, accelerated out-migration, high prevalence of poverty and food insecurity.
RAINFED CROPPING Semi-arid tropics	Smallholder farming in Western, Eastern and Southern Africa savannah region and in Southern India; agro-pastoral systems in the Sahel, Horn of Africa and Western India.	Desertification, reduction of production potential, increased crop failures due to climate variability and temperatures, increased conflicts, high prevalence of poverty and food insecurity, out-migration.
RAINFED CROPPING Subtropical	Densely populated and intensively cultivated areas, concentrated mainly around the Mediterranean basin.	Desertification, reduction of production potential, increased crop failures, high prevalence of poverty and food insecurity, further land fragmentation, accelerated out-migration. Climate change is expected to affect these areas through reduced rainfall and river runoff, and increased occurrence of droughts and floods.
RAINFED CROPPING Temperate	Highly intensive agriculture in Western Europe.	Pollution of soils and aquifers leading to de-pollution costs, loss of biodiversity, degradation of freshwater ecosystems.
	Intensive farming in United States, Eastern China, Turkey, New Zealand, parts of India, Southern Africa, Brazil.	Pollution of soils and aquifers, loss of biodiversity, degradation of freshwater ecosystems, increased crop failure due to increased climate variability in places.
IRRIGATED Rice-based systems	Southeast and Eastern Asia.	Land abandonment, loss of buffer role of paddy land, increasing cost of land conservation, health hazards due to pollution, loss of cultural values of land.
	Sub-Saharan Africa, Madagascar, Western Africa, Eastern Africa.	Need for frequent rehabilitations, poor return on investment, stagnating productivity, large-scale land acquisition, land degradation.
IRRIGATED Other crops	RIVER BASINS Large contiguous irrigation systems from rivers in dry areas, including Colorado river, Murray-Darling, Krishna, Indo-Gangetic plains, Northern China, Central Asia, Northern Africa and Middle East.	Increased water scarcity, loss of biodiversity and environmental services, desertification, expected reduction in water availability and shift in seasonal flows due to climate change in several places.
	AQUIFERS Groundwater-dependent irrigation systems in interior arid plains: India, China, central USA, Australia, North Africa, Middle East and others.	Loss of buffer role of aquifers, loss of agriculture land, desertification, reduced recharge due to climate change in places.

Global production systems	Cases or locations where systems are at risk	Risks
RANGELANDS	Pastoral and grazing lands, including on fragile soils in Western Africa (Sahel), North Africa, parts of Asia.	Desertification, out-migration, land abandonment, food insecurity, extreme poverty, intensification of conflicts.
FORESTS	Tropical forest-cropland interface in Southeast Asia, the Amazon basin, Central Africa, and Himalayan forests.	Cropland encroachment, slash-and-burn, leading to loss of ecosystems services of forests, land degradation.
Other locally important subsystems	DELTAS AND COASTAL AREAS: Nile delta, Red River delta, Ganges/Brahmaputra, Mekong, etc. and coastal alluvial plains: Arabian Peninsula, Eastern China, Bight of Benin, Gulf of Mexico.	Loss of agricultural land and groundwater, health-related problems, sea-level rise, higher frequency of cyclones (Eastern and Southeast Asia), increased incidence of floods and low flows.
	SMALL ISLANDS Including Caribbean, Pacific islands.	Total loss of freshwater aquifers, increased cost of freshwater production, increased climate-change related damages (hurricanes, sea-level rise, floods.
	PERI-URBAN agriculture	Pollution, health-related problems for consumers and producers, competition for land.

Source: this study

Map 3.2 highlights areas within agricultural systems where the rural population exceeds the capacity of land or water resources to provide food. This map shows where rural population density presents a challenge to agricultural systems, and where responses need to be crafted in combinations of sustainable intensification practices and reduction of demographic pressure on the environment.

Densely populated highlands in poor areas

These systems, which include areas such as the Himalayas, the Andes and high-land areas of sub-Saharan Africa (including the Rift Valley, the Ethiopian plateau and Great Lakes area), are characterized by extreme population pressure on fragile ecosystems. Expansion into marginal lands leads to high rates of erosion, increased risk of landslides and changes in patterns of runoff, with consequent degradation of water resources downstream. Negative impacts of erosion and desertification lead to declining productivity, and are expected to be exacerbated by climate change.

In these systems, there is almost no possibility of expanding the cultivated area. The scope for intensification is limited to non-marginal lands and requires heavy investments in soil and water conservation measures. Better land husbandry and

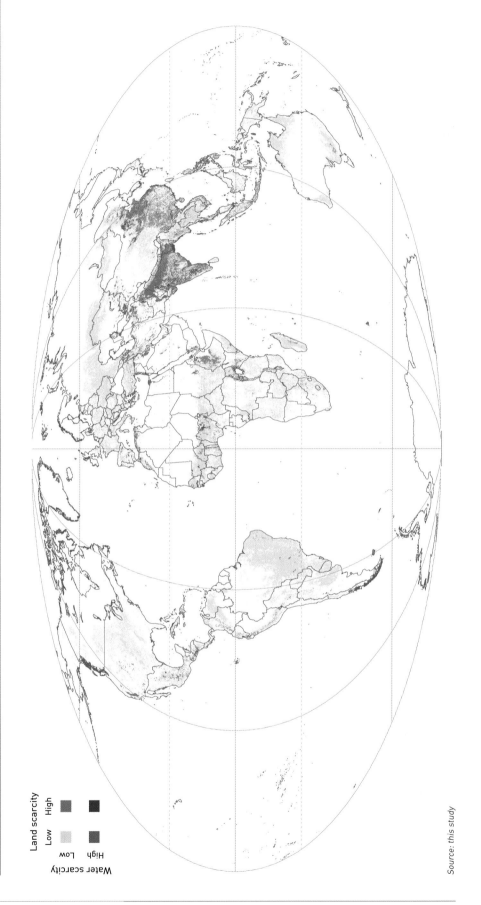

Land scarcity

Low   High

Water scarcity

Low   High

Source: this study

efforts to reduce pressure on fragile lands are needed, otherwise impoverishment and out-migration are likely to occur. Response options in such fragile ecosystems include soil and water conservation, watershed management practices, terracing, flood protection, and reforestation in most fragile areas. PES in watersheds, promotion of agri-tourism, planned out-migration and provision of basic services and infrastructure are among the non-agricultural options that need to be developed.

Rainfed systems in the semi-arid tropics

These include smallholder farming in sub-Saharan African savannahs and some agro-pastoral systems in Asia (western India) and Africa. They are currently characterized in many places by overexploitation of natural resources and fuelwood, and by expansion into more marginal lands. With low cropping potential and unimproved agricultural practices, productivity is low (and sometimes declining) due to depletion of soil organic matter and fertility, soil acidification, poor soil moisture-holding capacity, and wind and water erosion. Ecosystems are degrading, with biomass and biodiversity decline, frequent occurrence of fires and water shortages. Institutional failings contribute to problems of land tenure and access, and to agriculture–livestock conflicts. Many of these areas are characterized by widespread poverty and vulnerability to climate shocks, with highly variable production subject to climate variability. Issues of access to land and conflicts between agriculture and livestock are widespread.

The potential for expansion is low to medium, with some possibilities where lands are not too fragile and irrigation water is available. Potential for intensification varies, and depends on scarce water resources, presence of fragile lands and population density. Options for improvement include enhanced land tenure security, land reform and consolidation where possible, better integration of agriculture and livestock, investments in irrigation and water harvesting where possible, crop insurance, integrated plant nutrition, plant breeding adapted to semi-arid conditions, improved governance, and investments in infrastructure (markets, roads). These regions also offer potential for more systematic use of solar energy for agriculture and household consumption. In extremely pressurised systems, planned out-migration may be needed.

Subtropical systems

Subtropical systems include those found in the densely populated and intensively cultivated areas around the Mediterranean basin and in Asia. They suffer from overexploitation of land and water, leading to erosion, low soil fertility, vegetation and biodiversity decline, water shortage and fires. Socio-economic problems include land fragmentation and high rates of out-migration, in particular by male family members.

These systems have very little potential for expansion, as most agriculturally suitable land is already in use. Instead, reduction in cultivated areas is likely to happen, under the combined pressure on land and on water resources by other sectors. The potential for intensification is relatively low and likely to be constrained by further land fragmentation. Out-migration and progressive marginalization of agriculture are likely to continue. The pace of degradation and its impact on the livelihoods of rural populations will depend on agricultural policies and the effective implementation of better conservation programmes.

Response options will need to include plant breeding adapted to semi-arid conditions, improved soil and water conservation and integrated plant nutrition. On the institutional side, a combination of land reforms and consolidation and climate change adaptation planning, setting up of viable crop insurance systems, investments in rural infrastructure and services and planned out-migration will be necessary. These systems must be considered in the overall context of social development, where the necessary transition towards a more urbanized society will need to be anticipated and accompanied in order to ensure good balance and integration between urban and rural environment.

Intensive temperate agriculture systems

Most temperate systems are in high-income countries. Agricultural systems in Western Europe are characterized by the highest level of productivity, associated with high levels of intensification. Intensive farming also occurs in the United States, Eastern China, Turkey, New Zealand, parts of India, Southern Africa and Brazil. These systems are well integrated into global markets and include some of the most active food-exporting areas in the world. Some receive the highest levels of agricultural subsidies in the world.

Some systems do have potential for further expansion: set-aside land in Europe could be put into agricultural use again, and expansion is also possible in both Northern and Southern America. Potential for intensification is very limited in Europe, but still possible elsewhere. However, yield gaps are reducing rapidly in several regions, including Eastern China. Climate change may provide a warming effect in Europe, shifting agro-ecological zones further north and expanding the areas suitable for agriculture. However, less reliable rainfall patterns and more extreme events may cancel out any benefits.

These systems are productive, but often associated with environmental problems. Soil health degradation (compaction, organic matter decline, sealing), pollution of soils and aquifers (leading to health hazards and de-pollution costs), loss of biodiversity and the degradation of freshwater ecosystems are among the main challenges these systems face. The negative environmental impacts associated with such levels of intensification are likely to increase unless they are more carefully managed.

Response options include pollution control and mitigation, conservation agriculture, integrated plant nutrition and integrated pest management. Expansion and intensification will probably happen in response to market pulls, but they need to be carefully planned and monitored to avoid further negative impact on the environment.

Rice-based systems

Rice-based systems are concentrated mostly in Southeast and Eastern Asia, and to a lesser extent in sub-Saharan Africa (Madagascar, Western Africa, Eastern Africa). These regions show distinct characteristics and face quite different types of challenges. In Asia, rice-based systems have high but level productivity and suffer from fragile ecosystems, growing occurrence of droughts and floods, and soil and water pollution. Competition for land, water and labour, and a dynamic economic transition in most of the countries, are placing new stresses on these systems.

Irrigated systems in Asia are at high risk from many drivers. In the already intensive rice-based systems, there is little opportunity for further intensification or expansion, and stresses will grow due to strong competition for land, water and labour from urban settlements and industry. Increased demand for diversified production to serve urban populations, increased rainfall variability, and occurrence of droughts and floods are further challenges faced by these systems, together with land abandonment, loss of buffer role of paddy land, increasing cost of land conservation, health hazards due to pollution, and loss of cultural values of land. Improved water storage, mechanization, diversification (introduction of fish and vegetables), pollution control and PES are among the options that may help these systems respond to a rapidly changing economic environment and climate change.

Rice-based systems in sub-Saharan Africa are, by contrast, low in productivity, mainly due to institutional problems of poor management and governance (in particular in relation to irrigation and water user associations, rapid degradation of irrigation infrastructure and poor market development). These systems show a high potential for both intensification and expansion, but this would require solutions to the institutional and economic problems that have plagued operations up to now. These solutions need to consider market and technologies, better incentives to farmers, access to inputs and improved varieties, and improved governance, management and infrastructure. Several systems would benefit from adapted agronomic packages such as the system of rice intensification, where local systems of water control and topography are suitable. (Uphoff *et al.*, 2011)

Large contiguous surface irrigation systems in dry areas

Large contiguous systems found in the basins of Asia, Northern America, Northern China, Central Asia, Northern Africa and the Middle East suffer from water resource problems of scarcity, overexploitation and competition, and have major negative externalities, including sediment and salinity transport, and impacts on water-related ecosystems. For the large contiguous irrigation systems in dry areas, mostly in Asia, demographic pressure and urbanization will increase pressure on land and water. Very little expansion is expected. Further intensification and diversification are possible through modernization of irrigation service delivery and better soil and water management, but the negative impacts on the ecosystems are likely to deteriorate further with intensification unless corrective action is taken. Climate change is likely to modify the volume and patterns of river flows and increase crop water requirements, with possible imbalance between water availability and demand.

The scope for expansion is very low in many places that have already reached their limits in terms of land or water availability. Where it is still possible, irrigation schemes must be carefully planned, and environmental and social concerns incorporated. Modernization of irrigation schemes (both infrastructure and governance) is needed to improve water service and increase flexibility and reliability in water supply to support diversification. It will also be necessary to develop incentives for efficient use of water, as well as prepare and implement climate change adaptation plans.

Groundwater-dependent irrigation systems

Groundwater-dependent irrigation systems in interior arid plains are found in India, China, central USA, Australia, Northern Africa, the Middle East and elsewhere. They are characterized by the continuing depletion of high-quality groundwater, pollution and salinization in places, leading to the loss of the buffer role of aquifers, loss of agriculture land and desertification. They face competition from cities and industries for a source of good-quality water. Climate change is expected to affect the pattern and style of recharge of these aquifers.

In the places where aquifer depletion is already occurring, there is limited scope for expansion, and it is likely that the extent of agricultural land served by intensive aquifers will progressively shrink as water levels fall, while groundwater use in supplementary irrigation may increase in other areas. Regulatory measures for groundwater withdrawal, more effective water allocation and use, and enhanced water productivity in irrigation are the only options to avoid losing excessive production capacity.

Rangelands

Pastoral and grazing lands are found in all continents. In areas at risk, including West Africa (Sahel), North Africa and parts of Asia, these systems are characterized by decreases in traditional grazing and food use, livestock pressure on land, development of invasive species, fires, fragmentation, sedentarization, conflicts, extreme poverty, food insecurity and out-migration. Such systems are extremely vulnerable to climate variability, which affects the productivity of land. Climate change, through increased temperature and rainfall variability, is likely to accentuate this trend.

Possibilities for expansion are very limited because land is already near or beyond the limit of use, particularly in fragile lands in poor countries. Scope for better land husbandry, while limited, is possible, and depends on economic and climatic conditions and the adoption of better practices, which may include lowering or control of stocking rates, improved rangeland management, controlled grazing practices and better integration with agriculture.

Forest–cropland interface

Forest–cropland interface systems are found mostly in tropical areas (Southeast Asia, the Amazon basin, Central Africa) and in the Himalayas. The main risks are associated with encroachment of agriculture on tropical forests, include loss of biodiversity and forest ecosystem services, introduction of invasive species, pests and diseases, fires, erosion, sedimentation and soil degradation. It is also well established that conversion of forest to cropland represents a net positive contribution to global GHG emissions.

Expansion of cropland encroachment into forests is not desirable in most cases. Possibilities for intensification exist through improved management of forest resources, agroforestry and the establishment of incentives such as PES.

Deltas, coastal alluvial plains and small islands

Deltas, coastal areas and small islands share the characteristics of high population density and vulnerable coastal ecosystems. They are vital for regional food production. Highly populated deltas include the Nile, the Red River, the Ganges/Brahmaputra and the Mekong. Coastal alluvial plains include those in the Arabian Peninsula and Eastern China, Bight of Benin and the Gulf of Mexico. These systems are under heavy demographic pressure and have seen important losses of biodiversity, particularly mangroves. Competition for land and water from industry and urban settlements is growing. They are increasingly polluted (notably by arsenic), and suffer from alkalinization and compaction of soil, and from contamination of shallow alluvial aquifers and underlying systems by industrial causes. Saline intrusion in groundwater and rivers is increasing under the twin effects of reduced flow of freshwater from the rivers and sea-level rise. Groundwater depletion is a common problem of many small islands and coastal areas.

Climate change is expected to affect these systems by sea-level rise, higher frequency of cyclones (Eastern and Southeast Asia), increased incidence of floods and low flows. Risks include loss of agricultural land and groundwater (with possible total loss of freshwater aquifers in small islands) and health-related problems. There is generally no scope for expansion, as competition for land is already strong, and expansion is determined by physiographic considerations and sea-level rise.

The scope for intensification depends on existing levels of productivity, which are, in many places, already very high. Response options include land-use planning, control of groundwater depletion, the establishment of climate change adaptation plans, flood and pollution control, mitigation of arsenic contamination through improved irrigation practices, and implementation of integrated water management strategies at the river basin level.

Peri-urban agriculture

Peri-urban agriculture occurs all across all parts of the world, in response to increasing demand for agricultural products by urban centres. It suffers from scarcity of suitable land, poor land tenure security, limited access to clean water and pollution problems. Peri-urban agriculture will continue to expand where land and water are available, thus taking advantage of dynamic and fast-growing markets associated with urbanization. Health risks, both for producers and consumers, will need to be managed much more systematically than today, particularly where untreated waste-water is used. Better integration of urban and peri-urban agriculture in urban planning would allow such practices to efficiently and safely serve growing cities.

Conclusions

The world's agricultural systems, and the land and water resources on which they are based, have to respond to increasing demand for food and other agricultural products by a growing and richer population. Increase in production is likely to come primarily from sustainable intensification in temperate zones and in irrigated systems in large river basins; from extension of cultivated areas in parts of Latin America and Africa; from sustainable intensification in rainfed areas; and from progressive conversion of some rainfed land to irrigated production where it is economically and technically feasible. Groundwater-based supplemental irrigation will continue to serve an increasingly productive agriculture, where feasible.

Overall, the picture is also that of a world with increasing imbalance between availability and demand for land and water resources at local level: the number of regions reaching the limits of their production capacity is fast increasing. Food trade will compensate for some deficits, but this will have important implications for local

FIGURE 3.4: GLOBAL DISTRIBUTION OF RISKS ASSOCIATED WITH MAIN AGRICULTURAL PRODUCTION SYSTEMS – A SCHEMATIC OVERVIEW

Floods/sea-level rise
Water scarcity
Pollution
Loss of biodiversity
Deforestation
Desertification/droughts
Loss/low soil fertility
Erosion
Land scarcity
Cropland

Source: this study

and national food self-sufficiency, and for the livelihoods of rural communities. On the other hand, the intensive agricultural practices associated with past increases in productivity have been accompanied by severe degradation of ecosystems services. On-farm and downstream risks associated with demographic pressure and intensification will persist and worsen in several agricultural systems as long as corrective measures are not taken to reverse this trend. This represents a major challenge to the sustainability of land and water resource management.

Climate change will negatively affect farming systems, in the semi-arid and sub-tropical areas in particular, impacting water resources and irrigation systems in a number of ways, and requiring major adaptation efforts in most cases. Deltas and coastal areas will be doubly at risk of flooding from sea-level rise and more variable wet-season rainfall. Figure 3.4 gives a schematic overview of the global distribution of risks associated with main agricultural production systems.

In conclusion, a substantial share of the world's land and water resources, and their ecological integrity, are under stress from increasing demand and unsustainable agricultural practices. Further demand from agriculture and other sectors, taken with the anticipated aspects of climate change, will add stress and threaten their future production capacity.

TEMPERATE

SUB-TROPICAL

SEMI-ARID TROPICS

HIGHLANDS

Chapter 4

TECHNICAL OPTIONS FOR SUSTAINABLE LAND AND WATER MANAGEMENT

As discussed in Chapter 1, it is expected that more than four-fifths of the increased production to 2050 will come from existing land areas through increased productivity. Many systems are, however, already constrained either because of existing high productivity levels, or because there are technical, socio-economic or institutional constraints. In addition, as the intensity of farming increases, the risks and related trade-offs discussed in the previous chapter become more pressing. This chapter reviews technical options for moving towards 'sustainable land and water management' – that is, more intensive integrated management of soil, water, nutrients and other inputs to produce increased crop value while maintaining or enhancing environmental quality and conserving natural resources, both on-site and off-site.

Even though the growth in the area of rainfed agriculture has remained static, rainfed agriculture is still projected to produce one-third or more of the increase in global food output in the coming decades. Rainfed systems in temperate zones are already high-yielding, but face problems of nutrient and pesticide pollution. Smallholder rainfed systems in developing countries face far more problems of poor soil quality, soil moisture deficits and high levels of agro-climatic risk, exacerbated by climate change. They are also hindered by the absence of profitable market outlets and the resources to invest in improving productivity.

Improving rainfed productivity

Yield increases play a significant role in poverty reduction. It has been estimated that every 1 percent increase in agricultural yields translates into a 0.6–1.2 percent decrease in the numbers of absolute poor is households that cannot afford basic needs for survival (Thirtle *et al.*, 2001). However, the data also underline the risk that, if the enabling environment does not encourage change to farming systems in developing countries, cereals yields under traditional management could stagnate at less than 2t/ha. Several African countries, for example, have yields that are at around 20 percent of potential. Others, by contrast, realized gains of several percentage points in recent years (for example in Southern Africa). Trends over the five year period 2000–5 confirm that these potential productivity gains can be realized, with both more-developed countries (four percent increase) and less-developed countries (three percent increase) reducing the yield gap). The gap between actual and potential is largest in parts of sub-Saharan Africa, which even under low-input farming have the potential to almost double cereals yields. There is thus considerable scope to close the yield gap for some of the poorest parts of the world, with potential for developing countries to double average cereals yields from 2.9 t/ha to 5.7 t/ha (Fischer *et al.*, 2010).

Rapid increases in rainfed yields in some areas in recent years show that improvements are realizable if favourable conditions are in place (Molden, 2007). These conditions include institutional reform to deliver research and advisory services, efficient markets for inputs and outputs, road infrastructure, mechanization, improved use of fertilizer and high-yielding varieties, and better soil moisture management. These are the conditions that have allowed the rapid growth of productivity in rainfed systems across Asia and in the developed world. However, although all of these conditions are well known and have shown their value, rainfed yields in many smallholder production systems in the developing world have stagnated, particularly in sub-Saharan Africa, despite efforts that have been made for many years to improve performance. Rainfed yields in Eastern Africa have stagnated at 16 percent of potential for years.

One major challenge in rainfed farming is how to introduce accessible technical solutions to improve management without increasing risks. Rainfed systems in developing countries are often characterized by low productivity, caused by low and variable water availability, and by environmental and soil problems of salinity, temperature and lack of nutrients. The technological solutions available are characteristically low-yielding: the innovations of the green revolution depended largely on water availability. In addition, productivity-boosting improvements for rainfed systems typically heighten levels of risk. The insecurity of rainfed production is intensified by the risks associated with climate variability.

In some areas, these constraints have been overcome. In China, combined soil and water management investments have delivered good returns with manageable levels of risk. The Loess Plateau watershed rehabilitation project demonstrated on an area of 1.5 Mha that soil and water management improvements could be profitable (Box 2.7). Elsewhere in the world (Argentina, Australia, Canada, Kazakhstan and sub-Saharan Africa) a range of rainwater management technologies and conservation farming techniques have been introduced with some success, and there is increasing evidence that farmers are taking these up (Pretty *et al.*, 2011). One of the greatest problems is that some innovations take time to pay back investments.

Managing soil health and fertility

The challenges of low and depleting nutrients in soils and of poor soil structure are prevalent on rainfed croplands. The lowest average productivity of rainfed agriculture is found in sub-Saharan Africa, especially in small-scale systems, because of low inherent soil fertility of the land, compounded by severe nutrient depletion: cereal crop yields are often below 1 t/ha. Solutions that depend on large applications of fertilizers are often unaffordable and too risky within many low-potential rainfed cropping systems. In these cases, sustainable land and water management techniques, including conservation agriculture, may help to restore and improve soil fertility through integrated soil fertility management (Pretty *et al.*, 2011).

Benefits of keeping soils healthy

The direct and indirect benefits of improving soil management in agricultural systems can be assessed in economic, environmental and food security terms:

- Economic benefits: improved soil management reduces input costs by enhancing resource-use efficiency (especially decomposition and nutrient cycling, nitrogen fixation, and water storage and movement). Less fertilizer may be needed if nutrient cycling becomes more efficient and fewer nutrients are leached from the rooting zone. Fewer pesticides are needed where a diverse set of pest-control organisms is active. As soil structure improves, the availability of water and nutrients to plants also improves. It is estimated that nutrient cycling provides the largest contribution (51 percent) of the total value (US$33 trillion) of all 'ecosystem services' (including cultural, services waste treatment, disturbance regulation, water supply, food production, gas regulation and water regulation) provided each year (Costanza *et al.*, 1997).

- Environmental protection: soil organisms filter and detoxify chemicals and absorb the excess nutrients that would otherwise become pollutants when they reach groundwater or surface water. The management of soil biota helps to prevent pollution and land degradation, especially through minimizing the use of agrochemicals and maintaining or enhancing soil structure and cation exchange capacity (CEC). Excessive reduction in soil biodiversity, especially the loss of keystone species or species with unique functions (for example, as a result of excess chemicals, compaction or disturbance) may have catastrophic ecological effects leading to loss of agricultural productive capacity. The mix of soil organisms also partially determines soil resilience.

• Food security: improved soil management can improve crop yield and quality, especially through controlling pests and diseases, and enhancing plant growth. Soil biodiversity determines the resource-use efficiency, as well as the sustainability and resilience of agro-ecological systems.

Techniques for managing soil fertility

Low-input agriculture depletes the soil, mining soil nutrients and leading to decline of agricultural production, and ultimately to non-sustainable farming systems. When correctly applied, the use of mineral fertilizer in combination with other techniques for improving soil health has proved effective in restoring and enhancing soil fertility and in generating increased yields. However, mineral fertilizer is not affordable to many farmers, and in any case can form only one component of the solution to the challenge of soil fertility.

Organic sources of plant nutrients enhance soil fertility and improve soil structure, water retention and biological activity. They can be derived from incorporation of crop residues, application of animal manure, composting of organic wastes or from biological fixation through leguminous crops, green manures or nitrogen-fixing trees. However, these sources are by themselves not sufficient to sustain soil fertility. Recycling of crop residues does reduce losses, but it does not compensate for the nutrients exported in harvests, nor does it add to the total amount of nutrients originally available. Organic fertilizers need to be used in conjunction with other sources of nutrients.

The use of locally available rock phosphate can be an important component in integrated plant nutrient systems, as an essential phosphorus supply or as a strategy of phosphorus recapitalization. The effects of rock phosphate are beneficial primarily on acid and phosphorus fixing soils found mainly in the humid tropics, which are forested or used for perennial crops such as oil palm, cocoa or coffee. In order to be effective it has to be accompanied by a balanced supply of the other major plant nutrients.

For strongly acid soils, the application of soil amendments of lime or dolomite remedies deficiencies in calcium and magnesium, and neutralizes aluminium toxicity, constraints that limit root penetration and hence reduce access to other nutrients and water in subsurface layers. Without amendment, the effectiveness of other soil fertility-enhancing measures is very limited. The application required depends on land use (some crops are acid-tolerant) and soil characteristics. Liming in excess can reduce the availability of essential trace elements.

Plant diversity in cropping systems reduces the negative impact of monocropping on soils, and can bring positive advantages to soil health, improving soil quality, improving nutrient cycling and sustaining biodiversity. Biodiversity within the farming system can be achieved through intercrops (growing two or more crop species simultaneously on the same land), crop rotations (growing different crops sequentially on the same land) and relay crops (growing different crops with partially overlapping growing seasons). There is also evidence that using a diversity of crops can improve the effectiveness of mycorrhizal (fungal root symbioses) associations in a cropping system, provided that soils are not mechanically disturbed (e.g. through tillage, which has negative impacts on fungal life, as well as meso- and macro-fauna).

The use of legumes enhances biological nitrogen fixation. However, while the amounts of nitrogen fixed by legumes under experimental conditions have been well investigated, there is less data on the gains obtained in cropping systems under farmer conditions. Inoculation is often required, and the infrastructure and extension for this is often lacking. Furthermore, the effectiveness of nitrogen fixation is constrained by phosphorus deficiency in soil. As farmers grow many legumes for food (e.g. phaseolus beans, cowpeas, pigeon peas, groundnuts), relay or mixed cropping may prove to offer an economic return.

Agro-forestry systems have contributed to soil fertility. The use of *Faidherbia albida* (*Acacia albida*) provides a good example. Yields of grain crops are substantially higher under the tree crown than in the open field (Box 4.1). The beneficial effect is attributed to a higher content of soil organic matter and to the fertilizing effect of dung of animals grazing in the shade of the tree. Maintaining protective soil cover is also important, such as through minimum or zero tillage, the use of crop residues and mulch to reduce evaporation from bare soils, and optimization of rainwater infiltration and groundwater recharge. These practices have a positive impact on soil fertility, and hence on crop yields and water use efficiency. They also mitigate drought risk.

The need for improvement

Technical actions to enhance and restore soil fertility have to be selected and designed in accordance with the specific constraints and potentials of diverse environments. Advocating biological nitrogen fixation where legumes are not part of the

Maize growing under Faidherbia *trees in southern Tanzania*

The combination of trees in farming systems (agroforestry) with conservation farming is emerging as an affordable and accessible science-based solution to caring better for the land and increasing smallholder food production. Millions of farmers in Zambia, Malawi, Niger and Burkina Faso are restoring exhausted soils and increasing both crop yields and incomes with this approach. The most promising results are from the integration of fertilizer trees into cropping systems. These trees improve soil fertility by drawing nitrogen from the air and transferring it to the soil through their roots and leaf litter.

Scientists from the World Agroforestry Centre and national institutions have been evaluating various species of fertilizer trees for many years, including *Sesbania*, *Gliricidia* and *Tephrosia*. Currently, *Faidherbia albida* is showing promise. This indigenous African acacia is already a natural component of systems across much of the continent. Unlike most other trees, *Faidherbia* sheds its leaves during the early rainy season and remains dormant throughout the crop-growing period: the leaves grow again when the dry season begins. This reverse phenology makes it highly compatible with food crops, because it does not compete for light, nutrients or water during the crop-growing season.

In Zambia, 160 000 farmers now grow food crops within agroforests of *Faidherbia* over an area of 300 000 ha. Zambia's Conservation Farming Unit has observed that unfertilized maize yields in the vicinity of *Faidherbia* trees averaged 4.1 t/ha, compared with 1.3 t/ha nearby (but beyond the tree canopy). Similar promising results have emerged from Malawi, where maize yields increased up to 280 percent in the zone under the canopy of *Faidherbia* trees compared with the zone outside. In Niger, there are now more than 4.8 Mha of *Faidherbia*-dominated agroforests enhancing millet and sorghum production. Promising results have also been observed from research in India and Bangladesh.

Source: Garrity et al. (2010) Photo: © World Agroforestry Centre

CHAPTER 4

cropping pattern may face a low adoption rate. The use of rock-phosphate outside the acid soils of the humid and moist subhumid zones would have a limited impact. Liming may be effective in neutralizing aluminium toxicity in acid soils, but is superfluous on soils with fair calcium saturation. In order to be effective, applications of fertilizers in semi-arid areas need to be accompanied by water harvesting and water conservation, or by small-scale irrigation. Timing of fertilization needs to be designed for soils with low plant nutrient retention capacity. Relying on organic sources of plant nutrients in semi-arid areas, where biomass production is severely limited by water deficit, is unrealistic. The same applies to relying on animal manure in areas of severe tsetse infestation.

Cash inputs, in particular, are rarely adopted in subsistence systems. Despite significant growth in the use of fertilizers in a small number of countries in sub-Saharan Africa, the use of fertilizers has remained generally low as a result of unfavourable cost–benefit ratios, high risk and weak markets. However, in contrast with the past, staple food crops (e.g. maize, teff, barley, wheat) are now increasingly among the main crops that are fertilized (Morris *et al.*, 2007).

Packages also have to be designed for each local farming situation. Numerous attempts to improve soil fertility have failed because the proposed technology was not appropriate and because elementary information about the characteristics of the natural resource base was ignored. Recommendations that are formulated for entire countries or regions, without taking into account the great diversity that prevails at farmer level, are often counterproductive. Adapted packages are needed, with combinations of technical options tailored to meet site-specific ecological and socio-economic conditions.

There are many socio-economic constraints to adoption. Crop residues have alternative uses as fodder, fuel and building material, for which there are often no substitutes. Crop residues are also burnt in order to control weeds and pests. Applications of manure are effective in homestead gardens where farm animals are stabled, but elsewhere animals may be feeding on extensive rangeland from which manure cannot be collected. Composting is labour-intensive, and organic wastes on a small farm are limited. Grass and legume cover crops compete with food crops for land and for available water and nutrients. The same constraints apply to green manuring, which may require considerable labour for the incorporation of produced biomass. Major constraints to incorporating additional organic matter in the soil are the lack of draught power and the lack of short-term returns.

Packages thus need a 'feasibility and risk' assessment to build in incentives. Recent work in sub-Saharan Africa and Asia has developed packages that are designed to manage risk and provide incentives to farmers (Box 4.2). Some techniques, in fact,

Farmyard manure, Nepal

Integrated soil fertility management is a strategy to incorporate both organic and inorganic plant nutrients for higher crop productivity, prevention of soil degradation and reduction of nutrient loss. It relies on nutrient application through organic inputs such as compost, manure, inorganic fertilizer and/or the integration of nutrient-fixing crops. The integrated use of organic and mineral inputs in crop production has many positive interactions. However, for lasting positive effects on soil health, soil tillage should be avoided.

Source: CDE (2010) Photo: K. M. Sthapit

seem to offer several incentives. Plant diversity has the benefit of offering other advantages to farmers that make adoption attractive, including spreading market risks, increasing income opportunities, improving dietary balance, spreading labour requirements more evenly throughout the year, and decreasing risk from pests and adverse environmental factors such as drought.

Soil moisture management for rainfed areas

Improvement in rainfed agriculture is dependent on an adequate supply of water to plant roots. The first line of action in soil moisture conservation is to make the best use of the available rainfall. This involves minimizing unproductive water evaporation, increasing soil organic matter content and minimizing soil disturbances through appropriate techniques, including conservation agriculture.

Soil moisture management in high rainfall areas has traditionally been practised by a range of water-harvesting systems, including terracing and runoff diversion. There is considerable technical scope for improving agricultural water management in rain-fed cultivation through more water harvesting and better soil moisture conservation techniques – but also many technical and socio-economic constraints to adoption.

Rainwater harvesting aims to improve water control and ensure adequate soil moisture for crop roots during the growing season (Box 4.3). Such harvesting captures runoff from a managed catchment area and reserves it either in a storage area or in the soil profile. Technologies include simple on-farm structures diverting water to a planting pit, structures in the catchment that divert runoff to storage or run-on fields, permanent terraces and dams (CDE, 2010). Effective rainwater harvest-

BOX 4.3: RAINWATER HARVESTING

Furrow-enhanced rainwater (runoff) harvesting, Syria

Rainwater harvesting uses a range of technologies that gather runoff to make it available for agricultural production or domestic purposes. Rainwater harvesting aims to minimize variations in water availability and enhance the reliability of agricultural production. The basic components of a rainwater harvesting system are (1) a catchment area, (2) a concentration / storage area and (3) a cultivated area. When runoff is stored in the soil profile, (1) and (3) are synonymous. Rainwater harvesting covers a broad spectrum of different technologies, from simple measures such as V-shaped structures with a planting pit to more complex and large structures such as dams. The investment costs vary considerably.

Source: CDE (2010) Photo: F. Turkelboom

ing can boost yields by two to three times over conventional rainfed agriculture, especially when combined with improved varieties and minimum-tillage methods that conserve water. Several of the Consultative Group on International Agricultural Research (CGIAR) centres are researching issues of rainwater harvesting, and related issues of drought-tolerant and water-efficient germplasm and agronomic management for dryland conditions (World Bank, 2006: 170).

Farming on slopes comes with problems of rapid loss of moisture from the soil profile and erosion by runoff. Many vegetative and structural techniques for soil and water conservation on slopes are available, including vegetative strips on contours to retain moisture and prevent erosion (Box 4.4), and terraces and bunds that act as structural barriers (Box 4.5). Vegetative measures usually require lower investment and are more easily established, and farmers tend to give them priority over more demanding structural measures. Structural measures should be promoted where

BOX 4.4: VEGETATIVE STRIPS

Natural vegetative strip, Philippines

Vegetative strips may be composed of grass, shrubs and trees. These are often used along contours, helping to hold back excessive runoff, but may also be set perpendicular to the wind, to control wind erosion. Vegetative strips along the contour often lead to the formation of bunds and terraces due to 'tillage erosion' via the downslope movement of soil during cultivation. Compared with terraces and bunds they are thus much easier and cheaper to establish. Vegetative strips can also be utilized on flat land as shelterbelts, windbreaks or as barriers surrounding fields.

Source: CDE (2010) Photo: A. Mercado, jr

Establishment of small bench terraces, Thailand

Structural barriers are measures on sloping lands in the form of earth/soil bunds and stone lines for reducing runoff velocity and soil erosion. This is achieved by reducing the steepness and/or length of slope. Structural barriers are well known and are commonly prominent as traditional soil and water conservation measures. Structural barriers are often combined with soil fertility improvement (e.g. soil cover, manure or fertilizer application).

Source: CDE (2010) Photo: S. Sombatpanit

vegetative measures are not sufficient on their own, such as on very steep and erodible slopes. Ideally, structural measures are combined with vegetative or agronomic measures for protection, and to improve soil fertility and water management.

These techniques have traditionally relied on high levels of cheap or subsidized labour and animal draught. On marginal lands in low rainfall areas, the limited opportunities for on-farm control and related soil conservation still remain risky. Recent experience with introduced techniques in many countries is that they are often not profitable for farmers and can increase risk. They are thus rarely replicated in the absence of project support.

The best options are adaptable management practices that increase vegetative cover, and enhance retention of organic matter and soil moisture, along with adoption of adapted crop varieties. Strategies to provide yield stability in the face of climatic variability and to increase yields through improved soil, water and biological resource management will go hand in hand. Investment in improving agricultural water management needs to form part of a package that integrates soil, water and agronomy with a broader rural development and livelihoods approach, particularly to open access to input and output markets.

Integrated approaches to improving productivity in rainfed systems

Several integrated production approaches have developed that combine best practices in sustainable land and water management, adapted to both the local ecosystem and social circumstances as well as to a viable market demand (Neely and Fynn, 2010; CDE, 2010). They incorporate improved soil and water management techniques in a way that intensifies production through integrated soil fertility management, improved water-use efficiency and crop diversity. These approaches offer opportunities for farmers, particularly smallholder rainfed farmers, to improve productivity sustainably. Some of these approaches are also applicable in larger-scale farming.

Agro-ecological approaches

Agro-ecological approaches combine ecological knowledge and agriculture to promote a whole-systems approach to agriculture and food systems, using a range of traditional and modern approaches. Agro-ecological approaches use combined methods sourced from traditional knowledge, alternative agriculture, advanced science and technologies, and local food systems. Typically, the approaches employ minimum- and low-till methods, rotational grazing, intercropping, crop rotation, crop–livestock integration, intraspecies variety and seed saving, habitat management, and pest management rather than 'control'. Agro-ecological approaches also encourage beneficial predatory and parasitic insects, and the enhancement of beneficial biota including mycorrhizae and nitrogen-fixers, as well as conserving resources, including energy, water (through dry farming and efficient irrigation), stocks of soil nutrients and organic matter (Neely and Fynn, 2010; Pretty *et al.*, 2011).

Conservation agriculture

Conservation agriculture approaches seek to conserve natural resources while increasing yields and resilience. Conservation agriculture systems are grouped around three core technologies that, applied simultaneously, provide a basis for sustainable improvements in productivity through synergetic effects: minimal soil disturbance, permanent soil cover and crop diversity.

Conservation agriculture provides (1) improved rainwater infiltration (with reduced runoff, evaporation and erosion) (2) increased biodiversity and soil organic matter, and (3) improved soil structure. Labour requirements are reduced, and the use of synthetic fertilizer, pesticide and fossil fuels is minimized. Each of the technologies can serve as an entry point. However, only the simultaneous application of all three results in full benefits. Conservation agriculture is suited to both small- and large-scale farming. Its adoption is particularly attractive for situations facing acute labour shortages. Because of its proven track record, conservation agriculture is now being promoted by FAO globally, and there are currently around 117 Mha under conservation agriculture worldwide.

Organic agriculture

Organic agriculture avoids the use of synthetic input, conserves soil and water, and optimizes productivity by organic means. It is a holistic management system that minimizes or eliminates synthetic fertilizer, pesticides and genetically modified organisms, conserves soil and water, and aims to optimize the health and productivity of interdependent communities of plants, animals and people.

Organic agriculture includes a series of measures: crop rotations and enhanced crop diversity; different combinations of livestock and plants; symbiotic nitrogen fixation with legumes; application of organic manure; and biological pest control, such as 'push–pull'. All these strategies seek to make the best use of local resources. However, medium- and large-scale organic production often requires imports of organic material (in the form of compost, mulch, etc.) in order to maintain soil productivity. Medium- and large-scale organic production also often includes mechanical tillage.

Organic agriculture is a sustainable system that minimizes conflict with other ecosystem services, and has an enhanced economic value due to growing consumer preference for organic products. Over 32 Mha worldwide are now farmed organically by 1.2 million farmers, with organic wild products harvested on around 30 Mha (CDE, 2010; Neely and Fynn, 2010).

Agroforestry

Agroforestry is a land-use system in which woody perennials are integrated with agricultural crops and livestock in order to access beneficial interactions, and to balance ecological needs with the sustainable harvesting of tree and forest resources. Agroforestry provides many benefits and services – more productive and sustainable use of soil and water resources, multiple fuel, fodder and food products, and provision of a habitat for associated species. There are usually both ecological and economic interactions between the components of the system.

There are five main forms of agroforestry: alley cropping, forest farming, silvopastoralism (Box 4.6), riparian forest buffers and windbreaks. Agroforestry may

Silvopastoralism systems include the introduction of trees into grazing areas, providing shade and shelter, increased resilience, and in some cases improved forage quality. Silvopastoralism can bring dramatic results: 20 years ago in the Shinyanga region of Tanzania soil erosion was such that dust storms were common; today the activity of the Shinyanga Land Rehabilitation Programme (HASHI) means that woodlots yield firewood and building timber, while fruit orchards provide food and fodder trees supply protein-rich feed for livestock.

Source: Neely and Fynn (2010)

integrate a wide range of technologies: contour farming, multistorey cropping, (relay) intercropping, multiple cropping, bush and tree fallows, parkland, or home gardens. Many of the approaches form part of traditional land-use systems, which can be upgraded with the introduction of new or improved technologies.

Integrated crop–livestock systems

Mixed and integrated systems optimize the use of the biomass and nutrient cycles within a crop and livestock production system. Integrated crop and livestock systems can positively affect biodiversity, soil health, ecosystem services and forest preservation. Due to the integration of components, they are able to compete economically with intensive large-scale specialized operations. Variants include systems with or without trees or aquaculture, and agropastoral systems with or without trees.

The aim is for components to interact synergistically. For example, waste products such as manure from livestock are used to improve soil fertility for crop production, while crop residues provide supplementary feed for animals. Mixed systems diversify production, making resource use more efficient, and improve resilience to risks of climate change, market variability or production failure.

Traditional agriculture systems

Traditional agricultural systems comprise indigenous forms of ecological agriculture resulting from the coevolution of social and environmental systems. These systems are usually characterized by a high degree of complexity and plant biodiversity. Much can be learned from the very specific use of environmental knowledge and natural resources in these systems, because of their highly evolved synthesis between productive and natural systems. Some have now achieved the status of Globally Important Agricultural Heritage Sites (GIAHS). Careful introduction of management improvements to these systems, based on sustainable land and water management technologies, can result in higher yields, particularly from agroforestry and integrated crop and livestock practices. However, some forms of traditional agriculture are encountering pressures that may make them less sustainable, and changes may be needed (CDE, 2010; Neely and Fynn, 2010).

Sustainable agropastoral and pastoral practices

Healthy and productive grasslands are obtained in drylands by bunching the stock into large herds and moving them frequently. Controlled grazing allows for more even distribution of dung and urine that can enhance soil organic matter and nutrients for plant productivity. In fact, overgrazing is often more a function of time than of the absolute numbers of animals – it happens when livestock have access to plants before the above-ground parts and rooting systems have had time to recover. The holistic planned grazing method (Savory and Butterfield, 1999) should improve soil cover, plant diversity and biomass, increase water infiltration, and increase animal density to better distribute dung and urine, while limiting grazing time. It results in improved biomass production, as well as improved livestock quality and productivity.

Many researchers on pastoral systems have concluded that extensive livestock production on communal land is the most appropriate use of semi-arid lands in Africa (Scoones, 1995). Therefore, the conversion of de facto common property resources that are commonplace in rangelands into private user rights encourages short-term resource exploitation rather than the long-term conservation they require. Community managed conservancies in Kenya are utilizing holistic grazing of livestock to increase productivity of the livestock, as well as wildlife numbers (Box 4.7).

Key constraints stemming from lack of tenure, promotion of privatization, and minimal health and education services must be addressed to ensure that the synergistic relationship between livestock-based livelihoods and environmental health can be successful and sustainable (UNCCD, 2007). Improving pastoralists' capacities to move towards sustainable management of rangelands requires a combination of measures that include adaptive management approaches, social organization and tenurial arrangements that cover the common property resources upon which their livelihoods depend.

Constraints and challenges

The approaches described are all context-specific, and should be adapted to the local agro-ecological and socio-economic context. Major challenges are knowledge, incentives and resources. All approaches require knowledge and knowledge transfer, and the institutional basis for this has to be available. All of the approaches have their own economic rationale, but often financial costs are higher than in traditional systems, and overall profitability may be uncertain. Part of the benefit of 'ecologically adapted' agriculture goes off-site, to downstream or global beneficiaries,

In the land around Lake Baringo in Kenya's central Rift Valley, a quiet natural revolution is taking place to reverse devastating land degradation and re-establish grassland resilience. The Rehabilitation of Arid Environments (RAE) Trust recognized that, in pastoral areas, grass is the most important commodity. With community members, they are transforming the Baringo basin. Some 2 200 ha have been successfully rehabilitated using trees and grass plantings, and improved livestock management. Bringing back the grass has now positively impacted some 15 000–30 000 people – including individual families, pastoralists managing communal fields and group ranches, as well as self-help and women's groups. Grass seed is being harvested and is now sold throughout Kenya.

Getting the perennial grasses back has not just refurbished the ecosystem processes (land, nutrients, water and biodiversity) but has resulted in the confidence and competence for the communities to be self-sustaining. A focus on the drylands and grazing lands of Africa is indispensible to efforts for reversing degradation and reducing poverty.

Source: Elizabeth Myerhoff and Murray Roberts, RAE Trust. Photo: W. Lynam

whereas the farmer bears all of the cost. Even if the profit incentive is present, the investment costs and lead time before these approaches 'pay back' is a constraint for farmers, particularly poor smallholders.

CHAPTER 4

Sourcing water for irrigated agriculture

New diversions and multipurpose projects

Over the four decades to 2050, a net increase of water withdrawals for agriculture of about 150 km^3 is anticipated, with the largest gross increases in Southeast Asia, Southern America and sub-Saharan Africa. Most of this will have to come from surface water, as groundwater is already fully developed in most locations.

Opportunities for large storage dams are fewer than in the past, and low economic returns and environmental and safety considerations have reduced interest in the construction of large dams. High cost means that large dams can usually only be justified by hydropower benefits. However, projects are under way or under consideration in a number of countries, including China, Iran and several African countries. Some irrigation water may also be added by optimizing release rules on existing dams. Transboundary cooperation on water resources development and management could also increase water availability for irrigation. For example, hydropower dams on the Blue Nile in Ethiopia could provide extra irrigation water downstream.

But most new storage specifically for irrigation is likely to be at a small scale. In many countries there are options for such small structures. All such impoundments require social, economic and environmental assessment of the risks and trade-offs involved, and projects need to be studied within a basin-planning framework. At the policy level, diversion of extra water for agriculture would require decisions about locking in entitlements to agriculture over other, possibly higher value uses, and about downstream risks to the aquatic environment and wetlands. Where transboundary resources are concerned, governments would have to weigh the benefits of optimizing investment at the basin scale (which might, for example, suggest upstream investment in hydropower and downstream diversion for irrigation) against sovereignty and water security issues. A decision to invest in irrigation development rather than in rainfed agriculture or in other pro-poor assets and services would be conditioned by the impacts of possible investment alternatives.

Groundwater

Despite the problems of depletion and pollution, groundwater will continue to offer a key buffer in maintaining optimal soil moisture for irrigated crops, and this role will grow with increasing climatic variability (FAO, 2011d). In many countries, though, there are few opportunities for new groundwater development, so better use of existing groundwater resources is a vital priority.

But groundwater depletion as a consequence of intensive agriculture is unrelenting (Siebert *et al.*, 2010). Although introduction of management approaches is unlikely to restore many aquifers to complete sustainability, aquifer life and productivity can be improved. Recent experience with community self-management of groundwater is encouraging, where recharge of shallow aquifers is active and user interests in maintaining dependable levels of agricultural production are high (World Bank, 2010a).

Salinization of aquifers arises from percolation of polluted or saline waters from irrigated agriculture, and also when aquifer stocks are depleted and concentrations of salts rise. In addition, depletion of coastal aquifers can result in saline intrusion. The key solution is active management of aquifers, to reduce extraction to the sustainable yield. Aquifer health may also be restored by artificial injection of freshwater to dilute saline water or to create salt water intrusion barriers, but this can be costly and requires a high degree of control (Mateo-Sagasta and Burke, 2010).

Scope for investing in non-conventional sources of water

Globally, only about 60 percent of water withdrawn is actually consumed in direct evaporation – some 2 900 km^3 out of 5 200 km^3. The rest is returned to the hydrological system and is potentially recoverable for secondary uses, such as agriculture. If all this water were recovered, it would represent more than three-quarters of the present consumptive use in agriculture. Thus, particularly in water-short countries, investment in re-use of drainage water and municipal or industrial wastewater can offset scarcity.

Drainage water can be re-used either through loops in systems or by farmers pumping direct from drains. Use of these relatively saline waters poses agricultural and environmental risks due to soil salinization and water quality degradation downstream, and thus salinity risk assessment and monitoring are needed. Actions to prevent further salinization of land and water, or to remediate saline or sodic soils, also have to be implemented. Successes include in Egypt, which re-uses over 10 percent of its annual freshwater withdrawals without deterioration of the salt balance. Desalination of salty groundwater and brackish drainage water for agriculture is so far uneconomic due to high energy costs, with the exception of intensive horticulture for high-value cash crops, such as vegetables and flowers (mainly in greenhouses) grown in coastal areas, where safe disposal of the brine is easier than in inland areas (Mateo-Sagasta and Burke, 2010). However, desalinated water, including drainage water, is becoming a more competitive option, because costs are declining while those of surface water and groundwater are increasing.

As cities expand, more municipal and industrial wastewater will become available. Wastewater has the advantage of being rich in nutrients, and is available close to centres of population and markets, so is ideal for peri-urban market gardening and aquaculture. However, contaminants in wastewater pose risks for human health and the environment. To maximize benefits and minimize risks related to the use of wastewater, a robust policy and institutional framework has to be designed (WHO-FAO-UNEP, 2006). Decisions on *technical* aspects need to be taken up-front, because this will determine the treatment method for re-use of effluent. The *water resources allocation* aspects need to be planned: who will receive the water needs to be assessed and become subject to contractual arrangements. On the *environmental* side, rules and regulation are required to control contaminants at source, and to protect human health. Finally, on the *agricultural* side, restricted irrigation and cropping practices may need to be applied.

Modernizing irrigation systems

Improving water service in large irrigation schemes

The scope for efficiency gains and improved land and water productivity in irrigation is considerable. Efficiencies worldwide are well below technical maximums; pressurized systems and protected agriculture still occupy only a small area; low-value staples predominate in cropping patterns; and agricultural yields and farmer incomes are well short of potential (Molden *et al.*, 2010). Three elements can contribute to 'more value per drop': improving water service, improving on-farm water use efficiency (especially on-farm) and improving agronomic efficiency.

Pathways to improve productivity and bridge the yield gap in irrigation include increasing the flexibility, reliability and timing of water service through operation and maintenance of the diversion and canal system, or better distribution within the system (for example, by increasing supplies to tail-end areas). In principle, improved water service is feasible on almost all irrigation schemes.

An integrated approach is required to invest in the different inputs to the production system – soil, water, agronomy, along with economic and institutional improvements. The concept of large-scale irrigation scheme modernization embraces all the changes in the irrigation delivery system, in agronomic practices, and in the institutional and incentive structure needed to provide farmers with a sustainable, efficient and demand-responsive water delivery service that will underpin a high productivity and sustainable farming system (FAO, 2007e).

A second pathway is to improve water-use efficiency (consumptive use of water in irrigation as a proportion of water withdrawal for irrigation) so that a larger share of water diverted is used beneficially (for example, by reducing losses in the irrigation system, improving on-farm water management or recycling drainage water). The scope for increasing the beneficial use of water withdrawn for irrigation is demonstrated by the very low ratio in many areas between water required and water withdrawn, as up to three times as much water is withdrawn on irrigation schemes as is actually required for plant growth. However, the scope for saving water must be considered with caution, as a large part of unused water returns to rivers and aquifers through percolation and drainage.

Integrated modernization will require both 'hardware' and 'software' investments. Hardware investments will go beyond the simple rehabilitation of existing systems to include physical improvements to the system, such as the correct selection of gates and control structures, lining of canals with geosynthetics, construction of interceptor canals and reservoirs, and installation of modern information systems, as well as on-farm irrigation improvement technologies such as drip irrigation, and a drainage network that allows a non-polluting management of the salt balance. Modernization investments also include a range of 'software' improvements such as scheme management and institutional structures, on-farm water management practices, combined water and soil fertility management, drainage water management, and integrated approaches to combating drought, salinity and floods. Investment in irrigation modernization for sustainable, high-productivity agriculture requires an economic environment that provides undistorted incentives, manageable risk and market access.

The scope for improving productivity in small-scale and informal irrigation

The scope for improvements in irrigation productivity is not confined to large formal schemes. Many smallholders in Asia, Africa and the Middle East make their livelihoods from agriculture practised in small-scale and traditional irrigation systems. Often, small-scale irrigation is based on community-constructed water diversion and conveyance systems operated by user-managed institutions. These include flood-based systems (such as spate diversion or flood recession), spring and shallow well systems, small-scale perimeters lifting water from rivers, run-off/run-on systems, water-harvesting systems, and local market-gardening systems using wells, local runoff or even tap water.

Small-scale irrigation systems exist in almost all agro-ecological zones, and are important where water is a significant constraint on crop production and where water resources are limited or overused, particularly in semi-arid to subhumid zones. Often these schemes are partly (or even mainly) rainfed, using only supplementary irrigation. Typically, yields are well below those of larger formal schemes due to lack of economies of scale, lack of appropriate varieties and water control, and difficulties of accessing markets. Their strengths lie in well-developed traditional knowledge, sustainable management of land and water resources, and levels of local social capital.

The challenge is how to improve performance on these schemes without compromising their present sustainability. Some technologies are available – for example,

Drip irrigation system

The aim to increase returns to water, ('more crop per drop'), can be achieved through many ways, including more efficient water collection, abstraction, storage, distribution and application in the field. Drip irrigation schemes are water-efficient systems that apply small volumes of water at frequent intervals close to the root-zone. In drip irrigation systems, water flows through a filter into special drip pipes and is discharged directly onto the soil near the plants. When this technology is properly managed, the advantages include better water control, improved plant nutrition and reduction in labour requirement. It is well suited for high-value crops, including vegetables and fruit trees.

Source: CDE (2010) Photo: W. Critchley

canal lining for spring-fed schemes, or treadle pumps for market gardening. What is needed are mechanisms to transmit knowledge, technology and investment support, ensuring that change is introduced within the framework of traditional sustainable land and water management practices (Box 4.8).

Increasing on-farm water productivity

Water-use efficiency

Improving on-farm water-use efficiency (beneficial consumptive use by evapotranspiration as a proportion of water delivered) depends on the on-farm water management skills of farmers. Measures to improve on-farm water-use efficiency combine increasing the skills of farmers to better manage the timing and quantity of irrigation for their crops with investment in on-farm irrigation technology that provides better control over water deliveries and reduces wastage. Better control can be provided by piped distribution systems, and by precision delivery to wet the plant roots, (e.g. by drip or bubbler irrigation). These technologies will also reduce non-beneficial water consumption by reducing transmission losses to percolation and non-beneficial evaporation. Efficiency can be increased further by controlling the micro-climate around the crop, such as in protected agriculture under greenhouses.

Agronomic efficiency depends on the skills of farmers, though some constraints, such as climatic and socio-economic factors, are outside their control. Agronomic efficiency can be improved by:

- Water control and soil moisture management to ensure adequate availability of moisture to plant roots for optimal growth. Conservation agriculture, in particular, reduces significantly unproductive water losses.

- Water, soil and nutrient management to ensure timely availability of nutrients in the root zone and efficient nutrient uptake by plants. In particular, water, soil and input management to raise nitrogen availability is critical for high yield per unit of evapotranspiration.

- Crop husbandry to select the optimal cropping pattern, choose the best-performing varieties, align the cropping calendar with moisture availability, sow at the right time, and manage weeds, arthropod pests and diseases.

Water productivity

An additional route towards a more productive use of irrigation water is to increase agronomic or economic productivity so that more output is obtained per unit of water consumed. This can be obtained through better agricultural practices, leading to increased yields of irrigated crops (including by achieving a higher harvest index) and for which no additional irrigation water is needed, or through hanging cropping patterns and moving towards higher-value crops, bearing in mind the overall biophysical limits (Steduto et al., 2007).

Despite the considerable improvements in water productivity in recent years, a gap remains between the actual and attainable yield per unit of water consumed. Figure 4.1 shows actual recorded water productivity for both irrigated and rainfed crops, matched against the realizable potential water productivity. The data confirm that water productivity in irrigated agriculture is typically higher than in rainfed. For both irrigated and rainfed conditions, actual productivity falls well short of the potential. Wheat and rice show the largest gaps, indicating where water productivity can still improve substantially.

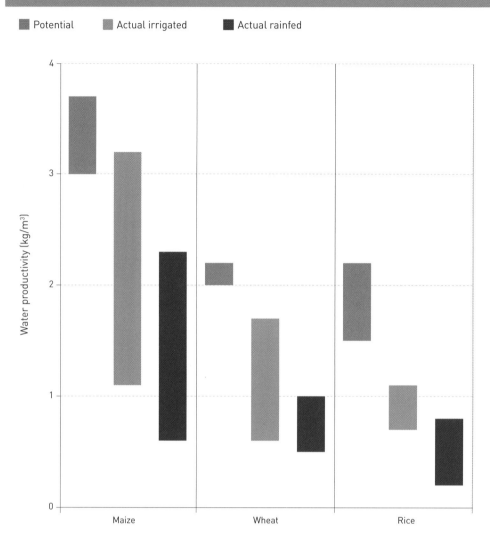

Source: Sadras et al. (2010)

It is generally observed that cropping patterns progressively change towards higher-value crops in water-constrained areas. In China, for example, there have been shifts, with a slight decrease in rice and wheat, and sharp increase in maize, vegetable and other high-value crops. The potential for closing the water productivity gap is considerable, but realizing higher levels of water productivity requires more intensive production techniques.

Many of the on-farm practices to increase crop water productivity are well known and could double water productivity. Situations vary widely across crops and production systems, and analysis and proposals for improvement need to be highly specific. Box 4.9 contains five case studies drawn from environmentally, technologically and culturally diverse regions, and covering farming systems ranging from subsistence to high-tech production systems. In most situations, adopting measures to improve soil moisture availability and raise the capacity of crops to capture water are the lowest-cost and quickest ways to raise water productivity. In addition, overall water productivity can be raised by improved methods to reduce harvest and post-harvest losses, which may add up to 30–40 percent of the yield originally produced at the farm (Lundqvist *et al.*, 2008).

BOX 4.9: FIVE CASE STUDIES OF IMPROVING CROP WATER PRODUCTIVITY

Rainfed **wheat** in southeast Australia, Mediterranean Basin, China Loess Plateau and North American Great Plains: a considerable gap between actual and maximum potential yield per unit of water was found. The average gap was 68 percent for the southern Great Plains of North America, 63 percent for the Mediterranean Basin, and 56 percent for China Loess Plateau, Northern Great Plains and southeast Australia. The reasons for these gaps included nutrition, sowing time and soil constraints. Soil moisture management was a key problem. Among the solutions identified were rapid ground cover to reduce evaporation, minimum tillage approaches and stubble management.

A similar yield gap exists for commercial rainfed **sunflower** in the western Pampas of Argentina, with nutrient and water availability and interaction at sowing time the most important leverage point to increasing yield and water productivity.

For **rice** systems in the lower Mekong River Basin, the yield gap is large, with actual productivity per unit of water consuming only 15–30 percent of maximum possible. The main opportunities for improvement include using high-yielding varieties, increasing application of fertilizer, herbicides and pesticides, and supplementary irrigation. Changing cropping patterns to higher-value crops such as coffee, vegetables and peanuts (which outperform rice in economic returns per mm of water use) may also be an option.

The irrigated commercial **maize** systems in the western US corn belt were only 10–20 percent below maximum productivity. Nonetheless, better management of water could still improve productivity; for example, irrigation scheduling based on real-time crop requirements and some water monitoring.

Environmental, management and plant-related factors contribute to very low water productivity of **millet** in the Sahel, averaging only 0.3 kg for each m^3 consumed. Improving water productivity of millet in dry, hot environments of Africa requires higher inputs, chiefly large fertilizer doses. However, the low harvest index of millet that contributes to its low water productivity needs to be considered in the context of a trade-off between grain production and valuable crop residues.

Source: this study

Where will improving crop water productivity make a difference?

Water productivity can improve, even over a relatively short timeframe, as recent progress in some systems shows. For example, the water productivity of rice in the lower Mekong River Basin is low (14–35 percent of potential), but has been increasing rapidly in recent years (Figure 4.2). The improvements arise from adoption of high-yielding varieties, better application of fertilizer, herbicides and pesticides, and supplementary irrigation. There are some straightforward technical gains for crops such as chickpea and sunflower, where large improvements in yield per unit of water

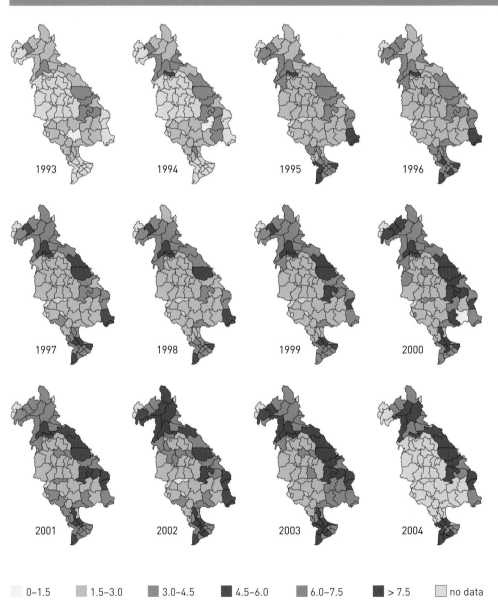

FIGURE 4.2: MEKONG RIVER BASIN YIELD PER UNIT EVAPOTRANSPIRATION OF RICE AT A REGIONAL SCALE (IN kg GRAIN/ha/mm)

0–1.5   1.5–3.0   3.0–4.5   4.5–6.0   6.0–7.5   > 7.5   no data

Source: adapted from Mainuddin and Kirby (2009)

China has made significant achievements in saving water used for agriculture, largely because of institutional and technological innovations. Between 1980 and 2004, while the total volume of water being used rose by 25 percent, the amount allocated to irrigation remained at 340–360 km^3. At the same time, the irrigated area increased by 5.4 Mha, food production capacity increased by 20 million tonnes and 200 million people gained food security. In the past decade, China's irrigation water use per hectare dropped from 7 935 to 6 450 m^3 nationwide.

Source: Wang et al. (2007)

consumed may result from simply shifting the growing season from spring–summer to autumn–winter, provided diseases and weeds are properly managed.

The technical scope for improving crop water productivity varies between crops, production systems and regions (Box 4.10). Among food grains, there is most potential for rice, but also considerable scope for improvement in wheat and some maize systems. Some parts of the world already exhibit high physical crop water productivity, with limited prospects for improvements with present technology. This is the case in many of the most productive regions, such as the Lower Yellow River Basin, and most of Europe, North America and Australia. The areas with the highest potential gains are sub-Saharan Africa, and parts of South, Southeast and Central Asia. In all these areas, increases in water productivity would increase land productivity and result in higher output from the existing cultivated area, with little change in overall water consumption. However, these productivity gains need to be considered in relation to overall river basin and aquifer balances. (Perry *et al.*, 2009).

Managing environmental risks associated with intensification

The techniques associated with higher productivity have to be accompanied by adequate and balanced use of fertilizers, to boost yields and to compensate for the removal of soil nutrients in crop yields. Intensive production also often requires further treatment of weeds, diseases and insects. But the use of inputs brings the associated risks of pollution from fertilizers and pesticides. Where the technical and socio-economic conditions are not in place for sustainable land and water management, on-site risks arise, and there are also significant risks to downstream water bodies and to human health. Management of inputs is essential to avoid these negative impacts (FAO, 1996).

In irrigation there may also be another spin-off in terms of improved health: malaria and bilharzia often plague irrigation schemes. Improved water management can reduce risks of infection (e.g. by reducing pools of standing water). In addition, modernization combined with water savings gives opportunities to extend schemes to supply water to local communities (Molden, 2007).

Fertilizer pollution and nutrient management

The largest quantities of fertilizer applied to crops are nitrogenous and phosphorous compounds. Nitrogen is required as nitrate for uptake by roots. The maximum achievable efficiency (uptake/application) is only around 50 percent, and in practice fertilizer efficiencies are rarely better than 20–30 percent. Because nitrogen fertilizers are highly water-soluble and are rapidly cycled in the soil, much of what is not taken up by the plant may be dissolved as nitrate in solution, finding its way into drainage systems, downstream watercourses and groundwater. Nitrogen is also released to the atmosphere as ammonia or nitrous oxide.

Managing nitrogen fertilizer loss can be achieved through a combination of (1) better application practices, (2) more efficient nitrogen take up by the plant and (3) better water management. Additionally, a healthy soil is needed to better hold nitrogen. Measures to improve the efficiency of application – and so reduce the release of nitrates – include such simple steps as:

- Split applications across the most responsive growth stages of a particular crop.

- 'Little and often' application in horticulture, using soluble fertilizers mixed into the irrigation water and applied with some precision. Farmers in Sunraysia (Australia), for example, have found that they achieve the highest fertilizer efficiency in fertigation by applying nitrogen at the end of an irrigation (in a 10–15 minute period, 25 minutes before the end of the watering).

- Placing the fertilizer in the root zone below and either side of the crop, at a shallow depth, where there is the highest concentration of roots.

- Deep placement of ammonia fertilizer as depot (CULTAN method). Nitrogen is partly taken up by the plants as ammonia, without passing through the state of nitrate, avoiding nitrate leaching.

Measures to promote higher uptake by plants include the use of protected and slow-release compounds, which release nitrogen progressively at a rate determined by soil moisture content, pH and soil temperature, thus creating a longer period of availability. These compounds have good commercial potential in high-value and shallow-rooted crops, and in areas where there is high potential for nitrate loss.

Biological additives may also be used to enhance nitrogen-use efficiency by encouraging stronger root growth and more active uptake, and by slowing the release of nitrogen as ammonia. Additives have resulted in 54 percent less ammonia volatilization in sugar cane and 79 percent less in wheat.

Soil management solutions include enabling the medium to hold nutrients and to convert them efficiently into plant nutrients. It is essential to pay more attention to soil health. This not only improves internal nutrient availability, and hence improves fertilizer efficiency; it also significantly reduces wastage of soil nutrients through erosion and leaching. It has been proven in several places (e.g. Brazil, Germany) that intake of nitrates and phosphates into water bodies is directly linked to soil tillage and that the reduction or avoidance of soil tillage could be crucial to significantly reduce the pollution to acceptable levels, without negatively impacting on production levels.

Although the fertilizer industry is innovating to improve fertilizer use efficiency and reduce environmental externalities, farmers may have neither the knowledge nor the incentives to reduce polluting behaviour. There are several policy options: (1) continue research, in partnership between the fertilizer industry, farmers and research bodies; (2) use selective regulation and incentives to encourage the use of slow release fertilizers wherever possible, and particularly in areas where risks of nitrogen being exported to water bodies are highest; and (3) farmer education (see Box 4.11).

Unlike nitrogen, phosphate is generally bound to soil particles and is made slowly available to plants. It is thus less likely to find its way into the drainage system or groundwater. A combination of good water management and soil incorporation of phosphate can reduce phosphate export to close to zero. Overall, where policies and

---

BOX 4.11: CHINA'S NITROGEN POLLUTION PROBLEM

The highest rates of nitrogen application in the world are now reported to be in China (around 550 to 600 kg N/ha/year in the east, southeast and North China Plain). Fertilizer use has increased rapidly between 1998 and the present, especially in the use of NPK fertilizers in horticulture and nitrogen fertilizers more generally. One consequence is that more than half of the nation's 131 large lakes are suffering from eutrophication. Surveys have revealed that most farmers are unaware of the efficiency of use and the environmental consequences of excessive fertilizer application. It has been suggested that price is too low and that this encourages overuse. But surveys reveal that farmers without access to irrigation water do not apply much nitrogen fertilizer, which indicates price sensitivity. Reducing nitrogen pollution thus depends on development and use of appropriate fertilizers, regulation and incentives, and farmer education.

Sources: Turral and Burke (2010); Jua et al. (2009)

---

programmes have been applied, there have been some successes in reducing pollution loads from agriculture, though most successes have been in reduction of urban loads.

Pesticide pollution

A range of IPM methods have been developed to address problems of pesticide pollution of water and risk to human health. IPM encourages rational and minimal use of inputs by regular monitoring and identification of pest numbers, and seeks to preserve healthy populations of natural predators and supportive habitats. IPM also incorporates the breeding and planting of pest-resistant varieties (bred by conventional or gene modification methods), strategic mixtures of varieties with different resistance characteristics, as well as crop rotation and fallowing. It may also include the introduction of natural predators of pests.

IPM approaches have been widely adopted by commercial farmers in developed countries in order to improve effectiveness and efficiency and in response to increasing environmental awareness. Take-up in developing countries has been slower, though farmer field schools have been highly effective at increasing farmer knowledge and uptake of IPM (Settle and Garba, 2011). Legislation, product approval requirements, farmer education and product price also play a role in restraining the use of pesticides. The lag in regulatory activity between developed and developing countries is a cause for concern, especially when cheap generic pesticides are produced locally after being removed from the market in richer countries.

Wider adoption of conservation agriculture, in which mechanical disturbance of the soil and other physical impacts are minimized, also has the potential to reduce the contamination of waters with pesticides due to erosion.

Many pesticides are soluble and mobile, and water management techniques are required to minimize their export to water courses (Box 4.12). Strict on-site regulation of compounds is needed when the risk of downstream contamination is high.

Minimizing risks from arsenic

Arsenic contamination of groundwater has been reported in more than 20 countries where contaminated shallow groundwater is used for both drinking and irrigation purposes. Additional industrial sources, such as from mineral extraction and processing wastes, poultry and swine feed additives, pesticides, and highly soluble arsenic trioxide stockpiles, have further contaminated soils and groundwater. Some 130 million people are at risk from arsenic toxicity (arsenosis), which causes skin lesions and various cancers. Arsenic accumulation in the food chain, such as arsenic transfer in rice in Asia, is a major concern (FAO, 2007d). Management options to prevent and mitigate arsenic contamination of food are being developed and tested. Strategies for management of arsenic that would enable rice production to continue in polluted areas include growing rice in an aerobic environment and switching to non-contaminated surface or deep groundwater to avoid further build-up of arsenic in the soil.

Salinity and drainage

In irrigated areas, the on-site and off-site risks from salinization and waterlogging have become a serious problem in many parts of the world (Mateo-Sagasta and Burke, 2010). Leaching and drainage are required to maintain salt balance in the soil profile and to sustain crop yields in arid areas. However, removal of salts from the soil through leaching and drainage increases the salinity of drainage water, which then might be up to 50 times more concentrated than irrigation water. Its disposal can raise the salinity of receiving water bodies to levels that make them no longer usable.

Solutions start with more efficient water use to reduce excess application and maintain the correct salt balance through tactical leaching doses. Subsequent drainage options are: (1) drainage water management; (2) drainage water reuse; (3) drainage water disposal; and (4) drainage water treatment. Each of these has differing impacts on the hydrology and water quality, and complex interactions and trade-offs occur when more than one option is applied.

Drainage water management is the primary method of controlling soil salinity. A drainage system should permit a small amount of the irrigation water (about 10–20 percent of drainage or leaching fraction) to be drained and discharged out of the irrigation project. This can be achieved by open ditches, tile drains or pumping from boreholes. The choice depends on the permeability of the soil, subsoil and underlying aquifer material, on the funds available for the capital works, on the resources of local communities for operation and maintenance, and on the energy costs of pumping.

Saline drainage water can be re-used downstream if blended with freshwater. These approaches require planning at the watershed scale to adapt agricultural practices and crops to the higher salt content. Here crop selection is important, as crops vary considerably in their ability to tolerate saline conditions: durum wheat, triticale and barley tolerate higher salinity than rice or corn. Irrigation with saline water can even improve the quality of some vegetables, as the sugar content in tomatoes or melons can increase.

Disposal options include direct discharge into rivers, streams, lakes, deserts and oceans, and discharge into evaporation basins. But such discharge of salty water can bring environmental problems to downstream areas. The hazards must be considered very carefully and, if necessary, mitigating measures taken. If possible, the drainage should be limited to wet seasons only, when the salty effluent inflicts the least harm. Constructed wetlands are a relatively low-cost option for protecting aquatic ecosystems and fisheries, either downstream from irrigated areas or in closed basins.

Land and water approaches in view of climate change

Agriculture and climate change

The relationship between land and water management and climate change has been identified across some of the key agricultural systems (FAO, 2011d). Land and water management practices have a strong impact on climate change drivers, both negatively and positively. Many past and current agricultural practices are among the causes of climate change, with agriculture and associated deforestation activities responsible for up to a third of total anthropogenic greenhouse gas emissions. At the same time, climate change is expected to have a considerable impact on land and water use for agriculture (IPCC, 2007; Fisher *et al.*, 2007), and the funding of adaptation strategies for increasing resilience of agricultural systems in the face of increasing climate threats, especially in poorer countries already at the margins of food insecurity, is now a global priority.

Sustainable land and water management can not only increase resilience of farming in the face of climate change but also have a positive impact on the drivers of climate change, offering cost-effective mitigation options (Tubiello *et al.*, 2008). Many management techniques that strengthen production systems also tend to sequester carbon either above or below the ground, as well as reducing direct greenhouse gas emissions.

Options for adaptation to climate change

Adaptation responses will require farmers and policy-makers to address key additional challenges: (1) from the farmer's side, the ability to implement new (or adapt previously known) technologies as the climate changes; and (2) from the policy-maker's side, the ability to develop the right incentives and deliver the necessary infrastructure in a planned and forward-looking fashion. *Autonomous adaptation* actions will be implemented by individual farmers on the basis of perceived climate change, and without intervention from above. *Maladaptation* (for example, pressure to cultivate marginal land, or to adopt unsustainable cultivation practices as yields drop) may increase land and water degradation, possibly jeopardizing future ability to respond to increasing climate risks. *Planned adaptation*, including changes in policies, institutions and dedicated infrastructure, will be needed to facilitate and maximize long-term benefits of adaptation responses.

From the technical perspective, adaptation options are largely similar to the existing activities that have been developed in the past in response to climate variability. Broadly speaking, adapting to changes will require farmers to (1) adapt management, (2) choose other more robust crop varieties, (3) select other crops and (4) modify water management practices. Such changes will come as a result of a combination of scientific knowledge and field experience. If widely adopted, these adaptations singly or in combination have the potential to offset negative climate change impacts and take advantage of positive ones. Adapting to increased frequency of extreme events, on the other hand, will be much harder, especially since such new regimes may not have historical analogues.

Options for cropping include: changes in crop varieties and species for increased resistance to heat shock and drought, flooding and salinization; adaptation of fertilizer rates; altering the timing or location of cropping activities; diversifying crop production; making wider use of integrated pest management; developing and using varieties and species that are resistant to pests and diseases; improving quarantine capabilities and monitoring programmes; and matching livestock stocking rates and grazing to pasture production. In particular, conservation agriculture, through simultaneous improvements in crop diversification, soil structure and organic matter content, can reduce the impacts of climate variability and represents a broad response to climate change adaptation.

Water management is a critical component of adaptation to climate pressures in coming decades. These pressures will be driven by changes in water availability (volumes and seasonal distribution), and in water demand for agriculture and other competing sectors. Practices that increase the productivity of irrigation water use may provide significant adaptation potential for all land production systems under future climate change. At the same time, improvements in irrigation performance and water management are critical to ensure the availability of water both for food production and for competing human and environmental needs (FAO, 2007e, 2011d). A number of farm-level, irrigation system-level and basin-level adaptation techniques and approaches are specific to water management for agriculture. They include: modification of irrigation amount, timing or technology; adoption of supplementary irrigation and improved soil moisture management techniques in rainfed cropping; adoption of more efficient water allocation rules; conjunctive use of surface water and groundwater; and adoption of structural and non-structural measures to cope with floods and droughts.

Better data and more attention to monitoring would support better climate forecasting, particularly seasonal forecasting. Forecasting technologies, even to the optimization of rainfall use, already exist and are commercially available in some countries. Much still needs to be done to improve the quality of forecasting and its communication in a user-friendly way if they are to have a positive adaptive benefit.

Government-level solutions should focus on developing new infrastructure, policies and institutions, including addressing climate change in development programmes, increasing investment in water control and irrigation infrastructure and in precision water-use technologies, ensuring appropriate transport and storage infrastructure, adapting land tenure arrangements (including attention to well-defined property rights), and establishing accessible, efficiently functioning markets for products and inputs (including water pricing schemes) and for financial services (including insurance).

Contribution to climate change mitigation

All action contributing to the protection of land and water resources, the efficient use of resources and inputs, reducing wastes and losses in agriculture, and making land- and water-use systems more resilient to the vagaries of weather and markets should all already facilitate mitigation and adaptation. The impact of more sustainable land and water management could be significant (Box 4.13). It is estimated that if

Pastoral systems hold great potential for synergies between climate change mitigation and adaptation. They occupy two-thirds of global dryland areas and their rural population is proportionally poorer than in other systems. They also have a higher rate of desertification than other land-use systems, which negatively affects the accumulation of carbon in the soils. Improved pasture and rangeland management in extensive dryland areas would contribute to substantial carbon accumulation and storage.

Improved grazing is a proven strategy for restoring soil and increasing land resilience while building the carbon pool. One of the most effective strategies for sequestering carbon is fostering deep-rooted perennial plant species on land used for agriculture, through rotations that include grass fallow or grass leys, and integrating fodder crops, trees or other perennial species into the cropping systems (i.e. maintaining mixed crop-livestock–tree systems).

Management practices that sequester carbon have the potential to generate economic benefits to households in degraded drylands, both through payments for carbon sequestration and, importantly, through co-benefits in terms of enhanced production, increases in ecosystem processes and sustainable resource use, thus enhancing climate change adaptation. While payments for carbon sequestration are currently limited to voluntary carbon markets, negotiations on future global climate change agreements as well as emerging domestic legislation in several developed countries may soon increase the demand for emission reductions from rangeland management activities in developing countries (Lipper *et al.*, 2010).

The economic feasibility of carbon sequestration in grasslands also depends on the price of carbon. IPCC (2007) note that, at US$20 per tCO_2eq, grazing land management and restoration of degraded lands have potential to sequester around 300 Mt CO_2eq up to 2030; at US$100 per tCO_2eq they have the potential to sequester around 1 400 Mt CO_2eq over the same period.

CHAPTER 4

action is taken on improved crop and livestock management and agroforestry practices, reduced tillage and land restoration, production of bio-energy from biomass, and forestry sector mitigation strategies, total CO_2 reductions could be 4–18 billion tonnes, sufficient nearly to offset sector emissions (Table 4.1).

Reducing methane and nitrogen emissions

Methane and nitrogen emitted by agricultural production have a high global warming potential. Mitigation of these non-CO_2 greenhouse gases is therefore very important. In addition to measures specific to livestock, which are outside the scope of this book, mitigation options for reducing methane from cultivation concern principally the development of more efficient rice cultivation systems, including lower require-

TABLE 4.1: MITIGATION POTENTIAL IN AGRICULTURE AND FORESTRY IN 2030

	Billion tCO_2eq
Global mitigation potential	15–25
Agriculture mitigation potential	1.5–5.0
Reduction of non CO_2 gases	(0.3–1.5)
Agroforestry	(0.5–2)
Enhanced soil carbon sequestration	(0.5–1.5)
Forest mitigation potential	2.5–12
REDD+	(1–4)
Sustainable forest management	(1–5)
Forest restoration*	(0.5–3)
Bio-energy mitigation potential	0.1–1.0
Total sector mitigation potential	4–18
Total sector emissions	13–15

* Including afforestation and reforestation.

Sources: FAO (2008); Tubiello and van der Velde (2010)

ments for water use (e.g. aerobic rice cultivation, in which flooding of cultivation fields is avoided), shifts from transplanted rice to direct-seeded rice systems and alternate wet–dry production system (FAO, 2006c).

In intensive agricultural systems with crops and livestock production, N_2O emissions from fertilized fields and animal waste can contribute more than half of total greenhouse gas emissions from farms. As these nitrogen emissions are diffuse over space and time, they are hard to mitigate. Current techniques focus on reduction of absolute amounts of nitrogen fertilizer applied to fields while minimizing soil compaction (which causes anaerobic conditions and thus increases nitrous oxide emissions), as well as on changes in livestock feeding regimes.

An effective strategy for mitigating non-CO_2 gases in intensive mixed crop–livestock farming systems, such as those in place in both Europe and North America, could involve a change in human diet towards less meat consumption, reducing both direct methane and N_2O emissions, and reducing the consumption of grain by livestock. However, patterns of development of cultures, tastes, lifestyles and demographic changes drive strongly in the opposite direction, towards major dietary changes – mainly in developing countries, where shares of meat, fat and sugar to total food intake continue to increase significantly (Tubiello and van der Velde, 2010).

Sustainable agriculture and forestry

Many of the sustainable agricultural and agroforestry management practices that have long been recommended for broader ecological and economic reasons also have a climate change mitigation impact, largely through carbon sequestration. Trees integrated into farming systems, whether as shelterbelts, for slope protection, or for woody biomass or fruit and nut production, not only form part of sustainable land and water management approaches for improved soil water retention and reduced erosion, but also have a carbon-fixing impact (Box 4.14). In addition, micro-climate improvement brought about through trees and shrubs in agroforestry systems combines with better soil cover to help regulate the climate and reduce the impact of extreme events (for example, reduced impact of strong winds in humid and dry areas, and protection against high temperatures and radiation, and against moisture loss in dry and warm areas).

Synergies between mitigation and adaptation

Many of the land and water management strategies discussed earlier link to both climate change mitigation and adaptation (Tubiello *et al.*, 2007). For example, reduced tillage, agroforestry and other 'best practice' soil and water management strategies not only improve productivity and sustainability by increasing the ability of soils to hold soil moisture and better withstand erosion, and by enriching ecosystem biodiversity through the establishment of more diversified cropping systems. They also enhance the long-term stability and resilience of cropping systems in the face of climate variability, helping cropping systems to better withstand climate-change-induced droughts and floods (adaptation). In addition, they contribute to soil carbon sequestration (mitigation). Box 4.15 illustrates how sustainable farming investments in vegetative sand barriers protect cropland against erosion (adaptation) and will also fix carbon (mitigation). Similarly, avoiding deforestation and improving techniques for forest conservation and management can not only lead to more resilient and healthy ecosystems, but also have important adaptation and mitigation effects.

CHAPTER 4

BOX 4.14: COMMUNITY REFORESTATION, BRAZIL: RESPONSE TO FLOODS AND LANDSLIDES

Many people from Brazil's interior have moved to cities such as Rio de Janeiro, and now live in slums (*favelas*) with poorly constructed houses on steep hillsides. The rapid growth of the *favelas* has led to deforestation, soil erosion and landslides, which in turn have caused sedimentation, flooding and wet areas with mosquitoes. The city created the Community Reforestation Project in 1986, which aimed to control erosion and reduce the associated landslide and flood risks through the reforestation of erosion-prone areas of the city. The project employs residents and is reintroducing native tree species that are suited to erosion control.

Source: CDE (2010)

Vegetative barriers

Northern China is suffering from severe land desertification, which brings economic losses to dryland agriculture – and also damage to the railway line. The railway department raised funds to construct tall living barriers. These consist of bushes and trees of an appropriate height and penetrability, suitable for dry and sandy conditions. It helps to protect fields and infrastructure from drifting sand.

Source: CDE (2010) Photo: Yang Zihui

Prospects for implementation

Increasing pressures on land and water resources will, in some regions, place severe constraints on efforts to appropriately intensify agricultural production in order to meet projected needs for food. The production systems 'at risk' where these conditions currently exist or are anticipated warrant appropriate remedial action. Remedial management actions should encompass not only the technical options to promote sustainable intensification and reduce risks as described in this chapter, but should also be accompanied by the enabling conditions required to eliminate institutional mechanisms that reinforce inefficiency, social inequity and the degradation of resources, as well as knowledge exchange and research, as addressed in other chapters of SOLAW (see also Box 4.16).

BOX 4.16: THE SUCCESSFUL SPREAD OF INDIVIDUAL PRIVATE IRRIGATION IN NIGER

In Niger, traditional small-scale irrigation using simple water-lifting techniques (*shaduf*, bucket) were long employed, but the introduction of pumps has led to rapid expansion and intensification. By 2006, the area covered by small-scale private irrigation was 16 000 ha. Plots are typically less than 1 ha (usually 0.1–0.75 ha). Most production is of horticultural crops for market. Producers in some areas are specializing (onions, peppers, garlic, tomatoes). Demand is strong for produce, both domestically and for export.

In 1996, the government took the decision to support the growth of small-scale private irrigation, and encouraged the establishment of an apex association for the private irrigation profession. With project support, the association has helped farmers acquire new technology (typically treadle pumps) and has promoted changes in husbandry and cropping patterns. An artisanal industry has emerged, comprising drillers, well technicians, and pump makers and repairers. Accessible microfinance, private sector farming advisory services and farmer-run input supply have also been promoted. Farmers' net annual income has increased from US$159 to US$560 (in a country where median annual per capita income is US$60). The distribution of benefits is broad: over 26 000 poor families have benefited. The programme makes a good contribution to growth, exports, household income and poverty reduction.

Source: World Bank (2008)

COMMERCIAL FARMERS

EMERGING FARMERS   COMMERCIAL

TRADITIONAL FARMERS

Photos: FAO Mediabase

Chapter 5

INSTITUTIONAL RESPONSES FOR SUSTAINABLE LAND AND WATER MANAGEMENT

The main food production systems are at risk of being degraded to the point at which global food security is compromised. Land and water management practice on these large areas of moderate– to high-potential lands needs to be improved urgently to reverse trends in degradation and maintain levels of productivity. Adaptation to climate change in the major food producing areas of the world will also be vital. Given these trends, what pathways towards more sustainable intensification can be set?

A focus on systems at risk will be a priority for certain countries and regions. But beyond this, sustainable land and water management will need to be translated into national agendas. This chapter sets a direction for the implementation of such agendas, given the current and projected state of land and water. It also indicates how national institutions can be strengthened to ensure that rights in use are protected; how knowledge and technology can be adapted in cooperation with users; and how mechanisms for planning and managing land and water resources can be effectively delegated.

The overall policy environment

The macro settings

The need for differentiated planning processes and implementation practices that can be scaled across systems at risk has been emphasized. The degree to which these processes and practices can be 'joined up' in a coherent approach to land and water management to achieve desired environmental outcomes will be determined by two factors. First, the urgency of the environmental problem and the political attention it attracts. Second, the competence of the institutional arrangement to address public good concerns. Contextual approaches that relate to specific scales may be nested and orderly in a well-defined and agreed planning framework. In practice, it has proved difficult to extend and sustain natural resource governance from national institutions down to local land and water management to the point where social and economic benefits can be spread and environmental trends can be reversed. Much of the 'blame' could be levelled at the institutions (public and private) that are responsible for making decisions over land and water use.

Farmers and agriculture policy-makers are under pressure to make choices between alternative approaches to natural resource management. The selection of a sustainable pathway will be scale-dependent. At the local level, livelihoods and ecosystem compatibility will determine patterns of use. At the subnational administrative scale (e.g. district or sub-basin level), considerations of land and water planning and environmental regulation will be factored in, setting norms and bounds for agricultural development. At the national level, policy objectives of economic development, food security, poverty reduction and conservation of nature will be important drivers. At the global level, concern for growth with equity in developing countries will be matched by the imperative of conserving global commons of freshwater across transboundary river basins, forest cover, marine environments, climate and biodiversity.

Prioritization from a neutral planning perspective will be driven by four main considerations. First, the priorities need to be clear with respect to national development objectives for sustainable, equitable and efficient growth. For low- and middle-income countries, they are likely to be pro-poor and promote local food security. Specific growth targets for the rural sector or for commodities (food, fibre), or socio-economic goals such as poverty reduction for marginalized groups or prevention of land and water conflicts, may also drive priorities. Second, the investments need to offer the best cost–benefit ratio. Third, the choices must offer the biggest ecological boost, including considerations of climate change mitigation and adaptation. Finally, priorities will need to be feasible in the light of national and local socio-economic and political realities, or at least there must be the possibility of adjusting the incentive structure so that local stakeholders are motivated to adopt sustainable practices.

Trade-offs between 'development' and 'conservation', and between commercial farming and staple production, between growth and income distribution, between urban and rural will be inevitable. What is vital is that the analysis should be explicit and decisions taken in the public interest where livelihoods and agricultural productivity are at risk.

The role of public investment

Public investment in research and development, in technology transfer, and in land and water infrastructure and roads may be the most politically acceptable and efficient means for governments to promote sustainable land and water management. One key role of government is to invest in pilot programmes that demonstrate the technology and economics of sustainable agriculture. This was successfully adopted in Brazil's Empresa Brasileira de Pesquisa Agropecuária (EMBRAPA) programme, which fostered conservation agriculture and demonstrated how it could be run on profitable lines as agri-business. Governments may also support farmer-based institutions through smarter agricultural services. Advisory services to farmers can now include a much broader array of information 'push', and even credit services through mobile technology. The adoption of information kiosks based on ATM models in rural India has been trialled together with dissemination of near-real-time remote-sensing products. These types of innovation will go beyond the conventional 'extension service' models used by agricultural and rural development agencies.

Setting incentives for sustainable land and water management

Incentives to promote or constrain agricultural production are most commonly transmitted through the tax regime, input subsidies, support prices, regulatory measures, infrastructure investment (e.g. in water-saving technology) and support measures such as extension or product market development. Policies that affect the price of production or consumption, such as trade policy to ban exports or impose import tariffs, can also quickly transmit new levels of demand for agricultural production, and hence feed directly through to land- and water-use decisions.

Removing distortions in the existing incentive framework that encourage less sustainable land and water management practices will be essential. An example is where low energy prices drive intensive groundwater abstraction. Governments typically control energy prices. Raising the price of energy to border parity levels will increase the cost of pumping groundwater, and should moderate over-extraction. However, altering a distorted incentive structure by raising prices can be politically unpalatable. Often governments opt to allow subsidies to dwindle through the unseen hand of inflation rather than to raise the price of politically sensitive commodities. In addition, knock-on effects may be hard to manage. Energy price rises will put up the cost of transport and increase consumer prices across the board. Higher-cost agricultural production will increase the cost of food or shrink the incomes of poor farmers. Resetting the incentive framework, therefore, has to be carefully designed and managed, with a clear political and economic strategy. A further problem is the impact on household incomes and the rural economy, which may be dependent on benefits generated by the existing incentive framework. Raising subsidized energy prices may save water, but it will also reduce farm incomes and employment. These risks underline the need to balance adjustments to distorted incentive frameworks with positive incentives designed to restore farm incomes.

For poor farmers living on the margin, change, including the adoption of appropriate technologies, can increase risk. The same is true of irrigation farmers being encouraged to take over the management of public assets for which operation and maintenance were previously under publicly funded agencies. The change has to yield tangible benefits. Clearly any incentive structure has to meet the combination of ecosystem conservation, intensified natural resource use and livelihoods objectives, with an eye on poverty-related impacts. Designing a structure that will achieve multiple objectives requires careful study and will inevitably involve trade-offs.

Dealing with externalities

Incentives to switch to more productive and sustainable land and water management practices may not be present in the market. One reason for this is the existence of strong 'externalities'. Costs of poor land and water management may be felt, for example, far downstream in dam siltation. Benefits of switching to alternative practices may be felt not by the farmer but by his neighbours in the community (e.g. reduced groundwater overdraft), or at basin level (e.g. reduced pollutant load), or at national level (reduced desertification or atmospheric dust), or even at global level (enhanced conservation of biodiversity or cultural landscape values, or reduced carbon emissions). Farmers will reason on the basis of their own livelihoods, and are unlikely to change attitude in the public interest unless returns to livelihoods (including household health) are apparent.

One of the key challenges in promoting more ecologically sound intensification is thus to design an incentive framework that can 'internalize' these externalities, and so correct the 'asymmetry of interest' among stakeholders. The framework has essentially to cope with this asymmetry both in the status quo, where the farmer garners the benefits and the remote stakeholder bears the costs, and in corrective measures (e.g. watershed management), where the farmer may bear the costs and the remote stakeholder (e.g. downstream urban dweller) gains the benefits. In addition, the incentive framework has to deal with the fact that time horizons are different – investing in corrective measures may bring benefit to the farmer, but only in a few years' time (terracing or tree planting, for example), and smallholders cannot wait to feed their families.

In some cases, productivity improvements that solve both the farmer's and the public good problem may be possible; for example, integrated approaches such as conservation agriculture or agroforestry, or improved irrigation and drainage management. In other cases, there may be a contradiction between the intensification path and public interest, as in increased use of chemical inputs. The incentive package needs to correct the mismatch between farmer interest and the public good.

One example of correction of this asymmetry of benefits is conservation of soil moisture, which extends the period of stress-free growth, but may be unattractive to a farmer because of the high cost of investment or of lag in benefits. Terraces, for example, require high initial investment in labour and materials, although they provide significant long-term benefits. However, investment in soil moisture conservation may also deliver downstream benefits. Mechanisms have been developed for PES, by which land users upstream are remunerated for their contribution to the provision of reliable water quantity and quality downstream.

An extension of this could be to soil carbon sequestration. Restoration of soil organic carbon will improve agricultural productivity. Farmers have an incentive to invest in this kind of agriculture, but may find it slower to yield and less financially profitable in the short run than less conservation-friendly approaches. However, soil carbon restoration also contributes to improving the agriculture carbon balance. Many forms of agriculture-based soil carbon sequestration are low-cost means of mitigating climate change that can be readily implemented through a range of proven land and water management technologies. In this sense, there is a justification for a mechanism to support farmers who invest in soil carbon.

The principle of PES is therefore based on the acceptance that practices adopted by one category of stakeholders benefit other stakeholders, either downstream (erosion or pollution control in watersheds) or at global level (carbon sequestration, biodiversity maintenance). PES can be used to encourage the adoption of more sustainable land- and water-use systems, and to enhance the economic viability of a given management system. Table 5.1 shows who benefits from a given practice (on- or off-site) – a first step towards recognition of environmental services.

Valuing costs and benefits and their distribution

In order to provide justification for adjusting the incentive structure to compensate for externalities and asymmetry of interest, it is necessary to have a method of calculating costs, benefits and their distribution, and also a mechanism for checking outcomes. However, at present methodologies are weak (Box 5.1). More work is required to develop widely accepted technical and economic approaches to measure and assess the cost of direct relationships such as those between soil loss

TABLE 5.1: INDICATIVE TRENDS IN THE DISTRIBUTION OF COSTS AND BENEFITS OF VARIOUS TECHNOLOGIES OR PRACTICES

Technology or practice	Short-term	Long-term	Benefit on-site*	Benefit off-site*	Comments
Conservation agriculture (CA)	+/–	++	++	+	The establishment of CA may have relatively low entry costs: hand tools, seed for new crops and cover crops. However, the availability and affordability of these tools and seeds can be a major obstacle, especially for small-scale land users.
Integrated soil fertility management	++	+++	+	++	Relatively small extra inputs in the form of organic and/or inorganic fertilizer can have a noticeable impact on crop production, so this technology can be introduced progressively, allowing testing and risk management. However, profitability depends on price.
Pollution control/ integrated pest management	+	+++	+/–	++	Integrated pest management and the control of pollution through pesticides requires more specialized skills and may not be seen as immediately attractive to users. Beneficiaries include both on-farm and downstream water users.
Groundwater monitoring and controlled extraction	–	+	–	+	Controlling and limiting groundwater extraction implies reduction of pumping by all users sharing a common aquifer. The short-term impact on individual farmers is negative, while the long-term impact on the community is positive. Such practices imply a good knowledge of aquifer recharge mechanisms and strong community management mechanisms.
Agroforestry, vegetative strips	+	+++	+/–	+	The establishment of seedling nurseries and distribution of plants at community/ catchment levels need to be taken into account, as well as community/individual costs of protecting planted trees from livestock and fire. Vegetative strips can be used as cost-effective contour farming measures for reduction of runoff or as wind barriers. They have similar effects as structural barriers and also require labour, but the investment cost overall is lower.
Structural barriers	+/–	+++	+	+/–	The establishment of structural measures such as terraces and stone lines requires high initial investments in material and labour. They may be very effective on steep lands and in dry conditions, but their construction often needs financial and or material support.

Key: Positive when benefits outweigh costs, negative otherwise.

* Benefits are on-site, when farmers benefit from proposed changes and off-site, when others benefit from the change.

In the wake of the original GLASOD study from 1987–1990, a debate developed on the cost of land degradation. One earlier argument contended that *'soil erosion is a major environmental threat to the sustainability and productive capacity of agriculture. During the last 40 years, nearly one-third of the world's arable land has been lost by erosion and continues to be lost at a rate of more than 10 Mha per year. With the addition of a quarter of a million people each day, the world population's food demand is increasing at a time when per capita food productivity is beginning to decline'* (Pimentel et al., 1995).

More recently a study on soil erosion and food security (den Biggelaar *et al.*, 2003) stated that *'production loss estimates vary across crops, soils, and regions but average 0.3 percent yr⁻¹ at the global level, assuming that farmers' practices do not change. Reducing production losses by limiting soil erosion would, therefore, go a long way to attain food security, especially in the developing countries of the tropics and subtropics'*.

However, there is no clear methodology for measuring the actual cost of the productivity losses incurred, as there are no consistent empirically demonstrated relations between soil losses and productivity (Eswaran *et al.*, 2001). In addition, most studies only estimate costs of soil erosion, not of land degradation, which may be magnitudes higher when biomass, water and biodiversity are considered. There is no accepted costing of other ecosystem services, or there are widely varying estimates – carbon markets, for example, show differences in carbon prices at a ratio of 1:10 in different markets. Unless the environmental cost (loss of carbon, decline in water resources, loss of cultural services) is correctly valued, economic valuation results will largely underestimate the costs. What is needed are both more developed approaches to measuring the soil loss/productivity relationship, and agreed methodologies for valuation of ecosystem goods and services. Until that is achieved, no progress will be made in accurately estimating the real global or national cost of land degradation.

Source: Nachtergaele et al. (2006d)

and production, and also the overall costs, benefits and trade-offs of action on degradation within the overall ecosystem (FAO, 2006d).

Securing access to land and water resources

The need for inclusive and stable land tenure

Per capita shares of land in low-income countries are expected to halve by 2050, creating pressures for opening of new lands for agriculture. Although there is considerable land theoretically suitable for cultivation, almost all of it is either in use for economic production or providing essential ecosystem services to both the local area and the biosphere. In addition, availability of land is not well matched with areas where demand is likely to be strongest. Nonetheless, some expectations are that 120 Mha of new land may be brought into cultivation by 2050.

At the level of global and national policy, expansion of the cultivated area has to be balanced with current use and the need to maintain existing ecosystem functions, protect global gene pools and enhance terrestrial carbon pools. Decisions to expand the cultivated area should be the product of well-reasoned and negotiated national policy, with involvement of the global community where appropriate. Careful evaluation of limitations and risks under alternative land uses is also a prerequisite.

Once policy is set and expansion of cropland is decided at the policy level, what then are the conditions for optimal use of new land? First, strategies for orderly management of pressures on land will become increasingly important. This requires well-functioning institutions, particularly for administering land tenure. Second, there needs to be policy and institutional support to ensure that when land conversion takes place, land and water use are appropriately regulated to retain the integrity of a sustainable and ecosystem-friendly production system. Incentives and regulatory frameworks that encourage managed development and sustainable farming are required. Research and technology transfer, farmer advisory services, access to capital and credit, and market development need to be in place. Finally, the crops and production system need to be profitable and sustainable, and compatible with sustainable land and water management principles and approaches. Farming should minimize trade-offs and mitigate loss of ecosystem services. Participatory monitoring and evaluation will be a useful support to decision-making.

Sustainable agriculture requires that the user of land and water resources have a long-term interest in the integrity of the resource base to ensure future production. In most countries, systems of individual freehold or long leasehold tenure provide this security. But where communal rights are poorly defined and not protected by law, clarity needs to be sought. Two options are most commonly applied. One is to assist communal land tenure systems to adapt (for example, by legal recognition and protection, demarcation of lands, and strengthening of the institutional capacity of landholders for self-management and self-regulation). This has been done in South Africa, Ghana, India and Brazil. Another solution is to introduce legal and institutional changes to enable the equitable conversion of communal rights to formal individual property rights. Individual plots inside communal areas or communities as a whole may convert to individual property rights. Land laws in some countries, for example in Mozambique and Tanzania, provide for such a negotiated process.

Land markets can help manage competing uses and growing scarcity. Land rental markets have been shown to enhance efficiency and equity in land allocation. However, rental markets have often been constrained by insecurity of land ownership, or by prohibitions or controls on land rental and share-cropping. For rental markets to reach their full potential, land tenure security and registration need to be improved, and regulation of rental markets needs to be eased. Land sales markets also require well-developed property rights and administration.

Land reform and redistribution have occurred periodically across most countries. State-owned land is hard to manage by governments, as it is often subject to invasion, settlement, historic ownership claims, and non-transparent and corrupt allocation via rental and sales. Often governments do not even know how much land they own and where, and if they do they are reluctant to dispose of it. Any reform initiative therefore needs to ensure the maintenance of an accurate cadastral register and the application of fiduciary safeguards on disposal of state assets. However, recent land reform has a mixed track record. Initiatives need to be accompanied by access to capital and credit, by beneficiary empowerment in planning and implementation, and by training and capacity-building.

Reforms are often opposed by existing right holders if they do not recognize their pre-existing rights. Beneficiaries of distortions, subsidies and other privileges will also staunchly defend them: *Even if new laws and regulations are enacted, they may remain unimplemented, opposed by powerful stakeholders, constrained by lack of institutional capacity or crippled by unworkable stipulation. Registration procedures may make it difficult or impossible for some existing users to have their rights recognized. Security for some users may come at a cost of reinforcing inequities and institutional rigidity that excludes others. Reforms may achieve economic gains, but leave environmental demands unmet* (Bruns *et al.*, 2005). It is therefore important to choose the objectives and sequencing of reforms carefully, as well as the specific policy, rights and institutional changes that are most likely to be adopted and implemented given the existing historical and political context.

Securing access to water and ensuring flexible water allocation

With water availability as the prime determinant of further intensification, physical and economic water scarcity will continue to pose a constraint to production and environmental management in areas which use a high proportion of their renewable water resources.

Setting up systems of modern water rights to enable responsible engagement with water resources, and at the same time promote responsible land use, may not be a realistic presumption in all cases (FAO, 2006e). But two principles emerge. First, that securing basic access to water for productive land use still requires effort to be inclusive of all users. Second, once secured, the ability to be flexible in use and regulation of that use will demand higher orders of knowledge on the part of both the user and the regulator.

Securing basic rights in use for agricultural users will still require progressive transformation of customary use into formally accepted and defendable rights where new resources are sought (FAO, 2009). Making use of water-use rights in a flexible manner is a key issue for WUAs. The scale of the association needs to be commensurate to the natural system and the level of practical networking to make effective resource allocation decisions and transfers among members. To be successful as an association, the primary prerequisite is information flow from the basin or water regulator and information flow among users. User associations thus have to be knowledge-rich.

These patterns of use happen in a basin or aquifer context for which the resource basin is changing on a day to day basis. Any basin manager or regulator has to find a way to relate to end users (the user associations), adjudicate over allocations, maintain levels of productivity derived from water and comply with environmental legislation. In the same way that WUAs can adjust within certain degrees of freedom, the regulator is also in a position to apply rules and regulations in a flexible manner. At the very minimum, irrespective of technology and investment levels, the flow of high-quality information is essential. Under conditions of competition, this information flow becomes even more important. Policy adjustments can correct the imbalance between supply and demand, improving the efficiency, equity and sustainability of water allocation and use. Integrated water management suggests four basic elements: a system of water allocation; incentives to efficient water use; promoting water efficient technology; and decentralization and partnership approaches to water management.

Most modern water administrations give the state powers to allocate water between uses, to regulate water rights and use in the public interest, to ensure maintenance of water quality, and to support users and local institutions with research and knowledge. Given the complexity of regulating local water management, decentralized solutions have begun to emerge for both surface and groundwater management on a partnership basis with local users. In the case of irrigation schemes, this has taken the form of participatory irrigation management, with users increasingly involved through WUAs in scheme management, operation and maintenance, and in financing the running of the scheme through user fees. For other forms of agricultural water management, initiatives have focused on reviving or creating communal water management institutions. For groundwater, the bypassing of traditional institutions and weak regulatory capacity have contributed to competition, with rapid depletion of groundwater stocks. Self-regulation and management by user groups has been shown to be effective in conserving groundwater resources. Support may be provided by official agencies, and the communal institutions may be linked to local government or to specific hydrological units (Box 5.2).

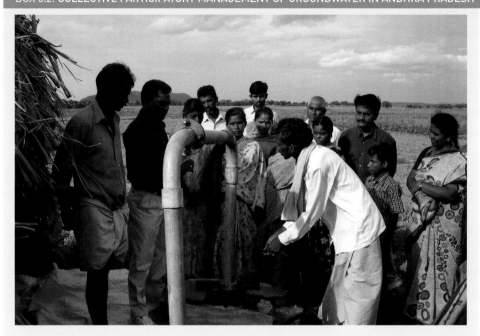

The Andhra Pradesh Farmer Managed Groundwater Systems (APFAMGS) project was supported by the government of the Netherlands and FAO between 2006 and 2010 in response to widespread drought and out-migration across the state. The project aimed to improve groundwater-use efficiency by empowering farmers in monitoring and managing groundwater resources. Groundwater management committees in each aquifer or hydrological unit came together to estimate the total groundwater resource available and work out the appropriate cropping systems to match. The committees then disseminated the information to the entire farming community and acted as pressure groups encouraging appropriate water saving/harvesting projects, promoting low-investment organic agriculture and helping to formulate rules that would ensure inter-annual sustainability of limited groundwater resources.

Some 6 500 farmers in 643 communities have been trained to collect data fundamental to the understanding the local aquifers. Farmers record daily rainfall at 191 rain gauge stations. At more than 2 000 observation wells, they carry out regular measurements of groundwater levels. In all, more than 4 500 farmers, men and women, are voluntarily collecting data. The data are maintained in registers kept at the groundwater management committee offices and are also entered on village display boards. At the aquifer level, 'hydrological unit members' are trained to use these data for estimation of groundwater recharge following the end of the summer monsoonal rains. In terms of cumulative water abstractions, 42 percent of the hydrological units have consistently reduced the *rabi* (dry season) draught over the three years of project operation, while 51 percent have reduced the draught intermittently, and only 7 percent have witnessed an increase in groundwater draught during this period. This impact is unprecedented, in terms of reductions actually being realized in groundwater withdrawals and, in terms of the geographic extent of this impact, covering dozens of aquifers, hundreds of communities, and approximate outreach of 1 million farmers.

Sources: FAO; www.apfamgs.org; World Bank (2010a) Photo: J. Burke

The absence of cooperation frameworks on some major transboundary rivers has led to suboptimal investment and to tensions between riparians. As demand for land and water grows, further unilateral development may take place, leading to loss of the added value that would have come from investments in land and water planned to optimize returns and to share benefits at the basin scale. Where possible, moves towards a cooperation framework may be taken, starting at the technical level and leading to mutually beneficial development and management and, ultimately, to agreements on international waters.

Defining national strategies

This section discusses institutional approaches that are likely to become increasingly important. Well-informed diagnosis and participatory planning approaches reflect the need for bottom-up identification of problems and solutions. For irrigation management, the search for production and environmental performance will remain a priority whether through public or private agencies.

Diagnosis

Packages for sustainable land and water management depend on the integration of knowledge stemming from research combined with local diagnosis to identify the appropriate entry points. Substantial knowledge already exists at the global, regional and national levels, and agricultural and land and water agencies need to bring this together and to work with farmers to match knowledge to need.

Choices of priority at the local level will need to be guided by knowledge of options, and have to be made on a partnership basis between local communities and public and other institutions. Private sector interests and investment opportunities have to be factored in. The balance between short-term revenue and long-term sustainability will need to be considered. Choices will be expressed through local and individual plans, supported where needed by public agencies and financing. Local priorities will be developed in interaction with national priorities, and in partnership between local and national institutions.

At system level and/or national level, mapping the spatial extent, including causes and impact of land degradation and conservation, indicates where investments can best be made, which practices have the potential to spread and what support is required. It also helps to set the agenda for further research and development. In many places, large-scale irrigation schemes are underperforming due to a combination of infrastructure degradation and outmoded management approaches.

Choices at the national level will also benefit from flexibility and open debate, and will be based on lessons learned and best practice from field experience and global knowledge. These choices will also need to find expression in laws, policies, programmes and investments. Diagnostic approaches can also be applied to more general agricultural variables. An example of one area of diagnosis is assessment of soil health and its relation to current and potential productivity in terms of crop yield and profitability. Box 5.3 describes how soil health can be evaluated within an ecosystem framework as a component of an integrated appraisal.

Setting strategies – invoking pluralism and participation

A key lesson from the past is that technical approaches in land and water management, however correct, cannot be imposed. Formal land and water management institutions rarely have monopolies over knowledge and capacity. A specific project may provide incentives to change behaviour for a period, but such approaches rarely produce sustainable improvements. More effective participatory planning approaches can engage local people and create lasting ownership. They can also tap local knowledge and match that with new ideas in order to identify solutions that can be integrated into sustainable farming practices. In this sense, pluralistic approaches to land and water management need both recognition and application. Additionally, while the concept of participatory planning is not new, its concrete application remains a challenge in many places where technological solutions prevail over a more balanced approach to problem-solving.

BOX 5.3: EVALUATING SOIL HEALTH WITHIN AN ECOSYSTEMS FRAMEWORK

An integrated appraisal of land and water, and their potential for sustainable agricultural development, would include an appreciation of the effects of soil life on soil physical, chemical and biological properties and processes, and on the air and water resources with which the soil interacts, as well as an assessment of the effects of agricultural practices on soil biota and their functions. Also, gauging the current and likely environmental effects from drainage, leaching, runoff and erosion is essential in order to evaluate the likely sustainability and externalities of various land and water management strategies. The diagnosis also needs to evaluate the impact of those interactions on soil degradation, and related effects on food production and environmental problems, including the greenhouse gas effect and water pollution. Improved understanding of the organisms and related processes and their interactions within the agricultural system, in regard to climate, soil type, plant species and diversity, and farm practices, will help build the appropriate land and water management package. The challenge is to develop approaches for assessing soil quality and health that are useful to producers, specialists and policy-makers. Soil health thresholds could then be used as tools to facilitate a change in direction towards more sustainable crop production intensification practices.

Participatory approaches and community watershed management plans have been used to reconcile the overlay of human activity on naturally defined watersheds. In wider watershed management projects, for example, participatory approaches have been employed to establish management plans. The participatory processes succeeded where there were common purposes that could interest all or most of the population, where the participatory process was flexible and provided for capacity-building and genuine empowerment, and where there were income and livelihoods incentives. Where communities could see the economic benefits, they were more willing to invest in long-term conservation.

Participation does not, however, guarantee outcomes. It involves shifts in decision-making power between the state and local communities, and also between different segments of the local community. Participatory processes therefore have to be designed for the intended development and distributional outcomes. Participatory approaches impose a demanding set of requirements – political commitment and equitable rules, time for the process to mature, inclusion of all stakeholders in the process, public agencies that understand the rationale and process of participation, and sustained capacity-building at all levels for both stakeholders and public agencies.

Experience in recent years has allowed certain practical lessons to emerge on how to introduce and scale up successful innovations, with particular focus on community action and partnerships. A set of basic principles includes the following:

- **Stakeholder involvement is critical.** This needs to start at the identification of the problem, followed by the planning and implementation stage, and to carry on to monitoring, evaluation and research. There are a variety of approaches that have been tested and documented on how to motivate land users to implement and further refine technologies.

- **The work has to start and end at the local level.** Local land and water users have detailed knowledge of their ecosystem. This needs to be complemented by access to knowledge from outside the local context through partners, as well as to advisory services, professional training, and technical and financial assistance. Partners can jointly identify, evaluate, select and implement potential strategies at the local scale. Once plans are agreed and support measures are in place, local stakeholders can take primary responsibility for implementation.

- **Knowledge and dissemination are key.** Stakeholders need easily accessible information that is based on sound knowledge and experience. For this purpose, decision support systems are essential. Mapping, monitoring and evaluation, and other decision support tools ensure that decisions about investments are based on facts, and implementation can be adjusted in the light of emerging impacts.

- **Permanent partnership approaches are required.** Changes require collaboration and partnership at all levels (land users, technical experts and policymakers) to ensure that the causes of the degradation and corrective measures are correctly identified. Partnerships involving governmental institutions, non-governmental organizations, civil society organizations, private sector and individual land owners and users foster mutual respect and allow negotiation among these diverse stakeholder groups for a common sustainable future. Expert networks are key to these partnerships.

- **Diagnoses and programmes have to cover not just technologies but the local- and higher-level enabling environment, including the key question of incentives.** 'No farm is an island', and it is necessary to broaden the scope of the diagnostic and related solutions through nested approaches, from the farm or household level upwards. Many conditions are essential if change is to take off; they range from the question of incentives and financial support to markets and prices, services and infrastructure, legislation and regulations, education and promotion, and documentation and knowledge management. Through partnerships and participatory approaches, these framework conditions have to be identified alongside the technical solutions.

Modernizing management in irrigation

Large-scale irrigation schemes offer a privileged entry point for intensification as they provide both a means to manage crop production at scale and a platform on which to concentrate transfer of knowledge, supply of inputs and access to output markets. However, many institutional and business models for managing large-scale schemes have given mixed results, with some achieving neither fiscal efficiency nor demand-responsive water service (World Bank, 2006; Molden, 2007). As a result, user involvement through WUAs, increasing delegation of water management functions and cost recovery, and progressive stages of irrigation management transfer have been on the agenda of many countries, with the purpose to relieve governments of both the fiscal burden and the responsibility for asset management and maintenance, and thus to improve efficiency by empowering farmers.

To this extent, success depend on the intrinsic profitability and physical sustainability of the scheme, as well as capacity-building for scheme management, operation and maintenance, secure land and water rights, and careful management of the WUA formation/management transfer process, including post-handover support. Where scale and complexity preclude full farmer management and there is no alternative to management by a professional agency, this needs to be financially self-sustaining.

Water service charges need to be adequate to cover the real costs of operation and maintenance, and overhead costs need to be kept to the minimum. Above all, the agency needs to be transparent and accountable to the users – a condition that can usually only be achieved when there is genuine participation of users in its management. Future stages in the process need to be designed after ample study and consultation, and to be well-adapted to the context. In some cases, governments have opted for continuing with state management, but with a new, service-oriented approach, as promoted by FAO's MASSCOTE programme (Box 5.4). Other countries are increasing farmer involvement either through assigning operation and maintenance responsibilities to farmers' organizations or through processes of irrigation management transfer.

BOX 5.4: FAO'S MASSCOTE: ENCOURAGING IRRIGATION STAFF TO MODERNIZE

FAO defines modernization of irrigation as a process of technical and managerial upgrading (as opposed to mere rehabilitation) with the objective to improve resources use productivity through better water delivery services. The MASSCOTE programme (Mapping System and Services for Canal Operation Techniques; FAO, 2007e), is a methodology for analyzing and evaluating different components of an irrigation system in order to develop a modernization plan. The plan consists of a set of physical, technical, institutional and managerial innovations to improve water delivery services and cost effectiveness of operations and maintenance.

The programme is introduced to engineers and managers in large irrigation systems to promote the concept of service-oriented management and to help them design their system's modernization plan. As an example, since MASSCOTE was introduced in Karnataka, India in 2006, staff have shifted their focus from being supply-oriented to service-oriented and have improved the way in which they target investment planning. This approach has been introduced more recently in other countries of South and Central Asia, the Middle East and North Africa.

Photo: R.Wahaj

CHAPTER 5

Increased private or user involvement in management may offer a further way forward. Often termed public–private partnerships (PPPs), these involve finding a viable 'third party' between farmers and governments. This could be a public entity, such as a reformed or financially autonomous government agency. Alternatively, it might be private, such as a contracting firm or WUA turned into a private corporation or a farmers' company. Such PPPs have arisen in the water and sanitation sector over the last two decades with mixed results, but are less widespread in the irrigation sector. A part of the PPP could involve unbundling management of large irrigation canal systems into, for example, reservoirs, main canals and distribution networks, in a way similar to reforms that have taken place in the power sector. PPPs could be useful in mobilizing financing, implementing investment programmes and improving the water delivery service. Morocco (Guerdane) and Egypt (West Delta) have successfully negotiated PPP arrangements for irrigation. China has experimented with using private contractors, with some success (Box 5.5). Sri Lanka has also experimented with a farmer-managed irrigation company. Experiences in Mali, France and New Zealand also support the notion that the private sector can efficiently manage irrigation systems and collect water charges, even in the absence of formal WUAs.

Developing national investment frameworks

Developing implementation approaches into national programmes that can mobilize and sustain public and private investment in land and water management requires another level of effort and institutional commitment. For instance, to be effective, national irrigation strategies may require a package of technical and managerial

---

BOX 5.5: SCOPE FOR INVOLVING THE PRIVATE SECTOR IN IRRIGATION MANAGEMENT

Transfer of responsibility to users has its limits, and PPP may be one way of bringing in efficient management skills and fresh funds, and relieving government of fiscal and administrative burdens. Experience in the water supply sector has shown that, under some circumstances, the private sector can help mobilize financing, implement investment programmes and improve performance of service delivery. Under PPP, governance functions typically remain with government, although there is some scope for contracting out. Operation, management and maintenance functions have proved the easiest functions to contract out. Regarding investment, the private sector is essentially risk-averse and, faced with relatively high levels of risk, is reluctant to commit investment capital unless government assumes much of that risk. Although efficiency and service delivery have certainly improved, charges have usually gone up at the same time, and there have been social problems over the need to downsize staff. Overall, experience in the water supply sector shows that PPP may not entirely relieve government's investment burden, but is useful to establish the principle of financial autonomy and to raise professional standards.

Sources: FAO (2007a); World Bank (2007b)

---

upgrading that ensures that they can respond to the needs of high-value agriculture through improved reliability, flexibility and equity in water services. Decisions over the allocation of public resources and the promotion of private investment need to be programmed and monitored. Investment frameworks can be used as a tool for programming public and private resources to restructure the irrigated subsector in line with national development objectives, and also allow the investments to be tracked. In this way, overall monitoring and evaluation of any national irrigation investment can be monitored and evaluated. Figure 5.1 illustrates how a notional

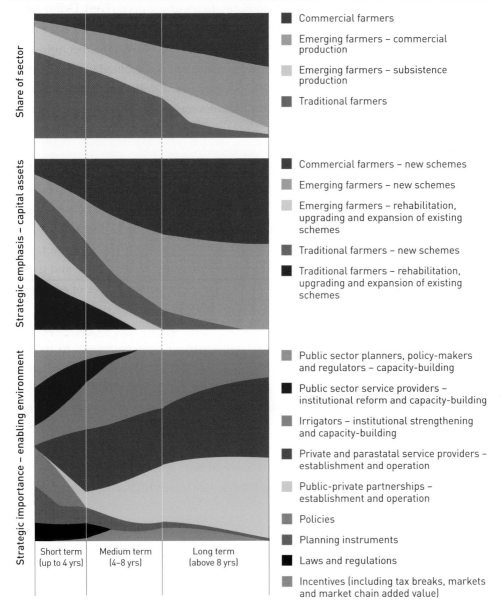

FIGURE 5.1: NOTIONAL STRATEGY MODEL FOR AN IRRIGATION INVESTMENT FRAMEWORK

Source: FAO Generic Investment Framework, Land and Water Division internal reports

strategy model for such a framework can be applied to a national irrigation strategy. Finally, monitoring and evaluation allow progress to be tracked, and technical and economic evaluations of outcomes and impacts to be made, which can then be fed back into improving and scaling up investment programmes. Within such investment programme, individual schemes can be appraised and 'benchmarked'.

The role of river basin agencies

In the future, the intensity of economic development across river basins and the degree of interdependence and competition over land and water resources can be expected to force a return to integration. However, despite the functional systemic integration of land and water, modern law and institutions now tend to deal with land and water separately. Even basin agencies, in principle dedicated to integrated resource management, deal primarily with a single resource, rather than with land and water jointly. Up to now, river basin management has had little direct influence over land use and land-use planning, except where it has contributed to remediation of non-point source pollution or has restricted agricultural water use. Basin management has largely been restricted to river functions such as hydropower, navigation and fish resources.

Current institutional trends in river basin management tend to be driven by either 'water development' or an 'ecosystem approach'. For example, major water transfer projects in China and India have been conceived within a water development planning framework, while the EU Water Framework Directive and Murray-Darling Basin planning follow an ecosystems conservation approach. In between, a range of solutions that respond to development priorities expressed at national and transboundary level have become apparent, with greater or lesser degrees of economic and environmental priority.

Irrespective of the agenda, whether development or environmental, to have a truly integrated effect on land and water use across a basin, planning and negotiation need to go beyond dealing only with in-stream water use along the course of the river. River basin audits offer an entry point. These audits give a basic account of land and water use throughout the basin in social, economic and environmental terms. This stage may be followed by the development of a vision for the basin in terms of feasible development and environmental outcomes. This requires extensive consultation with basin users to set measurable objectives for social, economic and environmental performance.

The range of policy tools now at the disposal of river basin agencies include: (1) statutory minimum environmental flow requirements to maintain a healthy ecology and fish populations; (2) requirements for environmental impact assessments (EIAs) as a precondition for granting licences for water use (most frequently surface and groundwater abstractions, and waste disposal); (3) declaration and supervision of reserves and protected areas (for example, wetlands) to maintain biodiversity and protect land and water quality; and (4) negotiation and supervision of measures to protect the watershed (e.g. through watershed management projects or other forms of PES).

The role of knowledge

The research and development agenda

Most research will have to be adaptive. For example, in rainfed agriculture, extending the positive environmental and soil moisture conservation benefits of conservation agriculture techniques will depend on mechanization capacity to respond rapidly to rainfall events. Techniques are known, but they need to be adapted to specific land and water and socio-economic settings. Where low-technology, opportunistic runoff farming is practised, which falls short of full water control over the whole cropping calendar, techniques to manage risk, particularly under more erratic rainfall regimes, need to be devised.

Sustainable intensification is more than improved land and water management. Agronomic practices such as earlier sowing, fertility management, weed control and the use of improved varieties play a key role too (Wani *et al.*, 2009). Efforts to stabilize production from existing rainfed systems in the face of climate change will need a better analysis of climate in relation to farming – rainfall patterns and soil moisture deficits linked to socio-economic vulnerability, not just in order to forecast food production volatility but also to structure inputs and services.

In irrigated systems, knowledge-based precision irrigation that offers farmers reliable and flexible water application will continue to form a major platform for intensification. In future, components like fertigation technology, deficit irrigation and recycling of treated wastewater, in particular for orchard crops (Winpenny *et al.*, 2010), are likely to become more widely used. All techniques are expected to become better integrated within irrigation systems that offer on-demand, just-in-time water delivery. Research and development will be needed to adapt these technologies to local farming practices.

Measures to modernize large-scale irrigation schemes will also require government intervention because of the scale and cost of investments. But in many cases, research and development may be best conducted by the private sector. Developing countries, for example, have already seen the promotion of low-head drip kits and pressurized subsoil drip for horticulture. In addition, the availability of cheap plastic moulded products and plastic sheeting for plasticulture will expand.

However, the broad-scale adoption of alternatives (e.g. solar technologies) or avoidance of polluting technology (plastic) will need to be led by government regulatory measures with effective policing of compliance.

Farming systems research will also be essential to determine intensification strategies. If rainfed production is to be stabilized with a contribution from enhanced soil moisture storage, the physical and socio-economic circumstances under which this can occur need to be well identified. There are also knowledge gaps that need to be filled, particularly on the economic and financial aspects, but also monitoring and evaluation of land and water degradation and of the positive impact of sustainable management measures.

Transferring the message

Sustainable intensification of land and water management will require inducing a very large number of farmers to improve their farming systems, adopting approaches to land and water productivity enhancement that fit their soils, water availability, labour force, access to inputs and markets, and also their income objectives. Thus, intensification packages must be accessible and feasible in technical and financial terms, and ensure an economic return on farmers' investment of labour and resources. There is ample evidence that technology-driven top-down approaches are non-sustainable. Therefore, this match of intensification packages with farmer endowment and objectives requires a 'demand-driven' approach that addresses the constraints as identified by the farmers themselves.

The capacity of existing extension systems to convey messages and technical packages to farmers is often limited. Site-specific behavioural changes would be best served by educational means (e.g. through Farmers' Field Schools, which reinforce farmers' decision-making capacities to adopt changes to land and water management). Flexible curricula need to be developed that specifically address problems of sustainable and environmentally sound land and water management for increased production. Where possible, indigenous knowledge and traditional practices should be integrated. Farmers should typically be addressed above the individual level, as land and water management generally requires cooperation.

Although a wealth of information exists on technologies and approaches, there is insufficient sharing of experiences at all levels, and between countries or regions. Existing knowledge bases are generally not widely accessible and may have sectoral or institutional biases. The knowledge is not always very user-friendly and is rarely directly accessible by the land users. Systems are largely 'passive', with few possibilities for regular updating. Key steps in putting in place an enabling environment will therefore be to develop the networks, forums and media for exchanging and disseminating knowledge, and for identifying and filling knowledge gaps.

Strengthening international partnerships

Resource inventory and use monitoring

As the challenges of sustainable land and water management mount, managers and users need accurate and timely data to monitor changes in land and water. New technologies, particularly remote sensing, are contributing to mapping and monitoring a wide range of parameters. A number of international programmes are developing resource inventory and monitoring tools. The potential of these spatial technologies for improving land and water management is enormous. One challenge is to ensure that there is access by all, and some programmes (such as the UNEP/FAO Digital Chart of the World and FAO's Geonetwork) have developed spatial data infrastructure and geospatial standards to increase data exchange between platforms.

New partnerships are sourcing data and interpreting it specifically for management purposes (Table 5.2). GEOSS initiatives (Box 5.6) comprise projects to support decision-taking on land and water across Asia and sub-Saharan Africa, including forest carbon tracking. The Millennium Ecosystem Assessment is a collaborative effort to track the impact of human activities on ecosystem services. In addition to its educational impact and influence on scientific research and policy, the coopera-

---

BOX 5.6: GLOBAL EARTH OBSERVATION SYSTEM OF SYSTEMS (GEOSS)

The global challenges posed by desertification, biodiversity loss and climate change have created an urgent need for an integrated system to monitor environmental changes and provide the information needed to move towards, a more sustainable management of natural resources. The group on Earth Observation (GEO), a voluntary partnership of governments and international organizations, was created in 2005 to build a Global Earth Observation System of Systems (GEOSS) to generate, disseminate and manage Earth observation data collected from a vast array of observation systems (oceanic buoys, hydrological and meteorological stations, and satellites), and to facilitate analysis in areas ranging from disaster risk mitigation to adaptation to climate change, integrated water resource management, biodiversity conservation, sustainable agriculture and forestry, public health, and weather monitoring.

In 2008 GEO launched the Forest Carbon Tracking Task (FCT) in collaboration with FAO, the European Space Agency (ESA) and the Committee on Earth Observation Satellites (CEOS). The goal of FCT is to develop a system of forest observation and carbon monitoring, reporting and verification based on satellites, airborne and *in situ* forest measurement data, and thus support countries that wish to monitor their forests, and create a system of carbon accounting.

Source: GEO (2010)

Programme	Goal related to land and water	URL
AQUASTAT (FAO)	Global information system on water resources, water uses and agricultural water management, with an emphasis on countries in Africa, Asia, Latin America and the Caribbean	www.fao.org/nr/aquastat
FAO Land and Water Digital Media Series	Provides a wide suite of data as well as educational resources on land and water issues	www.fao.org/landandwater/ lwdms.stm
FAOSTAT	The largest global source of agricultural data, with over one million time series	faostat.fao.org
Geonetwork	FAO's geospatial clearing house is a standardized and decentralized catalogue giving wide access to geo-referenced data, cartographic products and their metadata	www.fao.org/geonetwork/ srv/en/main.home
GEOSS	Earth geospatial data network	www.earthobservations.org
Global Soil Map Consortium	Soil analysis to inform land management practices	www.globalsoilmap.net
Global soil partnership (under discussion)	Harmonization of global soil databases	www.fao.org/nr/water/ news/soil-db.html www.iiasa.ac.at/Research/ LUC/External-World-soil-database/HTML/index.html
GTOS	Inter-agency coordinating mechanism for improving earth observation of natural resources	www.glcn.org
LADA	Land degradation assessment in drylands	www.fao.org/nr/lada/
UNEP/FAO digital charts of the world	Provide information on land cover and population density	www.fao.org/docrep/009/ a0310e/A0310E09.htm
UN-Water	Fostering information-sharing and knowledge-building across all UN agencies and external partners dealing with freshwater management	www.unwater.org/ flashindex.html
Wocat	Global network to disseminate knowledge on SLM practices	www.fao.org/ag/agL/agll/ wocat/default.stm

Source: Nkonya et al. (2010)

tion process itself has produced a deeper understanding of relationships between humans and natural systems.

But while progress has been made, efforts remain fragmented, financing for key functions has been dropping, and measures to ensure harmonization, accessibility and the sharing and use of data require further strengthening. On climate and water, global hydrological data and observation networks are still inadequate, and many countries have limited access to data. Data production needs to be further harmonized and dissemination needs to be broadened. Despite the potential of remote-sensing technologies, data are still not sufficiently tapped, and lack of data has been a key constraint to cooperation and investment. There is also a need for further effort to translate data into a usable format. International cooperation is required to facilitate the sharing of knowledge, and education and training in the application of information by decision-makers and managers needs strengthening (WWAP, 2009).

Coordinated policies and actions

Regional cooperation on land and water has been driven by the existence of multiple shared agendas – economic linkages, shared land and water resources, and common development challenges. There are numerous regional initiatives, with a particular concentration in sub-Saharan Africa, reflecting the poverty impact of the high levels of resource degradation prevailing in the region (Table 5.3).

International approaches for joint management and protection of land and water

Successive international conferences have resulted in international agreements relating to management and protection of aspects of land and water resources. Several UN agencies share responsibility for supporting their implementation, including FAO, UNEP and the World Bank. This section discusses the progress with implementation of some of these agreements.

In land, the UN Convention to Combat Desertification (UNCCD) supports national action plans and collaboration between donors and countries for combating degradation of land and water resources in dry areas. UNCCD has raised awareness and created some political momentum, but financial resources and a clearer mandate are needed to have significant impact.

The Global Environment Facility (GEF) was established in 1991. Its objective is to promote international cooperation to prevent global environmental degradation and to rehabilitate degraded natural resources. To date, the GEF has allocated US$8.8 billion, supplemented by over US$38.7 billion in cofinancing, for more than 2 400 projects. Through its Small Grants Programme, the GEF has also made more

TABLE 5.3: SELECTED REGIONAL COOPERATION EFFORTS ON LAND AND WATER MANAGEMENT

Regional cooperation	Activities related to land and water	Source
Cooperation institutions in Africa		
Comprehensive Africa Agriculture Development Programme (CAADP)	'Pillar 1' of the CAADP aims at extension of area under sustainable land management and reliable water control systems. Targets 6 percent growth in agricultural productivity and 10 percent public expenditure budget for agriculture.	www.africa-union.org/root/ au/Documents/Treaties/ treaties.htm
TerrAfrica	Partnership set up in 2005 that aims to address land degradation through country-driven sustainable land management (SLM) practices in sub-Saharan African countries.	www.terrafrica.org
Partnership for Agricultural Water in Africa (AgWA)	AgWA promotes and encourages investment in agricultural water management in Africa. Its five priorities are: advocacy; resource mobilization; knowledge sharing; donor harmonization; and capacity development. AgWA is a framework for coordination and for linkages with African subregional partnerships such IMAWESA, ARID and SARIA.	www.agwaterforafrica.org
AU (African Union)	Convention for the establishment of the African centre for fertilizer development; and African convention on the conservation of nature and natural resources	www.africa-union.org/root/ au/Documents/Treaties/ treaties.htm
SADC	Collaborative water management initiatives	Giordano and Wolf (2002)
Other cooperation institutions		
Association of Southeast Asian Nations (ASEAN)	Establish mechanisms for sustainable development through protection of the region's environment and natural resources	ASEAN Ministerial Meeting on Environment 2009 www.aseansec.org/19601.htm
Organization of American States (OAS)	Equitable and efficient land-tenure systems and increased agricultural productivity	www1.umn.edu/humanrts/ iachr/oascharter.html
EU	Convention on Environmental Impact Assessment in a Transboundary Context (1991); Convention on the Protection and Use of Transboundary Watercourses and International Lakes (1992); Water framework directive for integrated river basin management (2000).	Giordano and Wolf (2002)

Source: this study

than 10 000 small grants directly to non-governmental and community organizations. With US$792 million invested to date in sustainable land management, the GEF is the largest global grant investor in this sector (Box 5.7). Issues concern insufficient synergies among GEF's various focal areas, and constraints experienced in scaling up from projects to a programme approach.

- In the coffee fields of Central America, the GEF is working with farmers to raise incomes by increasing their harvest of shade-grown coffee. This helps protect biodiversity, reduces dependence on pesticides and sequesters carbon.
- GEF funding to restore degraded wetlands in Romania has resulted in the removal of an estimated 55 tonnes of phosphorus, 1 200 tonnes of nitrogen and 40 000 tonnes of sediment from the Danube River before it enters the Black Sea.
- GEF projects in the humid tropics, Amazonia, Guyana Shield, the Caucasus and the Himalayas collectively work to conserve the largest remaining tracts of tropical rainforests, home to millions of species.
- The regions of southern Mexico and Central America are helping to restore the Mesoamerican Biological Corridor through a GEF-supported project that combines nature conservation with improving the standard of living for people in the area.
- Under a GEF project, Brazilian technicians are designing a biomass gas turbine that runs on the residue and waste from sugar refining, including waste from harvesting and bagasse, a residue from processing. The new turbines provide efficient clean energy, reducing emissions.

Source: GEF (2011)

The International Land Coalition was set up as a 'convener' of civil society, governmental and intergovernmental stakeholders on land policies and practices. It has an advocacy mission to increase access to land resources by the poor, particularly through more secure land tenure.

In water, the Global Water Partnership (GWP) was established in 1996 to promote integrated water resource management and the coordinated development and management of land and water. GWP provides advice to governments on management approaches. The World Water Council (WWC) was established in 1996 to promote awareness and build commitment on sustainable water resources management, and is best known for its flagship conference, the World Water Forum.

All of these agreements and organizations are pursuing agendas defined within the broad principles agreed at international conferences. They have contributed to raising awareness and have prompted action on land and water issues by member states. In some cases, these initiatives have strengthened institutions and governance. GWP partners, for example, have contributed substantially to awareness of integrated water resource management and to its adoption into national law, strategy and practice. All the initiatives subscribe to an approach that in principle integrates land and water issues together. However, in practice, approaches remain largely sectoral. The GWP, for example, focuses mainly on water; the ILC on land. An international convention on sustainable land and water management could help to resolve these difficulties.

CHAPTER 5

Several of the organizations are working in the same field and with limited resources, which reduces focus and impact. There has been insufficient feedback on the successes and problems of these initiatives, so that the lessons of experience are not always being built in to new approaches. What is needed is a permanent forum and information exchange in which best practice and lessons can be pooled.

River basin cooperation

Although absence of a cooperative framework has been a constraint for the optimal development of many transboundary rivers, considerable progress has been made in recent years to reach varying degrees of cooperation. Cooperation on river basin development and management has usually started with technical cooperation, such as information exchange, leading over time to cooperation on planning, investment and benefit-sharing. The benefits of cooperation can be considerable: one study estimated that cooperation among Blue Nile riparian countries could increase net annual benefits from the river by US$5 billion (Whittington *et al.*, 2005).

The UN Convention on the Law of the Non-Navigational Uses of International Water Courses codified rules for equitable use, obligations of protection and conservation of international water bodies, information exchange, and settlement of disputes. The convention has not yet entered into force as insufficient members ratified it, but it provides a set of principles and standards to which riparians can refer.

In some basins, cooperation has resulted in a formal treaty and the legal establishment of a river basin organization: examples include the Mekong, the Senegal, the Volta and the Niger (Nkonya *et al.*, 2010). The Mekong River Basin Commission allowed planning to reduce flooding in the delta. Under the cooperative framework of the Lake Victoria Basin Commission, the water hyacinth problem in Lake Victoria was addressed (Foster and Briceño-Garmendia, 2010). However, experience shows that it may take decades before nations agree to joint development and management. For example, of the 18 initiatives for river basin cooperation in sub-Saharan Africa launched since the 1960s, only four have yet reached the stage of a legally established river basin committee (Grey and Sadoff, 2006). Some programmes are specifically addressing land and water management and degradation issues at the transboundary basin scale. Two GEF projects (the Fouta Djallon project in West Africa and the Kagera River Project in East Africa), as well as the Lake Chad Basin Sustainable Development Program (Box 5.8), are supporting environmental management and monitoring to improve land and water management, to mitigate carbon emissions and conserve biodiversity.

New partnerships and mechanisms

A number of recent initiatives and partnerships are likely to have positive effects on sustainable land and water management. Alongside traditional development

The Lake Chad Basin Sustainable Development Program (PRODEBALT) was designed in 2007 as a contribution to the implementation of the Strategic Action Plan and Vision 2025 of the Lake Chad Basin Commission (LCBC). It aims for the rehabilitation and conservation of the productive capacities of Lake Chad basin ecosystems through an integrated and judicious management of the basin, so as to adapt the production systems to climate change, thus reducing poverty among the populations living around the lake. The programme started in 2009 and has a duration of six years. Its cost of approximately US$97 million is jointly financed by an African Development Bank grant for about half of the total and the rest from other donors: GIZ, BGR, European Union, World Bank and Islamic Development Bank.

In particular, the activities carried out within PRODEBALT are:

1. Protection of Lake Chad and its basin: soil conservation; regeneration of grazing-land ecosystems; control of invasive aquatic plants in water bodies; conservation of the Kouri cow species; study and plan of optimal management of reservoirs and water supply points of the basin.
2. Adaptation of production systems to climate change: extension of the piezometric observation network; sustainable management of forestry, pasture and fishery resources; establishment of local development funds to finance basic community infrastructure.
3. Institutional support: improvement of stakeholder skills; building of LCBC institutional capacities, including strengthening of the Lake Basin Observatory; conduct of studies and research, including preparation of the erosion and silting control master plan; contribution to the final design of the project of transfer of the Oubangui waters to Lake Chad.

Source: AfDB (2008)

partners, the civil society, NGOs and the private sector and private foundations are playing an increasingly important role in the promotion of sustainable development (Box 5.9).

Public–private partnerships have emerged in land and water development and management. Recent examples include Guerdane in Morocco, where an international consortium entered into a 30-year concession for the construction, cofinancing, operation and management of an irrigation water supply and distribution network; and Brazil's semi-arid region where government invested in large-scale irrigation projects on 200 000 ha to demonstrate new cropping alternatives, technologies and productive processes, and so attracted private investment on a further 360 000 ha.

CHAPTER 5

Fairtrade: in addition to paying farmers a premium price for their produce, Fairtrade builds human and social capital in participating communities, as well as promoting good farm management practices with an emphasis on long-term sustainable production. Today, more than five million people across 58 developing countries benefit from Fairtrade. A good example is Thailand's Green Net Cooperative, which was established in 1993 by a group of producers and consumers. Farmers were suffering rises in their production costs and at the same time a decline in the prices of agricultural products. Meanwhile, Thai consumers were becoming increasingly conscious of the impact of pesticides on their health and on the environment. Green Net was the first (and is still the largest) wholesaler of fresh organic produce in Thailand. In 2002 Green Net was certified by Fairtrade Labelling Organizations International (FLO) and it now exports Fairtrade rice to Switzerland, Belgium, Germany, France, Italy, Austria, the Netherlands and Sweden (Fairtrade, 2011).

Green and organic labels and certifications: there are many examples of labels and certifications on the products of organic agriculture systems. Smallholder farmers can benefit from commodity-specific certification programmes (for example, by forming cooperatives or through participating in contract-farming arrangements). Products concerned include coffee, tea, cocoa, non-wood forest products and cotton.

Ecotourism: the key to sustainable ecotourism is sustainable ecosystem management with benefit-sharing among local populations. Functioning ecosystems are vital for ecotourism to thrive, and ecotourism is a key mechanism to provide incentives for sustainable agriculture and forestry within a whole-ecosystem context.

Environmental interest groups: many are actively engaged in partnerships to promote sustainable land and water management. They play both a financing and an advocacy role to promote policies and programmes to address climate change impacts and enhance biodiversity, and water quality and quantity. The Zambia Agribusiness Technical Assistance Centre helps small farmers in Zambia to invest in sustainable irrigated market gardening linked to wholesalers for export. Smallholders now grow irrigated fresh 'organic' vegetables for markets in Europe.

Foundations: private foundations such as the Rockefeller Foundation and Ford Foundation are supporting sustainable agriculture. The Bill & Melinda Gates Foundation focuses on areas with the potential for high-impact, sustainable solutions, including agricultural development. Recent grants in sustainable agriculture include funding for legumes that fix nitrogen in the soil, higher-yielding varieties of sorghum and millet, and research on crops that can withstand drought and flooding. The foundation also funds research for improved agricultural water management in support of smallholder enterprise.

TABLE 5.4: VIRTUAL WATER TRADE OF SELECTED COUNTRIES

	Total use of domestic water resources in the agricultural sector (km³/yr)	Water saving due to import of agricultural products (km³/yr)	Water loss due to export of agricultural products (km³/yr)	Net water saving due to trade in agricultural products (km³/yr)	Ratio of net water saving to use of domestic water
China	n.a.	79	23	56	0.08
Mexico	94	83	18	65	0.69
Morocco	37	29	1.6	27	0.73
Italy	60	87	28	59	0.98
Algeria	23	46	0.5	45	1.96
Japan	21	96	1.9	94	4.48

Source: Hoekstra (2010)

Globalization has also increased opportunities for trading virtual water – water used in the production of goods or services. The concept of virtual water suggests that a well-functioning global trade system would induce countries to export or import goods based on their natural resource endowment. Water- and/or land-poor countries would be net importers of agricultural commodities produced by water-abundant countries. It is argued that such a system would be more likely to achieve an optimal use of both land and water resources. Many countries are already net importers of agricultural goods, therefore importing large volumes of virtual water. Jordan, for example, imports about 6 km³ of virtual water per year and withdraws only 1 km³ from domestic sources (Hoekstra and Chapagain, 2007). Table 5.4 shows the level of water savings due to international virtual water trading.

It is argued that the virtual water content in trade of agricultural products from relatively land- and water-abundant to more land- and water-scarce areas has helped to increase water- and land-use efficiency. In fact, the realization of apparent 'comparative advantage' is hard to establish (Wichelns, 2010) since national economic policies appraise a range of factor productivities, not just water 'content'. The contribution of labour or energy can be much more significant in determining the comparative advantage in a specific crop. In this respect, it is important not to 'oversell' the importance of water in agriculture. It may be critical, but other factors of production can be equally important or dominant.

Enhancing international cooperation and investment

Investment in land and water is essential to increasing agricultural productivity and production sustainably. Investment in land and water has increased slightly in the last five years, but levels remain below those necessary to intensify production while minimizing negative impacts on the ecosystem. A particular concern is the low level of investment in the more vulnerable rainfed systems, where poverty and food insecurity are prevalent and risks of land and water resource degradation are high.

Growing interest but unmet needs

International cooperation on land and water has become a higher level of priority in many quarters. Continuing preoccupations over food security, poverty reduction and environmental protection have been heightened by growing concern over climate change, the recent food price crisis and associated land acquisitions. Interest in sustainable land and water management as a core development approach has also been heightened by a shift in thinking towards the possibilities of a new 'green economy' (Box 5.10). However, despite these positive trends, the level of investment is small compared with the levels needed to stem negative trends in land and water status and to develop higher productivity sustainably within an ecosystems context.

The case for a focus on sustainable land and water management

Agriculture is vital to poverty reduction, and strong agricultural growth has been a consistent feature of countries that have successfully managed to reduce poverty. GDP growth generated in agriculture is four times more effective in benefiting the

---

BOX 5.10: A GREEN AGRICULTURE FOR A GREEN ECONOMY

Faced with multiple crises, many questions have been raised about how to overhaul the global business model. One notion is that a low-carbon 'green economy', which recognizes and assigns value to natural capital, helps to mitigate climate change and adapt to its impacts, and reverses current negative trends in ecosystems (water resources depletion, pollution, land degradation, loss of social and cultural values, fisheries collapse). A green agricultural economy would incorporate the best elements of the old 'green revolution' (improved adapted crop varieties and livestock breeds) into more ecologically friendly land and water management that would take an ecosystem/landscape approach to respond to global environmental threats, land degradation, biodiversity loss and, in particular, climate change. This kind of green agriculture is becoming an important direction proposed by the Rio+20 programme.

The fiscal stimulus packages that many countries prepared to respond to the recent financial crisis contained funds dedicated to green projects, many related to energy efficiency and low-carbon technologies, river restoration and water management (World Bank, 2009a; Robins et al., 2009). This green stimulus showed that the economic turndown was taken as an opportunity for investing in the green sector (i.e. restoring growth through investing in a restructuring of the economic system). It also shows that a green economy requires substantial initial public investments and regulations, as well as a private sector ready to deliver on new technologies and markets.

Source: Salman et al. (2010)

---

poorest half of the population than growth generated outside agriculture (World Bank, 2007c). Increased agricultural productivity improves farmers' incomes, generates on-farm employment, lowers food prices, and has significant income and employment multipliers within the local non-farm economy, all of which reduce poverty, as the poor typically spend two-thirds of their income on food. Such increases in productivity will require increased investment in agriculture, and especially in land and water development.

The new focus on the green economy and on a win–win approach to productivity and maintenance of ecosystem services creates a powerful case for this strengthened focus on sustainable land and water management. Box 5.11 recapitulates the contribution of sustainable land and water management to multiple development goals. However, investment in these areas is decreasing, or at best stagnating. The drop-off in investment in agricultural land and water was mainly driven by the perception of a decline in rates of return compared to alternative investments in other sectors, but the recent surge in food prices and worsening of the food security situation show the limits of such short-sighted strategies. Moreover, the fact that the return on capital invested in agriculture rarely matches that in industry and urban services does not capture the multiplier and social benefits from rural investment, beyond the direct impacts on food security. Only a healthy agricultural sector, combined with a growing non-farm economy and effective safety nets and social protection programmes, will be sufficient to face the global recession, as well as to eradicate food insecurity and poverty.

Some successes and new initiatives

There are nonetheless encouraging signs. First, a policy favouring increased production by smallholders in food-deficit developing countries is being embraced at both international and national level. The Joint Statement on Global Food Security made at the 2008 G8 meeting in L'Aquila, Italy stressed the need to adopt a comprehensive strategy focusing on small farmers. Second, many countries have already made considerable steps towards hunger eradication. For example, Ghana, Malawi, Mozambique, Thailand, Turkey, Uganda and Vietnam have significantly reduced the number of undernourished people in their countries over the last five years. Although most have fallen short of the target, eight African countries have met the Maputo Declaration target of allocating 10 percent of the government budget to agriculture (Fan *et al.*, 2009). The foundations for increased agricultural productivity and production to foster food security have been laid: programmes, projects and plans already exist, and are simply waiting for the political will and financial resources to become operational.

Third, moves to increase aid efficiency and to align national programmes in accordance with the Paris Declaration on Aid Effectiveness and the Accra Agenda

Cooperation on land and water is not an end in itself. It is a means of achieving larger development goals – the MDGs, overall food security, poverty alleviation, conservation of local and global ecosystem services. Land and water investments are appropriate for financing from a large range of programmes and funds.

Key linkages between larger development goals and sustainable land and water management include:

- **Rural poverty reduction:** Reducing rural poverty depends directly on the productivity and profitability of land and water-based activities, all of which are threatened by land and water degradation.
- **Food security:** National-level food security depends heavily on sustainable production of food from land and water, which, in turn, requires sustainable land and water manage-ment. In addition, sustainable land and water management can reduce dependence on net food imports, and thus conserve important financial resources.
- **Provision of a range of livelihood products such as wood, fibre and biofuels:** Land and water degradation reduces the productivity of natural resources, not only for food production but also for the production of other outputs, such as fibre, building materials, bioenergy and non-timber forest products.
- **Mitigation and adaptation to climate change:** Poor land and water management contrib-utes to greenhouse gases. More sustainable land and water management practices increase soil carbon sequestration and reduce GHG emissions in agriculture. They also often contribute to adaptation to climate change by increasing resilience in the face of climate variability and extreme events.

for Action have led to more programmatic approaches to financing in support of national policies and strategies. In this context, several new financing facilities have been established, such as the African Fertilizer Financing Mechanism or the Global Agricultural and Food Security Program created after the G8 summit in 2008. However the establishment of dedicated funds with narrow targets, may be less efficient than fungible resources available for financing integrated national develop-ment programmes.

Attracting carbon sequestration financing for land and water strategies

One important innovation is the development of carbon markets. But although the potential for mitigation through agriculture is vast, the regulatory markets, such as the CDM under the Kyoto protocol and the EU emissions trading scheme, exclude agriculture. However, work is underway to reverse this. In addition, new initiatives are under discussion under the UN-REDD initiative (Box 5.12) to allow

- **Preserving biodiversity:** The trend towards monoculture and poor land and water management have negatively affected biodiversity. Matching of land and water use with land potential, thereby promoting diverse landscapes and products and adapted land use systems, is important to preserve remaining biodiversity levels.
- **Maintenance of other ecosystem functions:** Sustainable land and water management can also support other ecological functions or services, including the breakdown of waste products, pollination, soil biological activity that maintains nutrient and organic matter cycles, and biological control of pests and diseases. These important regulatory functions and the process of soil formation can only be maintained through appropriate land and water management practices.
- **Natural disaster prevention/mitigation:** Sustainable land and water management can increase the resilience of ecosystems, thereby reducing the risk and impact of natural disasters, such as floods, droughts, hailstorms or pest infestations.
- **Ecosystem health:** Overall, sustainable land and water management can not only arrest ecosystem degradation but can positively improve certain services: biomass, soil health, water storage and supply, and economic productivity. Amenity, tourism and cultural heritage values of landscape may also be improved.
- **Social stability:** Wellbeing and social stability in rural areas are directly related to the feasibility of earning a living from natural resources, and therefore to issues of access to land and water resources, security of tenure, and capacity to manage these resources in the most profitable and sustainable manner, through sustainable land and water management.

Sources: Nkonya et al. (2010); Salman et al. (2010)

reward for carbon sequestration in all landscapes, including 'agriculture, forestry and other land uses'. Pilot projects are being implemented in developing countries under voluntary carbon standards. A global survey of agricultural mitigation projects identified 50 agricultural projects focusing on climate change, of which 22 are developed specifically with a GHG mitigation objective.

However, problems both in the design of schemes and in the development of qualifying strategies in developing countries are not yet fully resolved. The basic difficulty is in quantifying and monitoring agricultural mitigation strategies and the resulting low-confidence, high-transaction costs and low prices of certified emissions. Problems on the side of developing countries are both in policy (lack of public commitment to invest in climate change adaptation and mitigation) and in implementation (weak property rights, low institutional capacity). Several pilot projects are being developed to try to overcome these hurdles (Box 5.13).

The United Nations Collaborative initiative on Reducing Emissions from Deforestation and Forest Degradation (UN-REDD) in developing countries is an effort to create a financial value for the carbon stored in forests, offering incentives for developing countries to reduce emissions from forested lands and invest in low-carbon paths to sustainable development. REDD+ goes beyond deforestation and forest degradation, and includes the role of conservation, sustainable management of forests and enhancement of forest carbon stocks. The UN-REDD Programme was launched in September 2008 as a collaboration between FAO, UNDP and UNEP. A multidonor trust fund was established to allow donors to pool resources, and provides funding towards programme activities. The Copenhagen Accord recognizes the role of UN-REDD and calls for 'immediate' establishment of a REDD+ mechanism. Developed countries committed to new and additional resources approaching US$30 billion to support enhanced action on mitigation, including 'substantial finance' for REDD+.

Source: UN-REDD (2011)

FAO is currently developing a sustainable grazing project in China in cooperation with Chinese national counterparts, which aims to increase the resilience of alpine grazing systems using carbon finance. In addition, FAO is currently developing through MICCA (Mitigation of Climate Change in Agriculture) several pilot projects to support efforts of smallholder farmers to mitigate climate change through agriculture and to move towards climate-smart agricultural practices. MICCA emphasizes supporting knowledge generation on GHG emissions and mitigation potential, and testing at country and field level how mitigation-promoting techniques can be integrated into agricultural practices.

Source: FAO (2010e)

There is also a voluntary carbon market financed by companies that wish to offset their carbon footprint (Box 5.14). If agriculture in developing countries can benefit from the carbon market, this has the potential to bring considerable funding to national and local sustainable land and water management strategies. Early research (Tennigkeit *et al.*, 2009) suggest that revenues from yield improvements through the improved management techniques far outweigh the payments to be received from carbon credits, so that carbon credits may simply have a complementary or catalytic role in well-designed land and water programmes.

If sustainable land and water management investments cannot be compensated under existing programmes or under possible future programmes such as

The voluntary carbon market, financed by companies that want to offset their carbon footprint as a way of corporate responsibility, can be separated into two categories, the Chicago Climate Exchange (CCX) and the 'over-the-counter' market. Currently, compliance markets (regulatory markets, such as CDM and the EU Trading Scheme) and voluntary carbon markets account for less than 2 percent of the global carbon market (Capoor and Ambrosi, 2009), but are increasing.

The CCX is the world's only voluntary cap-and-trade system, while the over-the-counter market is the non-binding offset market. The CCX is the only market with a considerable share of agricultural soil projects. However, from 2007 to 2008, this share fell from 48 to 15 percent. The drop in agricultural soil projects was due in part to the growth of the programme itself, and in part to modifications made to the agricultural soil protocol, which has led to a slowdown of the verification process (Hamilton *et al.*, 2009).

Source: Salman et al. (2010)

UN-REDD, an option is to set up special funds to finance adoption of sustainable land management practices by smallholder farmers, with specific rules and requirements, and linked to programmes designed to support policy, strategy and farmer-level implementation of sustainable land and water management along the lines recommended in this report.

Payment for environmental services

PES mechanisms have attracted interest and financing both within countries and from international investors. Systems exist for watershed services, biodiversity conservation, benefit-sharing in transboundary river basin development and reduction in carbon emissions (Box 5.15).

Lessons for the future

The prospects for the implementation of more forward-looking land and water management policies, to reverse degradation trends and conserve resources for the future, will only look bright if the institutional mechanisms prove adaptive to scale/environmental context and more comprehensive (pluralistic) engagement with users.

A combination of scale-specific policy responses, innovative institutional solutions and more inclusive (but more strategic) planning solutions can be packaged to meet human demand for agricultural production and environmental services. The test is whether any of these interventions will have a measurable impact in

In recent years, several mechanisms have been developed to overcome the problem that the costs of sustainable resource management may be borne by one party but the benefits reaped by another. The practice of contracting between the parties for payments for environmental services (PES) takes several forms.

Under PES for **watershed services**, watershed management programmes typically invest in sustainable development for poor communities in the upper catchment of river basins, justifying public investment subsidy on the grounds that the benefits largely accrue downstream, in the form of clean water, flood control and reduced siltation.

Under PES for **biodiversity**, financial incentives are provided for land users to conserve biodiversity. For example, in 1996 Costa Rica implemented an innovative programme under which forest and plantation owners were financially rewarded and legally acknowledged for the environmental services their forests provide nationally and globally. The early years of the PES scheme showed that it mainly benefited larger farmers and people using their forest for leisure purposes. Since then a number of measures have been taken to promote participation of small farmers and indigenous communities.

At a larger scale, **benefit-sharing in transboundary river basin development** compensates the country that bears an undue share of the costs with other benefits. For example, loss of water due to upstream abstractions might be compensated by hydropower benefits.

PES through the **carbon market** has an important potential. For example, the African agriculture sector has an estimated 17 percent of the total global mitigation potential. This could potentially translate into an annual value stream for African countries of US$4.8 billion. However, carbon markets still need to refine their implementation mechanisms in order to allow poor land users to benefit from them.

Source: Nkonya et al. (2010)

conserving or lengthening the life of Earth's natural endowments. In places where the natural capital is stretched, national institutions are more likely to be driven by environmental agendas in the future. The case for making the value of land and water explicit, and providing incentives to resource users and investors, is now well established (World Bank, 2009b).

In terms of water management, the 'more crop per drop' slogan will still apply, but the pressures from competing demands for water will necessitate 'more crop with less drop and less environmental impact'. This implies that water management for sustainable crop production and intensification will need to anticipate smarter precision agriculture. This will be technology-intensive and knowledge-intensive. It will also require agriculture to become much more adept at accounting for its water use in economic, social and environmental terms. But it is at farm level that farmers self-interest can be harnessed to improve environmental outcomes. In addition, private sector interests (including fertilizer and agro-chemical supply) can be regulated and incentivized to support more sustainable irrigation. All this suggests a shift from government roles in operating and maintaining irrigation schemes into the business of smart regulation, which can promote adoption of proven water management technologies combined with knowledge-rich agronomic practice.

The time is right to put sustainable land and water management in its rightful place at the centre of the global development debate. A first priority might be to develop and agree an integrated shared vision at the global, regional and national levels. This vision would need to be reflected in a strategy and investment framework, setting out how a shared vision might be operationalized, with tangible milestones, human and financial resource requirements, and responsibilities of the various actors. This strategy and framework could then be translated at the regional and national level into strategies and investment programmes.

At the global level, financing is required for increased levels of investment, and this might be linked to carbon credits. Investment is needed at the farm level, at the level of the basin, watershed or irrigation scheme, and at macro level, through government investment in institutions, knowledge and public goods, and through private investment in research and development and in productive capacity. Implementation would require a supportive enabling environment and incentive structure, institutional support, and a strong monitoring and evaluation mechanism.

There is scope for increased international cooperation on land and water, engaging with private sector partners, NGOs and international foundations. In this context, there is a need for international cooperation to establish 'rules of engagement', to ensure that foreign investments are beneficial to the host countries and that small farmers and the poor have access to increased economic opportunity as a result.

Chapter 6
CONCLUSIONS AND MAIN POLICY RECOMMENDATIONS

This book has traced three challenges facing the land and water resources upon which agriculture relies: to increase food production by almost 70 percent by 2050; to reduce hunger and improve livelihoods for the poorest; and to minimize or mitigate degradation of land and water and of the broader ecosystems. A range of technical and institutional solutions exist and have been discussed in previous chapters. They need to be adapted to local farming systems and socio-economic contexts. Improved planning, linked to smart incentive packages, can then establish a framework for investment that assigns agreed values to natural capital. On this basis, land and water management that is efficient, equitable and sustainable can be encouraged at all scales.

Movements towards this new 'green economy' have started. Increasingly, governments, civil society and the private sector are looking for technologies and approaches that can raise productivity while protecting the natural resource base and associated ecosystems. Packages for more sustainable farming are being adopted, and measures to overcome the technical and socio-economic constraints have been devised.

However, despite this progress, there remain considerable barriers to adoption. The proliferation of instruments, conferences and diverging commitments is time- and resource-consuming, with very little effect on the ground. Political commitment by nations and the international community to tackle issues in a synergetic manner is essential.

Moving to more sustainable pathways of intensification and ecological management will require additional efforts. Policies, institutions and implementation strategies will need adjustment at global, national and local levels to equip organizations and farmers with the knowledge, incentives and financial resources they need. With this support, farmers can raise productivity sustainably and strengthen the integration of their farming within local ecosystems, managing trade-offs to keep adverse effects to the minimum. A knowledge-rich engagement at local, national and global levels, focusing on land and water systems at risk, will ultimately spread socio-economic growth benefits far and wide, reducing food insecurity and associated poverty.

Ensuring sustainable production
in major land and water systems

Many major land and water systems are globally important and present substantial levels of risk, in terms of sustainability, productivity and capacity to address poverty and food security. This section summarizes how responses can be applied in the world's major land and water systems to promote expanded production within an ecologically sustainable framework, and with a focus on poverty reduction and food security.

Major land and water systems at risk

Although productivity improvements, and in some cases expansion of the cropped area, are possible in many land and water systems, all systems are at risk of degradation and loss of productive capability. The status varies. Among rainfed systems outside the temperate zones, desertification and land degradation are significant risks. In temperate zones there is considerable scope for expanding production, but at the risk of pollution and other degradation of ecosystems. In the vast productive basins of Asia, systems are generally highly developed, but with water scarcity and land deterioration problems. Delta systems will also suffer risks from sea-level rise, as well as rising pollution; in many locations, new infrastructure may be needed to improve water security and productivity in the face of likely increased but more variable rainfall patterns. All systems using groundwater are at risk from aquifer depletion and degradation.

Priorities for action include the areas from which the bulk of extra production will have to come (notably irrigated systems and rainfed production in temperate zones). In addition, priority has to go to geographical areas that are poor and vulnerable to degradation, and where agriculture, including livestock and forestry, plays a predominant role in poverty reduction and food security. Tackling the problems of production systems particularly vulnerable to degradation in every region is also a priority: for example, marginal mountain systems, marginal grazing lands converted to rainfed farming, or forest converted to quick-return commercial farming.

Options by major land and water system

Earlier chapters highlighted current problems and future risks in the world's major land and water systems as they face the challenge of greatly increasing output in the coming decades. This section summarizes the technical and institutional options that may be applied in each of these systems in order to manage the progress to higher levels of productivity and output, while minimizing negative impacts (Table 6.1).

TABLE 6.1: TECHNICAL AND INSTITUTIONAL RESPONSES TO SUPPORT IMPROVED LAND AND WATER MANAGEMENT

System	Technical responses to raise productivity through improved land and water management	Institutional responses to support sustainable improvements in land and water management
Rainfed		
Highlands	• Soil and water conservation • Terracing • Flood protection • Reforestation • Conservation agriculture	• Payment for environmental services (PES) in watersheds • Promotion of tourism • Planned outmigration • Provision of basic services and infrastructure
Semi-arid tropics	• Better integration of agriculture–livestock • Investments in irrigation and water harvesting • Integrated plant nutrition • Plant breeding adapted to semi-arid conditions • Conservation agriculture	• Enhanced land tenure security • Land reform and consolidation where possible • Crop insurance • Improved governance and investments in infrastructure (markets, roads) • Planned out-migration • Solar energy production • Farmer field schools
Subtropical	• Climate change adaptation • Plant breeding adapted to semi-arid conditions • Improved soil and water conservation • Integrated plant nutrition • Conservation agriculture	• Land reform and consolidation • Crop insurance • investments in rural infrastructure and services • Planned out-migration
Temperate	**Western Europe:** • Pollution control and mitigation • Conservation agriculture • Integrated plant nutrition and pest management **Elsewhere:** • Pollution control and mitigation • Integrated plant nutrition and pest management • Conservation agriculture	• Participatory planning for expansion and intensification

Options need to be adapted to both problems and opportunities. For land, changes in crop and land use, crop diversification, and measures to improve soil quality, such as soil fertility management and conservation agriculture, are needed to enhance productivity, sustainability and resilience of agricultural systems. Better-informed agronomic techniques are needed everywhere: minimum tillage, use of cover crops and nitrogen fixers in rotation cycles, managed application of fertilizers and organic amendments, soil water management improvements to irrigation and drainage, and a switch to improved varieties with higher water productivity. For water, a combination of supply-side measures coupled with demand management is needed to adjust

System	Technical responses to raise productivity through improved land and water management	Institutional responses to support sustainable improvements in land and water management
Irrigated		
Rice-based (Asia)	• Improved storage • Diversification (introduction of fish and vegetables • Pollution control	• Payment for environmental services (PES) • Farmer field schools
(Africa)	• System of rice intensification (SRI)	• Better incentives, markets, access to inputs and improved varieties • Improved governance management and infrastructure • Farmer field schools
River basin systems	• Modernization of irrigation schemes (infrastructure and governance) to improve water service, increasing flexibility and reliability in water supply to support diversification • Prepare and implement climate change adaptation plans	• Develop incentives for efficient use of water
Aquifer-based systems	• Enhanced water productivity	• Regulation of groundwater use • More effective water allocation
Other		
Deltas and coastal areas	• Climate change adaptation plans • Flood control • Pollution control • Mitigation of arsenic contamination through improved irrigation practices	• Land-use planning • Control of groundwater depletion
Peri-urban agriculture	• Pollution control	• Secured access to land and water • Better integration of peri-urban agriculture into urban planning

storage capacity and improve supply management, reduce the rate of groundwater depletion, promote more efficient conjunctive use and raise water productivity.

Rainfed systems in highland areas are particularly at risk in terms of impacts on poverty and food security. There will be a need to combat negative effects of erosion and desertification through soil and water conservation, terracing, flood protection measures, and tree planting. This will require outside support, as the areas are typically poor, and there are downstream benefits from these investments. PES schemes are very appropriate for these systems, where the conservation of landscape values will also generate tourism.

Rainfed systems in semi-arid areas can improve productivity through better integration of agriculture and livestock, and cropping productivity may be raised by integrated plant nutrition, better varieties and improved water control, employing supplementary irrigation or water harvesting. Institutional measures to improve land tenure and, in some cases, effect land reform and consolidation, combined with research, technology transfer and investment in rural infrastructure, are needed to help raise incomes and stem out-migration.

Rainfed systems in subtropical areas can exploit potential for intensification through soil and water conservation measures, integrated plant nutrition, and use of new, better adapted crop cultivars. Institutional support measures required include land reform and consolidation, and investment in rural infrastructure.

Temperate zone rainfed systems in some areas do have potential for both further intensification and expansion, but pollution risks need to be carefully regulated and managed, and integrated approaches to both plant nutrient and pest management are priorities. Institutional support measures should include research, regulatory mechanisms, and planning for orderly expansion of the cultivated area.

The irrigated systems are generally a higher risk. In the Asian **rice-based systems**, priorities are improved storage for water control and flood prevention, diversification into higher value crops and multifunctional systems (e.g. rice/fish), and control of downstream pollution impacts. For **irrigated systems in Africa**, the key will be improved market access, combined with improved governance and management of irrigation.

Across **river basin systems**, modernization of infrastructure and institutions can improve water service and support intensification and diversification. Incentive structures will need adjustment to promote water-use efficiency. Climate change adaptation planning will be required. **Groundwater systems** can continue to support intensification, but only if users can be encouraged to moderate demand to within the limits of aquifer replenishment. The at-risk **delta and coastal plain systems** will need to give high priority to climate change adaptation and related strategies and investments for adaptation and flood control. Technical and institutional measures for control of pollution will also be a high priority to restore degraded systems and prevent further impact. Finally, **peri-urban agriculture** will require a regulatory framework for re-use of wastewater.

Policies and strategies for sustainable land and water management

The systems at risk present regional and global targets, but the real work of fixing them through better land and water management starts at local and national levels, where sovereign policies and investment can be applied. Bearing these overall system targets in mind, what practical steps can be taken at national level to structure support and implement more effective management?

The macro-policy setting

At the national level, governments have a role to ensure an enabling environment that is favourable to sustainable, efficient and equitable agricultural development. This includes the framework set by trade and price policy, fiscal policy and budget allocations, legislation and institutional set-ups for land and water administration, and producer services. Ideally, policy frameworks are developed by transparent, participatory processes of shared analysis, and result in policies and institutions that are efficient, pro-poor and favourable to ecosystem sustainability.

One key task is to encourage the multiple synergies and decide upon the trade-offs involved in intensification of production or in expansion of the cultivated area – synergies between sustainable production systems and food security, conservation and sustainable use of biodiversity, and climate change adaptation and mitigation. Trade-offs to consider include those between the short term and the longer term, between production and the conservation of existing ecosystem services, between food crops and biofuel feedstocks, between commercial farming and smallholder farming, between resource allocation to agriculture or to urban and industrial sectors, and between local benefits and global goods.

Setting the incentive framework

Programmes to encourage sustainable management have to be technically appropriate, and the knowledge, financing and markets need to be in place. Most importantly, incentives, investment support or subsidies will need to be pitched at levels that encourage farmers to choose sustainable practices over the less sustainable.

A supportive incentive structure is vital, but it needs to be match to user interests. Incentives are often quite different at local, national and global levels, and equitable and fair distribution of costs and benefits is essential for sustainable land and water management. Some form of smart subsidy to farmers who bear costs but do not receive benefits may need to be designed, for example through PES contracts. Incentives may also need to be built in to compensate farmers for the lag between investment and the arrival of benefits. Care needs to be taken to ensure that any subsidies are targeted to policy objectives, environmental conservation and are pro-poor.

Securing access to land and water resources

Farmers adopt new measures and technologies if they are assured stable engagement with land and water resources. Hence systems of land tenure and water-use rights that can allow farmers to exploit comparative advantage in food staples and cash crops are foundational, and require analysis and adjustment at the outset. Promotion of rural credit and finance that suits specific agricultural systems is also a necessary precondition, but needs to be based not only on annual production credits but also longer-term finance for investment in land and water resources. These initiatives will have to be complemented by dissemination of technology and good practices, and thus require adequate levels of public investment.

National strategies for sustainable land and water management

Assuming the necessary enabling policy environment is in place, local and national agendas for sustainable land and water management need to be translated into strategies and investment programmes. These would need to be supported by sound cost–benefit analyses to identify strategic investments that will facilitate adoption of best practices in land and water management. Box 6.1 summarizes steps involved in the preparation of a national strategy for sustainable land and water management. Such planning has to be done with the full participation of local people.

Institutional support

Sustainable land and water management requires strong institutional support, with sustained budget allocation to regulate natural resource use in the public interest. Institutions need to be adaptable to take into account changing needs, and to have access to the knowledge resources essential to the task. Institutional reforms that may be required at the country level to support sustainable land and water management include:

- Reform of land and water institutions to support more equitable tenure and responsible management. Stable access to land and water, incentives for responsible management, and obligations not to pollute are key.

- Development and strengthening of institutions for integrated land and water management at the project or scheme level, including programmes for modernization of irrigation institutions and infrastructure, with full participation of users in decision-making and financing.

- Where regional development agencies or river basin authorities exist, the adoption of programmes that tightly integrate land and water management across regions or basins. Watershed management programmes may be

Diagnostic. An in-depth participatory diagnostic and situation analysis is needed as a reference point for developing the strategies.

Implementation strategy. The strategy would spell out how the shared vision for sustainable land and water management can be implemented. The strategy would have tangible milestones, human and financial resource requirements, and detailed roles and responsibilities of the various actors (public, community organizations, NGOs and private).

Strong and adaptable institutional support for implementation. Cooperation for sustainable land and water management requires strong institutions with sustained budgetary support, strong monitoring and evaluation, conflict resolution mechanisms, and other mechanisms for accountability. Good databases and knowledge-sharing mechanisms on land and water are essential. Institutions also need to be adaptable in order to take into account changing needs.

Taking to scale – use of investment frameworks. The investment framework would be supported by a sound cost–benefit analysis, and would identify strategic investments that will lead to a rapidly increasing adoption of best sustainable land and water management practices. Investment frameworks in land and water management can be used to target beneficiaries and structure support.

Disseminating knowledge. Knowledge sharing and dissemination is a key element in a strategy for sustainable land and water management. It must make best use of local knowledge, complemented with research, and exchanges at regional and international levels. Global catalogues can play an important role when adapted to local situations, in partnership with local people, and consistent with national objectives and policies.

Monitoring and evaluation. Implementation strategies and investment frameworks need to be accompanied by a simple, comprehensive and transparent monitoring and evaluation (M&E) framework that focuses on both performance and impact aspects of the strategy.

required, and these need to be implemented over long timeframes, with good monitoring and evaluation to measure changes in the complex upstream–downstream interactions.

- Framework conditions put in place for the efficient working of competitive input and output markets.

- Research and extension packages, and outreach programmes such as Farmer Field Schools, working in partnership with local farmer groups, NGOs and the private sector.

Also important are community and farmer organizations that can work with the local administration, technical agencies, NGOs and the private sector on a partnership approach to local sustainable resource management.

Taking to scale – delivering investments where they are most needed

A combination of public and private finance is needed at the national level, strengthened through strategic international financial support. Recent increases in resource allocation to agriculture by some African countries have been encouraging, but policy-level commitments to sustainable land and water management would need to be matched by increased and more strategic allocation of public resources, along with mechanisms to engage private sector financing. The investment framework approach elaborated in Chapter 5 can be used to programme public and private financial resources to achieve a well-structured agricultural sector that is responsive to both national development objectives and changing demand for production and environmental services.

Three areas of investment can be identified in countries. At the national level, government investments can be geared to local markets so that they can become effective in meeting local demands and contribute to growing regional markets. This will require investment in public goods such as roads and storage, but will also involve a large role for private investment. In addition, governments need to invest in the institutions that regulate and promote sustainable land and water management: context-specific research and development on good practices for sustainable intensification of crop, livestock and aquatic systems; integrated nutrient management (INM) and integrated pest management (IPM); incentives and regulatory systems that promote sustainable intensification; and land-use planning and water management, including negotiating cooperative agreements on transboundary water resources, where appropriate.

At basin or irrigation scheme level, an integrated planning approach will drive a sequenced programme of land and water investments. For irrigation schemes, a focus on modernization of infrastructure and institutional arrangements is needed to improve productivity of individual schemes and reduce resource degradation and externalities. To encourage local management and ease pressure on limited public finance, the development of WUAs, operational cost recovery and progressive irrigation management transfer will be a priority. These institutional fixes would be as important as investment in more water efficient technology and husbandry, but they are more likely to succeed if they are clustered and context-specific.

At the local level, support can put in place the knowledge, incentives and resources (including credit) to enable farmers and pastoralists to adopt sustainable management practices, but in the end land users will decide. Any package has to be tailored to fit the environmental and socio-economic context, and its adoption and modifications have to be monitored and adjustments made if needed.

Application of knowledge

Translating principles and finance into action needs knowledge development and transfer. A wealth of information exists on technologies and approaches for sustainable land and water management, including local knowledge, but there is insufficient sharing of experiences among stakeholders at all levels, and between countries or regions. Key steps in putting in place an enabling environment will therefore be to strengthen, through better synergy, the existing networks and media for exchanging and disseminating knowledge, and for identifying and filling knowledge gaps.

Farming systems research will be essential to determine strategies, looking not only at production technology and data but also at socio-economic factors such as farm size, family size, food security, and access to capital and markets. If rainfed production is to be stabilized with a contribution from enhanced soil moisture storage, the physical and socio-economic circumstances under which this can occur need to be well identified.

Monitoring and evaluation

The progressive impact of institutional reform and investment need to be monitored and evaluated carefully. This can be done as part of an investment framework. Indicators to be measured would draw from the inventory on supply and demand of land and water, and could include: status and changes of land use, land cover and land degradation; changes in water and soil health; indicators of biodiversity and carbon stocks below and above ground; changes in access to land and water by the poor; changes in agricultural productivity; changes in rural poverty; and rates of adoption of sustainable land and water management practices. The GEF and the UNCCD have developed sets of standard indicators that could be adapted for use at the country programme level.

Reforming international cooperation in land and water management

Agreement on principles and approaches

There is so far no agreed framework at international level for the sustainable management of land and water. However, the vision and strategies developed by several global programmes could form building blocks for principles and practices around which major initiatives for sustainable land and water management could be aligned.

Such an agreement could include definition of common priorities and broad development objectives and strategies to be addressed by sustainable land and water management in the context of systems at risk. This could cover enhanced food security, improved rural livelihoods, sustainable conservation, improvement of ecosystem services, carbon sequestration and reduction of agricultural greenhouse gas emissions. A shared vision agreed at the international level could then be reflected in institutions, policies and programmes at the national and local levels.

To move from shared vision to action, agreement would need to be accompanied by a multisector strategy and investment framework, setting out how the shared vision for sustainable land and water management could be made operational, with tangible milestones, human and financial resource requirements, and detailed roles and responsibilities of the various actors: public bodies, international organizations, non-governmental organizations, community organizations and the private sector.

New entry points for international cooperation

The potential for international cooperation has increased recently as a result of several drivers, including concern over climate change, the recent food price crisis and the world recession, as well as global moves towards a greener economy. All these factors have raised awareness of the need for cooperation and heightened interest in the mechanisms of cooperation. There are many areas of current and emerging international cooperation on land and water. Some of these may represent entry points for increasing cooperation and scaling up support to the adoption and implementation of sustainable land and water management approaches (Box 6.2).

Financing

While it is clear that considerable financial resources will be needed for sustainable land and water management, it is the quality of investment that will count. Attention will be required on the most efficient mechanisms for financing increased levels of investment, whether through existing funds such as GEF or the International Development Association (IDA), or private and market sources. Financing would have to be consistent with the principles of the Paris Declaration on Aid Effectiveness and, for Africa, the Accra Agenda for Action. The possibility of a dedicated fund to support sustainable smallholder land and water management might be evaluated, possibly within the context of global climate change negotiations over adaptation or carbon sequestration financing. Mechanisms to provide incentives for farmers (and particularly for enabling smallholders and poorer farmers to adopt sustainable management practices) need to be built into financing arrangements.

Programmes in support of sustainable land and water management need to be designed and financed with incentives and mechanisms to promote local-level, pro-poor adoption, to promote global goods such as reforestation and carbon capture,

Many of the current and emerging cooperative activities on land and water represent entry points for scaling up. These include:

- Private sector partnership opportunities such as Fairtrade, green and organic labels and certifications, ecotourism.
- Partnerships with international foundations such as the Ford, Rockefeller and Gates foundations.
- PES for watershed services, biodiversity conservation, benefit-sharing in trans-boundary river basins and reduction of carbon emissions.
- Concerns over climate change: the technical, institutional and financial support mobilized around this issue and that may be available globally, regionally and at country level could have large positive spill-over effects for the land and water agenda (for example, in the shape of carbon credits).
- Financing for the new 'green economy': global thinking is moving towards support for 'green economy' approaches, and this is receiving impetus from the Rio+20 programme. Green economy rationales may thus strengthen the case for sustainable land and water practices to access a range of funding sources, and may also lead to the setting up of new facilities from which land and water management improvements might benefit.
- Foreign direct investment (FDI) in developing country agriculture brings both risks and opportunities. There is scope for international cooperation to establish 'rules of engagement' to ensure that foreign investments are beneficial to the host countries, and that small farmers and the poor have access to *increased* economic opportunity as a result. Cooperation through international law and government policies, and the involvement of civil society, the media and local communities, would help ensure that these win–win outcomes are reached.

and to reduce negative environmental impacts, including GHG emissions. Adopting the concept of PES would help to improve the balance of incentives in favour of ecological management, and could facilitate adoption by farmers otherwise unable or unwilling to implement sustainable management approaches.

Acknowledging the important role played by foreign direct investments and their rapid increase in the past decade, it will be fundamental to establish rules of engagement in order to ensure that foreign investments are beneficial to the host countries and the land users.

Knowledge

A key element for the implementation of international cooperation for land and water could be an Inventory of the World's Land and Water Systems, with focus on systems at risk, and a capacity for regular monitoring and reporting on their status

Considerable investment of intellectual and financial capital has gone into the development and dissemination of knowledge instruments on land and water. These need to be brought together and articulated in an Inventory of the World's Land and Water Systems. Such an inventory would include: (1) a shared **diagnostic** between cooperative partners on the situation and status of land and water resources in major farming systems; (2) an **inventory** of the demand for goods and services derived from land and water; and (3) **an analysis of constraints and opportunities** for the adoption of sustainable land and water management technologies at institutional, budgetary and policy level. It should be simple, transparent and scientifically validated, and should serve as a reference and platform for knowledge exchange and international cooperation.

To complement the inventory and to equip governments, planners and practitioners with best practice tools, existing catalogues of approaches for sustainable land and water management should be enhanced and disseminated. They would include best practice knowledge on solutions, options and lessons for sustainable land and water management, including what works, where and how, as well as conditions for success, bottlenecks for uptake and scaling up, best approaches (landscape, participative, watershed management), best-bet basket of technologies (conservation agriculture, agroforestry, organic farming, crop–livestock integration), new opportunities and promising technological developments, together with benefit and risk assessment.

and trends (Box 6.3). The global inventory could guide choices at the international, regional and national levels, help setting principles and approaches, and assist countries and their partners in priority setting. Existing catalogues of best practices, success stories and approaches for sustainable land and water management could be enhanced and more widely disseminated. Knowledge synthesis done at the international level can be adapted for use at the level of farming systems, and at national and local levels.

Further work is needed on the issue of ecosystem services valuation in the framework of natural resources accounting. Although considerable research is under way, particularly in complex rainforest systems, no agreed method of assessing and valuing ecosystem services has yet emerged, and tools to classify the priority of land for conversion or protection and to assess and validate outcomes are still lacking. Building on the global Inventory of Land and Water Systems at Risk, a monitoring framework needs to be developed for tracking of degradation and SLM trajectories and pace, together with methodologies for valuation of ecosystem goods and services. These methodologies would measure and cost direct relationships such as those between soil health and production. They would also quantify and cost externalities, and would assess the overall costs and benefits, and the synergies and trade-offs of degradation, and of measures to prevent, mitigate or reverse it. Governments and the global community will need to pursue this research agenda, which will then provide the means to make these difficult assessments of trade-offs and evaluate externalities.

Institutions

Current approaches of global and regional organizations tend to be sectoral, focusing only on specific aspects of land or water management. Several conventions and initiatives of direct relevance to land and water management provide a more integrated framework for action, but the synergies between them need to be strengthened to avoid duplications of efforts and make tangible impact. An international agreement on sustainable land and water management would indicate pathways for more integrated approaches and lend impetus to these needed changes.

For international river basins, cooperative frameworks and basin-wide management institutions will continue to optimize economic value and ensure negotiated, equitable benefit-sharing. For major basins under threat, concerted economic, institutional and agro-engineering plans will need to be developed and implemented to slow or reverse trends in land and water degradation and overcome constructed scarcity. Private and market-based institutions to promote sustainable land and water management, such as Fairtrade and ecological labelling, should be encouraged, and global trade agreements should favour sustainable agricultural practice.

Looking ahead

The challenges facing agriculture and the land and water resources upon which they depend are clear and multiple: to produce at least 70 percent more food by 2050, reconcile the use of land and water resources with the conservation of the broader ecosystem, and improve food security and the livelihood of the rural poor; all this in the context of a changing climate and associated risks.

This book has set out the evidence that large parts of the world's land and water resources are under stress or vulnerable from current and emerging patterns of agricultural practice. There is a risk, as demand rises, that current trends will deteriorate further, with consequent threats to local food security and the resource base on which production and livelihoods depend. The possible repercussions for global food security are not negligible. The risk for the world's poor is acute. This book has therefore proposed accelerated uptake of more sustainable land and water management that can expand production efficiently while limiting impacts upon the ecosystems on which the world depends.

This will require adjustments in policies, institutions, incentives, programmes, financing and knowledge at national and global levels. Above all, it will require the world's farmers to acknowledge that many current intensification patterns and practices of extending the cultivated area are unsustainable, and need to change for their own long-term benefit. Promoting such a shift will require the global community and all nations to have the political will to adopt paths to sustainable intensification and to put in place the necessary institutional and financial support. Only by these changes can the world feed its citizens in the short and long term, through a sustainable agriculture that supports, not harms, the ecosystems on which it depends, and that ensures fair and equitable access to resources to those who manage it.

Annexes

A1 – Country groupings used

- Pacific Islands
- Australia and New Zealand
- Eastern Europe and Russian Federation
- Western and Central Europe
- Southeast Asia
- East Asia
- South Asia
- Central Asia
- Western Asia
- Southern America
- Central America and Caribbean
- Northern America
- Sub-Saharan Africa
- Northern Africa

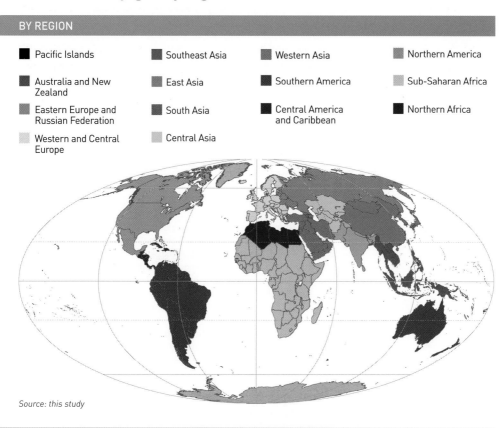

Source: this study

- High income
- Middle income
- Low income
- Not available

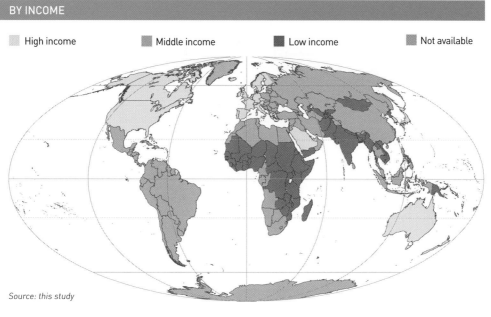

Source: this study

A1-1: Subregional country groupings

Continent Regions	Sub-region	Countries
Africa		Algeria, Angola, Benin, Botswana, Burkina Faso, Burundi, Cameroon, Cape Verde, Central African Republic, Chad, Comoros, Congo, Côte d'Ivoire, Democratic Republic of the Congo, Djibouti, Egypt, Equatorial Guinea, Eritrea, Ethiopia, Gabon, Gambia, Ghana, Guinea, Guinea-Bissau, Kenya, Lesotho, Liberia, Libyan Arab Jamahiriya, Madagascar, Malawi, Mali, Mauritania, Mauritius, Morocco, Mozambique, Namibia, Niger, Nigeria, Rwanda, Sao Tome and Principe, Senegal, Seychelles, Sierra Leone, Somalia, South Africa, Sudan, Swaziland, Togo, Tunisia, Uganda, United Republic of Tanzania, Zambia, Zimbabwe
Northern Africa		Algeria, Egypt, Libyan Arab Jamahiriya, Morocco, Tunisia
Sub-Saharan Africa		Angola, Benin, Botswana, Burkina Faso, Burundi, Cameroon, Cape Verde, Central African Republic, Chad, Comoros, Congo, Côte d'Ivoire, Democratic Republic of the Congo, Djibouti, Equatorial Guinea, Eritrea, Ethiopia, Gabon, Gambia, Ghana, Guinea, Guinea-Bissau, Kenya, Lesotho, Liberia, Madagascar, Malawi, Mali, Mauritania, Mauritius, Mozambique, Namibia, Niger, Nigeria, Rwanda, Sao Tome and Principe, Senegal, Seychelles, Sierra Leone, Somalia, South Africa, Sudan, Swaziland, Togo, Uganda, United Republic of Tanzania, Zambia, Zimbabwe
	Sudano-Sahelian	Burkina Faso, Cape Verde, Chad, Djibouti, Eritrea, Gambia, Mali, Mauritania, Niger, Senegal, Somalia, Sudan
	Gulf of Guinea	Benin, Côte d'Ivoire, Ghana, Guinea, Guinea-Bissau, Liberia, Nigeria, Sierra Leone, Togo
	Central Africa	Angola, Cameroon, Central African Republic, Congo, Democratic Republic of the Congo, Equatorial Guinea, Gabon, Sao Tome and Principe
	Eastern Africa	Burundi, Ethiopia, Kenya, Rwanda, Uganda, United Republic of Tanzania
	Southern Africa	Botswana, Lesotho, Malawi, Mozambique, Namibia, South Africa, Swaziland, Zambia, Zimbabwe
	Indian Ocean Islands	Comoros, Madagascar, Mauritius, Seychelles
Americas		Antigua and Barbuda, Argentina, Bahamas, Barbados, Belize, Bolivia (Plurinational State of), Brazil, Canada, Chile, Colombia, Costa Rica, Cuba, Dominica, Dominican Republic, Ecuador, El Salvador, French Guiana (France), Grenada, Guatemala, Guyana, Haiti, Honduras, Jamaica, Mexico, Nicaragua, Panama, Paraguay, Peru, Puerto Rico (United States of America), Saint Kitts and Nevis, Saint Lucia, Saint Vincent and the Grenadines, Suriname, Trinidad and Tobago, United States of America, Uruguay, Venezuela (Bolivarian Republic of)

(Continued)

Continent Regions	Sub-region	Countries
Northern America		Canada, United States of America
	Northern America	Canada, Mexico, United States of America
	Mexico	Mexico
Central America and Caribbean		Antigua and Barbuda, Bahamas, Barbados, Belize, Costa Rica, Cuba, Dominica, Dominican Republic, El Salvador, Grenada, Guatemala, Haiti, Honduras, Jamaica, Nicaragua, Panama, Puerto Rico (United States of America), Saint Kitts and Nevis, Saint Lucia, Saint Vincent and the Grenadines, Trinidad and Tobago
	Central America	Belize, Costa Rica, El Salvador, Guatemala, Honduras, Nicaragua, Panama
	Greater Antilles	Cuba, Dominican Republic, Haiti, Jamaica, Puerto Rico (United States of America)
	Lesser Antilles and Bahamas	Antigua and Barbuda, Bahamas, Barbados, Dominica, Grenada, Saint Kitts and Nevis, Saint Lucia, Saint Vincent and the Grenadines, Trinidad and Tobago
Southern America		Argentina, Bolivia (Plurinational State of), Brazil, Chile, Colombia, Ecuador, French Guiana (France), Guyana, Paraguay, Peru, Suriname, Uruguay, Venezuela (Bolivarian Republic of)
	Guyana	French Guiana (France), Guyana, Suriname
	Andean	Bolivia (Plurinational State of), Colombia, Ecuador, Peru, Venezuela (Bolivarian Republic of)
	Brazil	Brazil
	Southern America	Argentina, Chile, Paraguay, Uruguay
Asia		Afghanistan, Armenia, Azerbaijan, Bahrain, Bangladesh, Bhutan, Brunei Darussalam, Cambodia, China, Democratic People's Republic of Korea, Georgia, India, Indonesia, Iran (Islamic Republic of), Iraq, Israel, Japan, Jordan, Kazakhstan, Kuwait, Kyrgyzstan, Lao People's Democratic Republic, Lebanon, Malaysia, Maldives, Mongolia, Myanmar, Nepal, Occupied Palestinian Territory, Oman, Pakistan, Papua New Guinea, Philippines, Qatar, Republic of Korea, Saudi Arabia, Singapore, Sri Lanka, Syrian Arab Republic, Tajikistan, Thailand, Timor-Leste, Turkey, Turkmenistan, United Arab Emirates, Uzbekistan, Viet Nam, Yemen
Middle East – Western Asia		Armenia, Azerbaijan, Bahrain, Georgia, Iran (Islamic Republic of), Iraq, Israel, Jordan, Kuwait, Lebanon, Occupied Palestinian Territory, Oman, Qatar, Saudi Arabia, Syrian Arab Republic, Turkey, United Arab Emirates, Yemen

(Continued)

Continent Regions	Sub-region	Countries
	Arabian Peninsula	Bahrain, Kuwait, Oman, Qatar, Saudi Arabia, United Arab Emirates, Yemen
	Caucasus	Armenia, Azerbaijan, Georgia
	Islamic Republic of Iran	Iran (Islamic Republic of)
	Near East	Iraq, Israel, Jordan, Lebanon, Occupied Palestinian Territory, Syrian Arab Republic, Turkey
Central Asia		Afghanistan, Kazakhstan, Kyrgyzstan, Tajikistan, Turkmenistan, Uzbekistan
Southern and Eastern Asia		Bangladesh, Bhutan, Brunei Darussalam, Cambodia, China, Democratic People's Republic of Korea, India, Indonesia, Japan, Lao People's Democratic Republic, Malaysia, Maldives, Mongolia, Myanmar, Nepal, Pakistan, Papua New Guinea, Philippines, Republic of Korea, Singapore, Sri Lanka, Thailand, Timor-Leste, Viet Nam
	South Asia	Bangladesh, Bhutan, India, Maldives, Nepal, Pakistan, Sri Lanka
	East Asia	China, Democratic People's Republic of Korea, Japan, Mongolia, Republic of Korea
	Southeast Asia	Brunei Darussalam, Cambodia, Indonesia, Lao People's Democratic Republic, Malaysia, Myanmar, Papua New Guinea, Philippines, Singapore, Thailand, Timor-Leste Viet Nam
Europe		Albania, Andorra, Austria, Belarus, Belgium, Bosnia and Herzegovina, Bulgaria, Croatia, Cyprus, Czech Republic, Denmark, Estonia, Faroe Islands, Finland, France, Germany, Greece, Holy See, Hungary, Iceland, Ireland, Italy, Latvia, Liechtenstein, Lithuania, Luxembourg, Malta, Monaco, Montenegro, Netherlands, Norway, Poland, Portugal, Republic of Moldova, Romania, Russian Federation, San Marino, Serbia, Slovakia, Slovenia, Spain, Sweden, Switzerland, The former Yugoslav Republic of Macedonia, Ukraine, United Kingdom
Western and Central Europe		Albania, Andorra, Austria, Belgium, Bosnia and Herzegovina, Bulgaria, Croatia, Cyprus, Czech Republic, Denmark, Faroe Islands, Finland, France, Germany, Greece, Holy See, Hungary, Iceland, Ireland, Italy, Liechtenstein, Luxembourg, Malta, Monaco, Montenegro, Netherlands, Norway, Poland, Portugal, Romania, San Marino, Serbia, Slovakia, Slovenia, Spain, Sweden, Switzerland, The former Yugoslav Republic of Macedonia, United Kingdom
	Northern Europe	Denmark, Faroe Islands, Finland, Iceland, Norway, Sweden
	Western Europe	Andorra, Austria, Belgium, France, Germany, Ireland, Liechtenstein, Luxembourg, Netherlands, Switzerland, United Kingdom
	Central Europe	Bosnia and Herzegovina, Bulgaria, Croatia, Czech Republic, Hungary, Montenegro, Poland, Romania, Serbia, Slovakia, Slovenia
	Mediterranean Europe	Albania, Cyprus, Greece, Holy See, Italy, Malta, Monaco, Portugal, San Marino, Spain, The former Yugoslav Republic of Macedonia

(Continued)

Continent Regions	Sub-region	Countries
Eastern Europe		Belarus, Estonia, Latvia, Lithuania, Republic of Moldova, Russian Federation, Ukraine
	Eastern Europe	Belarus, Estonia, Latvia, Lithuania, Republic of Moldova, Ukraine
	Russian Federation	Russian Federation
Oceania		Australia, Cook Islands, Fiji, Kiribati, Micronesia (Federated States of), Nauru, New Zealand, Niue, Palau, Samoa, Solomon Islands, Tonga, Tuvalu, Vanuatu
Australia and New Zealand		Australia, New Zealand
Pacific Islands		Cook Islands, Fiji, Kiribati, Micronesia (Federated States of), Nauru, Niue, Palau, Samoa, Solomon Islands, Tonga, Tuvalu, Vanuatu
World		Afghanistan, Albania, Algeria, Andorra, Angola, Antigua and Barbuda, Argentina, Armenia, Australia, Austria, Azerbaijan, Bahamas, Bahrain, Bangladesh, Barbados, Belarus, Belgium, Belize, Benin, Bhutan, Bolivia (Plurinational State of), Bosnia and Herzegovina, Botswana, Brazil, Brunei Darussalam, Bulgaria, Burkina Faso, Burundi, Cambodia, Cameroon, Canada, Cape Verde, Central African Republic, Chad, Chile, China, Colombia, Comoros, Congo, Cook Islands, Costa Rica, Côte d'Ivoire, Croatia, Cuba, Cyprus, Czech Republic, Democratic People's Republic of Korea, Democratic Republic of the Congo, Denmark, Djibouti, Dominica, Dominican Republic, Ecuador, Egypt, El Salvador, Equatorial Guinea, Eritrea, Estonia, Ethiopia, Faroe Islands, Fiji, Finland, France, French Guiana (France), Gabon, Gambia, Georgia, Germany, Ghana, Greece, Grenada, Guatemala, Guinea, Guinea-Bissau, Guyana, Haiti, Holy See, Honduras, Hungary, Iceland, India, Indonesia, Iran (Islamic Republic of), Iraq, Ireland, Israel, Italy, Jamaica, Japan, Jordan, Kazakhstan, Kenya, Kiribati, Kuwait, Kyrgyzstan, Lao People's Democratic Republic, Latvia, Lebanon, Lesotho, Liberia, Libyan Arab Jamahiriya, Liechtenstein, Lithuania, Luxembourg, Madagascar, Malawi, Malaysia, Maldives, Mali, Malta, Mauritania, Mauritius, Mexico, Micronesia (Federated States of), Monaco, Mongolia, Montenegro, Morocco, Mozambique, Myanmar, Namibia, Nauru, Nepal, Netherlands, New Zealand, Nicaragua, Niger, Nigeria, Niue, Norway, Occupied Palestinian Territory, Oman, Pakistan, Palau, Panama, Papua New Guinea, Paraguay, Peru, Philippines, Poland, Portugal, Puerto Rico (USA), Qatar, Republic of Korea, Republic of Moldova, Romania, Russian Federation, Rwanda, Saint Kitts and Nevis, Saint Lucia, Saint Vincent and the Grenadines, Samoa, San Marino, Sao Tome and Principe, Saudi Arabia, Senegal, Serbia, Seychelles, Sierra Leone, Singapore, Slovakia, Slovenia, Solomon Islands, Somalia, South Africa, Spain, Sri Lanka, Sudan, Suriname, Swaziland, Sweden, Switzerland, Syrian Arab Republic, Tajikistan, Thailand, The former Yugoslav Republic of Macedonia, Timor-Leste, Togo, Tonga, Trinidad and Tobago, Tunisia, Turkey, Turkmenistan, Tuvalu, Uganda, Ukraine, United Arab Emirates, United Kingdom, United Republic of Tanzania, United States of America, Uruguay, Uzbekistan, Vanuatu, Venezuela (Bolivarian Republic of), Viet Nam, Yemen, Zambia, Zimbabwe

Low-income food-deficit countries (LIFDC)

An FAO classification of a country, based on: (1) whether the per capita income is below the 'historical' ceiling used by the World Bank to determine eligibility for international development assistance; (2) the net (i.e. gross imports less gross exports) food trade position; and (3) whether a country specifically requests FAO not to be included in the LIFDC category.

Africa:

Angola, Benin, Burkina Faso, Burundi, Cameroon, Central African Republic, Chad, Comoros, Congo, Côte d'Ivoire, Democratic Republic of the Congo, Djibouti, Egypt, Equatorial Guinea, Eritrea, Ethiopia, Gambia, Ghana, Guinea, Guinea-Bissau, Kenya, Lesotho, Liberia, Madagascar, Malawi, Mali, Mauritania, Morocco, Mozambique, Niger, Nigeria, Rwanda, Sao Tome and Principe, Senegal, Sierra Leone, Somalia, Sudan, Swaziland, Togo, Uganda, United Republic of Tanzania, Zambia, Zimbabwe

Asia:

Afghanistan, Armenia, Azerbaijan, Bangladesh, Bhutan, Cambodia, China, Democratic People's Republic of Korea, Georgia, India, Indonesia, Iraq, Kyrgyzstan, Lao People's Democratic Republic, Mongolia, Nepal, Pakistan, Philippines, Sri Lanka, Syrian Arab Republic, Tajikistan, Timor-Leste, Turkmenistan, Uzbekistan, Yemen

Europe:

Republic of Moldova

America:

Haiti, Honduras, Nicaragua

Oceania:

Kiribati, Papua New Guinea, Solomon Islands, Tuvalu, Vanuatu

More-, less- and least-developed countries or regions

(a) More-developed regions comprise Europe, Northern America, Australia/ New Zealand and Japan.

(b) Less-developed regions comprise all regions of Africa, Asia (excluding Japan), Latin America and the Caribbean, plus Melanesia, Micronesia and Polynesia.

(c) The group of least-developed countries, as defined by the United Nations General Assembly in its resolutions (59/209, 59/210 and 60/33) in 2007, comprises 49 countries, of which 33 are in Africa, 10 in Asia, 1 in Latin America and the Caribbean, and 5 in Oceania.

(d) Other less-developed countries comprise the less-developed regions, excluding the least-developed countries.

Source: United Nations (2009)

A2 – Environmental externalities associated with irrigated agriculture

Cause	Location	Nature of externality
Depletion of stream flow by crop water use in irrigation system	In-stream, downstream	• Reduced flow • Changed flow pattern, especially low flows • Possibly resulting in: anoxic conditions, high temperature, salt accumulation • Loss of habitat, flora and fauna: fish stocks → livelihoods
	Riparian zone	• Loss of riparian vegetation, wetlands, billabongs • Increased bank erosion and sediment inflow from adjacent land • Loss of near-bank fauna • Loss of buffering capacity of riparian zone • Salinization of banks and adjacent water bodies
	Wetlands	• Changed wetting patterns and reduced inflow • Loss of wetland area and associated livelihoods • Loss of tree and vegetation – amount and species composition
	Flood Plain	• Loss of stream power → poor definition of natural channels and floodways • Channel sedimentation • Loss of groundwater recharge
	Estuary	• Loss of inflow, and changed habitat; changed pattern and range of saline intrusion
Additional impacts of storage of stream flow or runoff in dams or reservoirs	In-stream	• Loss of low and medium frequency flood flows → reduced flushing of river • Loss of sediment (deposited in dam) → downstream erosion (higher erosive capacity) • Flow reversal: higher than natural flows in irrigation season (dry season) and lower flows in wet season
	Upstream–downstream	• Barrier to fish migration for spawning → population decline
	Estuary	• Radically changed habitat flows and sediment
Upper catchment development	Downstream waterways, existing storages and diversions	• Reduced runoff and water availability • Possible reductions in groundwater recharge
Groundwater mining (average extraction exceeds average recharge)	Across aquifer	• Declining water table → increased pumping cost • Where latent, emergence of arsenic and fluoride contamination • Where relevant, mixing of saline and fresh aquifer water • Land subsidence • Loss of groundwater-dependent wetland area • Loss of tree cover, where dependent on water table
	Downstream	• Reduced baseflow in rivers • Increased seepage from river system to shallow aquifer (streamflow 'loss')

Cause	Location	Nature of externality
Irrigation in areas with saline soils or saline groundwater close to soil surface	Within irrigation system	• Severe salinization requiring remediation, drainage and leaching • Yield penalty • Soil structure damage • Loss of biodiversity (excepting salt tolerant plants)
	Downstream	• Regional salinization (soil and water) • Episodic saline flushes in river network (typically after heavy rainfall) → loss of flora and fauna • Salinization of riparian vegetation, wetlands etc. • Loss of trees in landscape • Degraded quality of water for irrigation downstream
Development of irrigated land	Various	• In flood plain (dyking, levees, polders) – loss of flood function • Loss of wetlands (drainage) – loss of livelihoods • Rice paddies have limited flood mitigation function, but rice will not survive submergence for more then 4–5 days • Loss of native fauna, trees and habitat
Irrigation when annual $ET_0 >$ rainfall on non-saline soils	Within irrigation system	• Salt accumulation • Potential salinization • Restricted yield and crop pattern choice • Manageable by leaching and limited drainage
Irrigation of sodic soils	Coastal zones	• Soil dispersion and sediment export → degradation of coastal ecosystems, such as coral reefs, especially if accompanied by adsorbed phosphate
Excess or inefficient N fertilizer application	Within irrigation system	• Long term soil acidification (rice soils with ammonium compounds: dryland soils with a range of compounds)
	Downstream	• Nitrate contamination of waterways and water bodies → eutrophication, predisposition to (toxic) algal blooms • Excessive aquatic weed growth (e.g. water hyacinth)
	Groundwater	• Nitrate contamination of potable water (public health), especially in shallow wells; possible eutrophication
Excess or inefficient P fertilizer application	Downstream	• Episodic phosphate flushes associated with vegetation changes (weed control, senescence) in sediment in drains and rivers • Eutrophication and predisposition to toxic algal blooms
	Groundwater	• Rarely documented, but occurs through preferential flows and soluble phosphate; consequences uncertain
Herbicide application	Groundwater	• Long term contamination of groundwater – limits abstraction for drinking water (e.g. Atrazine in the USA)
Poorly managed Insecticide use	Landscape	• Loss of biodiversity, and natural predators • Accidental death or chronic illness • Accumulation in food chain (now rare)
	Stream network and groundwater	• Fish and fauna loss • Contamination of drinking water (streams, groundwater, shallow wells)

Cause	Location	Nature of externality
Application of organic wastes and partially treated wastewater	Locality	• Smell • Faecal coliform contamination of produce and encysted parasites – public health • Heavy metal accumulation (typically copper from intensive pig production) • Groundwater contamination – faecal coliforms, encysted parasites
Long term monoculture	Landscape	• Progressive loss of biodiversity: loss of pollinators • Episodic insect and plant disease epidemics due to progressive loss of natural predators • Accelerated soil nutrient and micro-nutrient depletion
Poor cultivation and livestock management	Wet soils	• Loss of structure, aeration • Pugging • Reduced productivity
Excess water application through poor irrigation (technology/ management)	Within system, shallow groundwater, streams	• Perched water table • Salinization (if connected to deeper saline groundwater) • Water logging and crop loss • Drainage flows that transport pollutants to streams
Excessive flow rate or slope furrow irrigation	On farm and downstream	• Erosion, sediment export, topsoil loss at site

A3 – Country programmes for sustainable land management

Country SLM programmes can be built through a series of steps: (1) stakeholder engagement and partnerships; (2) stocktaking and diagnostics; (3) prioritization and programming; (4) investment formulation; and (5) implementation and M&E. These steps are presented below. The steps are not intended as a blueprint, but as a 'template' of actions that can be adapted to each country and local situation (TerrAfrica, 2009).

The five steps are designed to build an '**SLM investment framework**', which will specify the principles, policies and institutional approaches involved, as well as the priorities, the investment and financing programme, and implementation arrangements.

Usually, SLM activities fit within existing programmes and are implemented through on-going programmes and instruments by mandated agencies and bodies (public, communal and private) at national or local level. SLM is thus not treated as a separate 'sector' of activity but as a complement to the policy, institutional and implementation structures already in place.

Step 1: Stakeholder engagement and partnerships

Under step 1 the aim is to set up a broad-based SLM coalition and platform, including central and local-level public agencies, civil society, donors and – most importantly – the land users themselves. Such a coalition, which could be associated in a **'country SLM team'**, should operate in a flexible manner, avoid excessive formality and provide the basis for implementing the following activities:

- Development of a common vision on SLM among technical ministries (e.g. agriculture, environment, energy, local government, finance and planning), the donor community, the private sector and NGOs/civil society organizations (including farmer organizations and WUAs), and land users' representatives. The involvement of civil society and a range of private sector representatives is key, as dominance of government representatives may weaken the partnership approach.
- Ensuring effective and long-term political commitment to SLM, from the highest level (e.g. president, prime minister, cabinet).
- Raising awareness of the need of a programmatic approach to SLM.
- Developing better coordination, harmonization and alignment between partners. Agreed practices might be summarized in a 'code of conduct on SLM'.

Step 2: Stocktaking and diagnostics

A wide-ranging participatory **diagnostic study** would need to be implemented to identify existing programmes and activities across all sectors and to identify the main bottlenecks and opportunities for scaling up and mainstreaming SLM. This diagnostic is structured around five different components:

Technical component: through a review and assessment of the past SLM experiences and lessons learnt, this component identifies best practices that can be recommended for scaling up, with options for different land-use types and geographical areas.

Ecosystem/spatial component: through an assessment of the main agro-ecological and land uses, this component identifies bottlenecks and opportunities for improving productivity and sustaining or improving other ecosystem services (including reversing land degradation), and highlights options for introducing or scaling up SLM.

Policy and incentive framework component: based on a review of constraints and opportunities in sectoral and cross-sectoral policies and strategies related to land and water resources, this component would place SLM within national policies and identify changes that would facilitate the introduction and scaling up of SLM. A key element here will be analysis of the incentive framework driving land and water management practices, and of the opportunities for recalibrating the incentives to favour the adoption of SLM.

Institutional component: through analysis of relevant private and public institutions at national and subregional level concerned by land and water issues, this component would identify agencies responsible for land and water and associated areas, identify what is or could be their role in SLM delivery, assess gaps and weaknesses, and propose recommendations for strengthening and streamlining.

Financial component: through an assessment of existing funding for SLM, this component would identify the main existing and potential financing mechanisms, bottlenecks and opportunities for scaling up. The objective would be to ensure that financing is in place that would promote SLM adoption at the farmer level. The component would cover local-level financing mechanisms (e.g. through credit schemes), national-level programmes and global programmes such as carbon credits.

On the basis of the diagnostic study, the country SLM team might prepare a **'strategy note'** that identifies main **SLM priorities** (technologies, areas, partners), as well as the main thrusts of the SLM investment framework that will be developed (see step 3). The strategy note should be prepared in a fully participatory way, ensuring that the perspectives of land users and civil society are fully integrated.

Step 3: Programming and the investment framework: decision on priorities

The main thrusts identified by the diagnostic study (and captured in the strategy note) should be assessed against national development priorities for synergies, gaps, contradictions and links. They should then be ranked according to which offer the highest synergies and complementarities. Based on the results, a preliminary investment framework is then prepared. Through a series of consultations, validation workshops and the assessment of any pilot projects or other catalytic field activities under way, the investment framework can then be finalized. This step should include some negotiation with land users and communities, to make sure that their needs and priorities are well taken into account, in particular as far as land tenure and territorial issues are concerned.

Step 4: Investment formulation and costing

This phase includes detailed formulation of SLM activities and investments with the participation of all the beneficiaries, and in coordination with the development partners and donors. The investment proposals will be matched to financing sources, ideally within long-term national programmes with sustained external financing, rather than through short-term and one-off projects.

Step 5: Implementation and M&E

When possible, first investments should be those that can be implemented rapidly and demonstrate quick results – for example, where local demand is strong, there are champions, and the agro-economic and land and water situation favours success. Early demonstrations of success will feed back lessons into the programme and prepare the ground for rolling out SLM on a wider scale.

Monitoring and evaluation should concern both performance and impact indicators, collected preferably through simple, cost-effective and rapid assessment, using multimedia technologies (combination of ground photos, global positioning system, data sheets, georeferenced on maps).

Timescale and cost

Overall, it is expected that the preparation of an investment framework (steps 1 to 3) may take between six and twelve months and cost between US$100 000 and US$200 000. This cost is small 'seed money' for a programme that can contribute to the achievement of multiple national and household-level objectives through the adoption of SLM on a large scale.

A4 – Core land and water indicators
by country or region

A4-1: Arable land in use, cropping intensities and harvested land

Continent / Regions	Year	Total land in use			Rainfed use			Irrigated use*		
		A	CI (%)	H	A	CI (%)	H	A	CI (%)	H
Africa	2009	251	85	214	239	83	199	12	131	15
	2050	342	79	270	326	77	250	15	129	20
Northern Africa	2009	28	74	21	22	54	12	6	149	9
	2050	27	92	25	19	70	13	7	149	11
Sub-Saharan Africa	2009	223	87	194	217	86	187	6	112	6
	2050	315	78	245	307	77	237	8	111	9
Americas	2009	395	69	273	356	66	233	40	102	40
	2050	468	82	384	427	80	340	41	106	44
Northern America	2009	253	58	146	224	52	117	29	100	29
	2050	241	80	192	214	77	165	27	100	27
Central America and Caribbean	2009	15	64	10	14	56	8	1	162	2
	2050	15	80	12	13	73	9	2	120	3
Southern America	2009	127	93	118	118	92	108	10	100	10
	2050	213	85	181	200	83	166	12	117	14
Asia	2009	542	109	588	357	94	335	185	137	253
	2050	541	118	641	340	101	344	201	148	297
Western Asia	2009	64	66	43	47	47	22	18	117	21
	2050	55	93	52	31	80	24	25	110	27
Central Asia	2009	39	69	27	28	56	15	12	100	12
	2050	33	94	31	20	90	18	13	100	13
South Asia	2009	204	113	232	126	108	136	78	122	95
	2050	212	115	243	135	97	131	77	145	112
East Asia	2009	133	133	176	74	99	74	58	175	102
	2050	133	144	191	67	116	77	66	172	114
Southeast Asia	2009	101	109	111	82	107	88	19	118	23
	2050	107	115	124	88	106	93	19	156	30

Continent Regions	Year	Total land in use			Rainfed use			Irrigated use*		
		A	CI [%]	H	A	CI [%]	H	A	CI [%]	H
Europe	2009	293	63	184	280	60	168	13	119	16
	2050	264	83	219	245	82	200	19	100	19
Western and Central Europe	2009	125	76	94	113	73	83	12	100	12
	2050	125	89	111	111	87	97	14	100	14
Eastern Europe and Russian Federation	2009	168	53	89	167	51	85	2	249	4
	2050	139	78	108	134	77	103	5	100	5
Oceania	2009	46	57	26	42	52	22	3	100	3
	2050	58	83	48	55	82	45	2	101	2
Australia and New Zealand	2009	45	56	25	42	53	22	3	100	3
	2050	58	83	48	55	82	45	2	101	2
Pacific Islands	2009	1	70	0.4	1	–	–	0.004	–	–
	2050	–	–	–	–	–	–	–	–	–
World	2009	1527	84	1286	1274	75	958	253	130	327
	2050	1673	93	1562	1393	85	1179	279	137	382
High-income	2009	368	61	225	326	56	182	42	102	43
	2050	353	86	302	314	83	261	39	108	42
Middle-income	2009	444	136	603	331	132	436	114	147	167
	2050	769	95	728	628	84	528	141	142	200
Low-income	2009	714	64	458	617	55	341	97	121	117
	2050	551	97	532	451	87	391	100	141	140
Low-income food-deficit	2009	642	107	685	476	95	453	167	139	232
	2050	766	104	794	587	89	524	179	151	270
Least-developed	2009	173	94	163	159	92	146	14	118	17
	2050	227	82	187	211	78	164	16	145	24

A = cultivated area (million ha); CI = cropping intensity (percent); H = harvested land (million ha).
* Refers to around 2006.

Source: FAO (2010a,b)

A4-2: Per capita land by major current land cover type for years 2000 and 2050 populations (ha/person)

Regions	Cultivated land		Grassland and woodland		Forest land		Sparsely vegetated and barren land		Settlement and infrastructure	
	2000	2050	2000	2050	2000	2050	2000	2050	2000	2050
Northern Africa	0.13	0.08	0.23	0.13	0.04	0.02	3.36	1.99	0.02	0.01
Sub-Saharan Africa	0.33	0.13	1.61	0.62	0.77	0.29	0.80	0.31	0.03	0.01
Northern America	0.62	0.45	1.77	1.28	1.61	1.17	0.66	0.48	0.04	0.03
Central America and Caribbean	0.21	0.13	0.33	0.20	0.40	0.25	0.01	0.01	0.02	0.01
Southern America	0.37	0.27	1.89	1.36	2.45	1.76	0.28	0.20	0.03	0.02
Western Asia	0.24	0.13	0.39	0.21	0.07	0.04	1.66	0.91	0.02	0.01
Central Asia	0.60	0.30	1.82	0.90	0.07	0.04	3.44	1.71	0.03	0.02
South Asia	0.15	0.09	0.04	0.03	0.06	0.03	0.03	0.02	0.02	0.01
East Asia	0.10	0.09	0.26	0.24	0.15	0.14	0.24	0.22	0.02	0.02
Southeast Asia	0.19	0.13	0.24	0.16	0.46	0.31	0.00	0.00	0.02	0.01
Western and Central Europe	0.26	0.25	0.30	0.28	0.33	0.31	0.02	0.01	0.03	0.03
Eastern Europe and Russian Federation	0.80	1.03	2.71	3.52	3.84	4.99	0.65	0.85	0.03	0.04
Australia and New Zealand	2.21	1.49	22.14	14.97	4.24	2.87	5.53	3.74	0.05	0.04
Pacific Islands	0.32	0.19	0.55	0.32	2.26	1.32	0.04	0.03	0.03	0.02

Source: adapted from Fischer et al. (2010)

A4-3: Share of currently cultivated land suitable for cropping under appropriate production systems

Regions	Prime (Mha)	Good (Mha)	Marginal (Mha)	Total (Mha)
Northern Africa	3	9	7	19
Sub-Saharan Africa	71	128	26	225
Northern America	94	136	28	257
Central America and Caribbean	7	8	2	16
Southern America	41	77	10	129
Western Asia	4	34	23	61
Central Asia	0.3	32	13	46
South Asia	57	84	60	201
East Asia	25	72	53	150
Southeast Asia	28	54	16	98
Western and Central Europe	50	54	27	131
Eastern Europe and Russian Federation	59	102	12	173
Australia and New Zealand	4	26	21	51
Pacific Islands	0	0	0	0
Total (Mha)	442	816	298	1 556
Total (%)	28	53	19	100

The columns shown as 'Marginal' include both marginal land and land not suitable for crop production.

Source: adapted from Fischer et al. (2010)

A4-4: Soil and terrain constraints for low-input farming of current cultivated land (as a percentage share of region)

Regions	No or slight constraints	Soil nutrients	Soil depth	Soil drainage	Salinity/ sodicity	Calcium carbonate/ gypsum	Soil workability	Terrain slopes	Perma-frost
Northern Africa	57	13	5	5	2	1	7	9	0
Sub-Saharan Africa	41	37	3	6	1	0	9	2	0
Northern America	64	14	2	13	2	0	2	2	1
Central America and Caribbean	47	18	1	3	0	1	17	14	0
Southern America	36	42	2	6	2	0	8	4	0
Western Asia	49	7	16	3	4	4	4	14	0
Central Asia	68	12	2	5	6	3	0	4	0
South Asia	49	12	3	6	6	1	20	3	0
East Asia	41	22	6	14	2	1	2	12	0
Southeast Asia	20	46	5	17	0	0	6	6	0
Western and Central Europe	47	16	14	12	1	2	5	3	0
Eastern Europe and Russian Federation	73	15	2	7	3	0	0	0	1
Australia and New Zealand	41	20	1	17	17	0	3	1	0
Pacific Islands	58	8	15	1	0	0	0	18	0
Low-income countries	44	24	3	7	3	1	14	3	0
Middle-income countries	49	24	4	9	2	1	4	6	0
High-income countries	56	17	6	13	3	1	2	1	0

Note: ☐ Highest values are highlighted.

Source: adapted from Fischer et al. (2010)

Glossary of terms and definitions used in this report

Adsorption: Process whereby molecules are attracted and retained on the surface of a substance (liquid or solid).

Agricultural land: Land used primarily for agricultural purposes. FAOSTAT defines agricultural area as the sum of areas under (a) arable land, (b) permanent crops (land cultivated with long-term crops that do not have to be replanted for several years), and (c) permanent meadows and pastures.

Agroforestry: Land-use systems or practices in which trees are deliberately integrated with crops and/or animals on the same land management unit.

Alkalinization: A net increase of alkali salts in the (top) soil, leading to a decline in agricultural productivity.

Anthropogenic activities: Activities related to human beings.

Arable land: Land under temporary agricultural crops, temporary meadows for mowing or pasture, market and kitchen gardens, and land temporarily fallow (less than five years). The abandoned land resulting from shifting cultivation is not included in this category. Data for 'arable land' are not meant to indicate the amount of land that is potentially cultivable.

Baseflow: Part of streamflow, which results predominantly from groundwater discharged into a stream.

Carbon sequestration: The process of removing carbon from the atmosphere and depositing it in reservoirs such as oceans, forests or soils through physical or biological processes.

Conjunctive use (of surface water and groundwater): The coordinated management of surface water and groundwater supplies to maximize overall water yield.

Conservation agriculture (CA): An approach to managing agro-ecosystems for improved and sustained productivity, increased profits and food security, while preserving and enhancing the resource base and the environment. CA is characterized by three principles: continuous minimum mechanical soil disturbance; permanent organic soil cover; and diversification of crop species grown in sequences or associations.

Conservation tillage: An approach to soil management that excludes conventional tillage operations that invert the soil and bury crop residues. Five types of conservation tillage systems: no-tillage (slot planting), mulch tillage, strip or zonal tillage, ridge till (including no-till on ridges), and reduced or minimum tillage.

Consumptive use of water: The part of water withdrawn from its source for use in agriculture, industry or domestic purposes that has evaporated, transpired, or been incorporated into products. The part of water withdrawn that is not consumed is called return flow.

Cropland (or cultivated land): In SOLAW, the term cropland is used to indicate land which is under agricultural crops. In statistical terms, cropland is the sum of arable land (see definition above) and permanent crops.

Desertification: The degradation of land in arid semi-arid, and dry subhumid areas due to various factors, including climatic variations and human activities.

Drylands: Arid, semi-arid and dry subhumid areas (other than polar and subpolar regions) in which the ratio of mean annual precipitation to mean annual reference evapotranspiration ranges from 0.05 to 0.65.

Ecosystem: A dynamic complex of plant, animal and microorganism communities, and the nonliving physical components of the environment (such as air, soil, water and sunlight), interacting as a functional unit.

Ecosystem services (or environmental services): The benefits people obtain from ecosystems. These include provisioning services (such as food and water), regulating services (such as regulation of floods, drought, land degradation and disease), supporting services (such as soil formation and nutrient cycling) and cultural services (such as recreational, spiritual, religious and other non-material benefits).

Eutrophication: The enrichment of freshwater bodies by inorganic nutrients (e.g. nitrate, phosphate), typically leading to excessive growth of algae.

Evapotranspiration: The combination of evaporation from the soil surface and transpiration from the plants.

Externality: A consequence (positive or negative) arising from the production and/or consumption of goods and services that is experienced by unrelated third parties and for which no appropriate compensation is paid.

Fertigation: The application of fertilizer with irrigation water.

Freshwater: Naturally occurring water on the Earth's surface in lakes and rivers, and underground in aquifers. Its key feature is a low concentration of dissolved salts. In this report, when not otherwise specified, the term *water* is used as synonym of freshwater.

High-level inputs/advanced management: Under the high input, advanced management GAEZ scenario (IIASA/FAO, 2010), the farming system is mainly market-oriented. Commercial production is a management objective. Production is based on improved high-yielding varieties, is fully mechanized with low-labour intensity, and uses optimum applications of nutrients and chemical pest, disease and weed control.

Integrated nutrient management (INM): (or integrated plant nutrition management, IPNS). Approach by which plant nutrition is obtained by optimizing the benefits from all possible sources of nutrients. The basic objectives are to reduce the inorganic fertilizer requirement, to restore organic matter in soil, to enhance nutrient-use efficiency, and to maintain soil quality in terms of physical, chemical and biological properties.

Integrated pest management (IPM): An ecosystem approach to crop production and protection that combines different management strategies and practices to grow healthy crops while minimizing the use of pesticides.

Intermediate-level inputs/improved management: Under the intermediate input, improved management GAEZ scenario (IIASA/FAO, 2010), the farming system is partly market-oriented. Production for subsistence plus commercial sale is a management objective. Production is based on improved varieties, on manual labour with hand tools and/or animal traction, and some mechanization. It is moderately labour intensive, and uses some fertilizer application and chemical pest, disease and weed control, adequate fallows and some conservation measures.

Internal renewable water resources (IRWR): The conventional measure of freshwater available to a nation (surface water and groundwater), comprising resources deriving from the rainfall within a nation's boundaries. It excludes transboundary and fossil water resources.

Land degradation: The reduction in the capacity of the land to provide ecosystem goods and services over a period of time for its beneficiaries.

Low-level inputs/traditional management: Under the low-input, traditional management GAEZ scenario (IIASA/FAO, 2010), the farming system is largely subsistence-based and not necessarily market-oriented. Production is based on the use of traditional cultivars (if improved cultivars are used, they are treated in the same way as local cultivars), labour-intensive techniques, no application of nutrients, no use of chemicals for pest and disease control, and minimum conservation measures.

Mixed level of inputs: Under the GAEZ scenario of mixed level of inputs (IIASA/FAO, 2010), only the best land is assumed to be used for high-level input farming; moderately suitable and marginal lands are assumed to be used at intermediate- or low-level input and management circumstances.

Modernization: In irrigation, modernization is defined as a process of technical and managerial upgrading (as opposed to mere rehabilitation) of irrigation schemes combined with institutional reforms, if required, with the objective to improve resource utilization (labour, water economics, environment) and water delivery service to farms.

Mycorrhiza: Fungus that forms a symbiotic association with the roots of particular plants and through which these plants benefit from greater availability of nutrients.

Organochlorines: Chemicals characterized by carbon and chlorine components. Some environmentally persistent pesticides (like DDT) are organochlorines.

Payment for environmental services (PES): A voluntary transaction whereby a service provider is paid by (or on behalf of) beneficiaries for land-use practices that are expected to result in continued or improved environmental service provision beyond what would have been provided without the payment.

Qanat: Excavated underground channels tapping groundwater from upslope aquifers.

Rangeland: Land on which the indigenous vegetation (climax or subclimax) is predominantly grasses, grass-like plants, forbs or shrubs that are grazed or have the potential to be grazed, and which is used as a natural ecosystem for the production of grazing livestock and wildlife.

Riparian: Relating to land adjoining a stream or river.

Runoff: Part of the water from precipitation or irrigation that flows over the land surface in stream flow and is not absorbed into the ground.

Salinization: The process by which salt accumulates in or on the soil. Human-induced salinization is mostly associated with poor irrigation practices.

Shaduf: An irrigation tool, consisting of a pole with a bucket at one end and a weight at the other end.

Silvopastoralism: Land-use systems and practices in which trees and pastures are deliberately integrated with livestock components.

Sodic soil: A soil that contains sufficient sodium to adversely affect the growth of most crop plants (sodic soils are defined as those soils which have an exchangeable sodium percentage of more than 15).

System of rice intensification (SRI): An integrated rice production system where yield increase is obtained through changes in management practices rather than by increasing inputs. Central to the principles of SRI are soil moisture management (no use of continuously saturated soils), single planting and optimal spacing, and trans-plantation within 15 days after germination.

Vertisols: Dark-coloured clay-rich soils with characteristic shrinking and swelling properties.

Wadi: The bed or valley of a seasonal stream in arid or semi-arid areas that is usually dry except for a short time after spate flow events (a few hours to a few days).

Water accounting: A systematic method of organizing and presenting information relating to the physical volumes and flows of water in the environment, as well as the economic aspects of water supply and use.

Water audit: A systematic study of the current status and future trends in both water supply and demand, with a particular focus on issues relating to accessibility, uncertainty and governance in a given spatial domain.

Water demand management: A set of actions consisting in controlling water demand, either by raising the efficiency of its use (see definition below) or operating intra- and intersectoral reallocation of water resources.

Water harvesting: A technology by which rainwater is collected, and either directly applied to the cropped area and stored in the soil profile for immediate uptake by the crop (runoff irrigation), or stored in a water reservoir for future productive use (for example used for supplementary irrigation).

Water productivity: The amount or value of output (including services) provided by water, in relation to the volume of water used. Crop water productivity refers to the ratio between crop yield and water supply. Economic water productivity is expressed as the ratio between added value of a product and water supply.

Water resources assessment: Water resources assessment focuses on the supply side of water accounting and provides a systematic assessment of water resources, including their variability and trends. See also water accounting.

Water right: In its legal sense, a legal right to abstract or divert and use water from a given natural source; to impound or store a specified quantity of water in a natural source behind a dam or other hydraulic structure; or to use or maintain water in a natural state (ecological flow in a river, and water for recreation, religious/spiritual practices, drinking, washing, bathing or animal watering).

Water-use efficiency: The ratio of the amount of water actually used for a specific purpose to the amount of water withdrawn or diverted from its source to serve that use.

Water withdrawal: Water abstracted from streams, aquifers or lakes for any purpose (e.g. irrigation, industrial, domestic, commercial).

Waterlogging: State of land in which the water table is located at or near the soil surface, affecting crop yields.

Explanatory note for the global maps presented in this report

SOLAW contains a limited set of carefully selected global maps, which support the main messages of the report. While some of these maps have been previously published, several have been prepared specifically for first publication in SOLAW. These notes provides brief methodological explanations on the newly prepared maps as well as references for those previously published. Detailed documentation is available on the SOLAW website: http://www.fao.org/nr/solaw/.

Map 1.1: Dominant land cover and use

This map shows a global distribution of major land cover classes, which includes elements of land use in which cropland has been separated from natural grass and shrub categories. It is extracted from the Global Agro-Ecological Zones (GAEZ v3.0) database maintained by FAO and IIASA, and used as a basis for agricultural perspective studies.

Source: IIASA/FAO, 2010.

Map 1.2: Global distribution of physical water scarcity by major river basin

This map provides a representation of levels of water scarcity by major river basin, expressed in terms of the ratio between irrigation water that is consumed by plants through evapotranspiration and renewable fresh water resources. In contrast to earlier water scarcity maps, this map uses consumptive use of water rather than water withdrawal. Renewable freshwater resources, as well as net irrigation water requirements in the river basin, are calculated through a water balance model, using data on climate, soils and irrigated agriculture as inputs.

Source: this study

Map 1.3: Major agricultural systems

This map, which builds upon work done by Dixon *et al.* (2001) in mapping major farming systems, is used as the basis for the analysis of SOLAW's systems at risk. The map is based on an interpretation of global land cover data, as well as thematic datasets showing irrigated land and the extent of paddy rice.

Source: this study

Map 1.4: Dominant soil and terrain constraints for low-input farming

This map shows dominant soil and terrain constraints for low input farming conditions. The map is part of the IIASA/FAO Global Agro-Ecological Zones version 3.0.

Constraining soil and terrain-slope conditions are accounted for and factored into the analysis by means of soil quality ratings.

Source: IIASA/FAO, 2010.

Map 1.5: Yield gap for a combination of major crops

This map presents, for a combination of major crops, the ratio between actual crop production in the year 2000 and that potentially achievable under advanced farming in current cultivated land. It represents the productivity gap due to low levels of inputs and management, or the potential gains that could be obtained when moving from current to advanced farming.

Source: IIASA/FAO, 2010.

Map 1.6: Area equipped for irrigation as a percentage of land area

This map shows the extent of land area equipped for irrigation around the turn of the 20th century according to the Global Map of Irrigation Areas (version 4.0.1), together with areas of rainfed agriculture obtained from Map 1.3.

Source: Siebert et al., 2007

Map 1.7: Percentage of irrigated area serviced by groundwater

Most irrigation systems in the world are serviced either by surface water, by groundwater or by a combination of the two (conjunctive use of water). This map is based on a combination of Map 1.6 and a global dataset of groundwater irrigation. Both areas serviced by groundwater and areas under conjunctive use of surface water and groundwater are represented.

Source: Siebert et al., 2010

Map 2.1: Prevalence of stunting among children

This map is adapted from a global GIS database maintained by FAO on food insecurity, poverty and the environment. It is based on stunting data among children under 5 years of age, around the year 2000.

Source: FAO, 2007c.

Map 2.2: Distribution of poor population in developing countries, based on stunting among children

Stunting among children is used by FAO as an indicator of food insecurity and poverty. By overlaying stunting rate (Map 2.1) and population density, this map shows the density distribution of poor populations in developing countries.

Source: this study

Map 3.1: Proportion of land salinized due to irrigation

This map represents the spatial distribution of land under irrigation that is affected by some degree of salinization. It was produced by combining FAO AQUASTAT country statistics regarding irrigated areas affected by salinization with spatial information on irrigated areas where precipitation is not sufficient to leach away salt residues that have built up in the soil due to irrigation.

Source: this study

Map 3.2: Agricultural systems at risk: human pressure on land and water

This map shows the extent to which rainfed and irrigated agricultural systems, as identified on Map 1.3, are constrained by land and/or water scarcity. Land scarcity in rainfed agriculture was assessed by comparing the rural population density with the suitability for rainfed crops, assigning a distinctive population carrying capacity to each suitability class. Water scarcity in irrigated areas was assessed by combining Map 1.2 with the global map of irrigation areas. Land-scarce areas in dry climates are considered both land- and water-scarce.

Source: this study

All FAO publicly available input datasets, including references, are available at FAO's GeoNetwork metadata repository (http://www.fao.org/geonetwork).

References

AfDB 2008. *Lake Chad Basin Sustainable Development Programme (PRODEBALT).* Appraisal Report, October 2008. Abidjan and Tunis, African Development Bank Group. (Available at: http://www.afdb.org/fileadmin/uploads/afdb/Documents/Project-and-Operations/30771454-EN-LACTCHAD-DEC-2008.PDF)

Aguilar-Manjarrez, J., Kapetsky, J. M. and Soto, D. 2010. The potential of spatial planning tools to support the ecosystem approach to aquaculture. Expert Workshop. 19–21 November 2008, Rome, Italy. FAO Fisheries and Aquaculture Proceedings. No.17. Rome, FAO.

Akroyd, S. & Smith, L. 2007. *Review of public spending to agriculture.* London/Washington, DC, DFID/World Bank. (Available at: http://www1.worldbank.org/publicsector/pe/pfma07/OPMReview.pdf)

Alexandratos, N. 2005. Countries with rapid population growth and resource constraints: issues of food, agriculture, and development. *Population and Development Review,* 31(2): 237–258.

Alexandratos, N. 2009. World food and agriculture to 2030/50: highlights and views from 2009. 32 pp. In: *How to feed the world in 2050.* Proceedings of an expert meeting, FAO, Rome, 24–26 June 2009. (Available at: ftp://ftp.fao.org/docrep/fao/012/ak542e/ak542e04.pdf)

Batchelor C. H., Rama Mohan Rao, M. S. Manohar Rao, S. 2003. Watershed development: A solution to water shortages in semi-arid India or part of the problem? *Land Use and Water Resources Research* 3:1–10. (http://www.luwrr.com)

Bates, B. C., Kundzewicz, Z. W., Wu, S. and Palutikof, J. P. 2008. *Climate change and water.* Technical Paper VI of the Intergovernmental Panel on Climate Change. IPCC Secretariat. Geneva, 210 pp. (Available at: http://www.ipcc.ch/publications_and_data/publications_and_data_technical_papers.shtml)

Bhattarai, M. and Narayanamoorthy, A. 2003. Impact of irrigation on rural poverty in India: an aggregate panel-data analysis. *Water Policy,* 5(5–6): 443–458.

Bickel, M. and Breuer, T. 2009. Foreign direct investments in land in developing countries. *Rural 21 – The International Journal for Rural Development,* 43(2), April.

Bingham, G., Wolf, A. and Wohlgenant, T. 1994. *Resolving water disputes.* Washington, DC, USAID. (Available at: http://www.beyondintractability.org/articlesummary/10049/)

Binswanger, H. P. 1991. Brazilian policies that encourage deforestation in the Amazon. *World Development,* 19(7): 821–829.

Blench, R. 1999. Extensive pastoral livestock systems: issues and options for the future. Rome, FAO. (Available at: http://www.smallstock.info/reference/FAO/kyokai/document2.pdf)

Blomquist, W. 1992. *Dividing the waters: governing groundwater in southern California.* San Francisco, CA, Institute for Contemporary Studies.

Boonman, J. G. and Mikhalev, S. S. 2005. The Russian Steppe. In: Suttie, J. M., Reynolds, S. G. & Batello, C. (eds.) *Grasslands of the World.* Rome. FAO Plant Production and Protection Series No. 34, 381–416.

Bostock, J., McAndrew, B, Richards, R., Jauncey, K., Telfer, T, Lorenzen, K., Little, D., Ross, L., Handisyde, N., Gatward, I. and Corner, R. 2010. Aquaculture: global status and trends. *Philosophical Transactions of the Royal Society B* 365: 2897–2912. (doi:10.1098/rstb.2010.0170)

Brismar, A. 1999. Environmental challenges and impacts of land use conversion in the Yellow River basin. Interim Report IR-99-016. Laxenburg, IIASA. (Available at: http://www.iiasa.ac.at/Publications/Documents/IR-99-016.pdf)

Bruinsma, J. 2003. *World agriculture: towards 2015/2030. An FAO perspective.* London/Rome, Earthscan/FAO. (Available at: ftp://ftp.fao.org/docrep/fao/005/y4252e/y4252e.pdf)

Bruinsma, J. 2009. *The resource outlook to 2050: by how much do land, water use and crop yields need to increase by 2050?* Expert Meeting on How to Feed the World in 2050. Rome, FAO and ESDD. (Available at: ftp://ftp.fao.org/docrep/fao/012/ak542e/ak542e06.pdf)

Bruns, B. R., Ringler, C. and Meinzen-Dick, R. 2005. Reforming water rights: governance, tenure and transfers. pp 283–309. In: *Bruns et al.* (eds) *Water Rights Reform.* Washington, DC, IFPRI. (Available at: http://www.ifpri.org/sites/default/files/publications/oc49.pdf)

Caponera, D. A. 1992. *Principles of water law and administration: national and international.* Rotterdam/Den Haag, Balkema.

Capoor, K. and Ambrosi, F. 2009. *State and trends of the carbon market 2007: a focus on Africa.* Washington, DC, World Bank. (Available at: http://siteresources.world-bank.org/INTCARBONFINANCE/Resources/State___Trends_of_the_Carbon_Market_2009-FINAL_26_May09.pdf)

Carpenter, S. and Bennet, E. (2011) Reconsideration of the planetary boundary for phosphorus. *Environmental Research Letters.* 6: 014009 (12pp).

CDE 2010. Coping with degradation through SLWM. Centre for Development and Environment. SOLAW Background Thematic Report – TR12. Rome, FAO. (Availlable at: http://www.fao.org/nr/solaw/)

Charalambous, A. N. and Garratt P. 2009. Recharge–abstraction relationships and sustainable yield in the Arani–Kortalaiyar groundwater basin, India. *Quarterly Journal of Engineering Geology and Hydrogeology,* 42: 39–50. (doi:10.1144/1470-9236/07-065)

Chorley, R. C. (ed) 1969. *Water, earth and man.* London, Methuen.

Costanza, R., d'Arge, R., de Groot, R., Farber, S., Grasso, M., Hannon, B., Limburg, K., Naeem, S., O'Neill, R. V., Paruelo, J., Raskin, R. G., Sutton, P. and van den Belt, M. 1997. The value of the world's ecosystem services and natural capital. *Nature,* 387. (Available at: http://www.uvm.edu/giee/publications/Nature_Paper.pdf)

Cotula, L. 2010. Land tenure issues in agricultural investment. SOLAW Background Thematic Report TR05B. Rome, FAO. (Available at: http://www.fao.org/nr/solaw/)

Cotula, L., Vermeulen, S., Leonard, R. and Keeley, J. 2009. *Land grab or development opportunity? Agricultural investment and international land deals in Africa.* Rome/London, Food and Agriculture Organization of the UN (FAO)/International Fund for Agricultural Development (IFAD)/International Institute for Environment and Development (IIED). (Available at: http://pubs.iied.org/pdfs/12561IIED.pdf)

Coudouel, A., Hentschel, J. and Wodon, Q. 2002. Poverty measurement and analysis. In: Klugman, J. (ed.) *A sourcebook for poverty reduction strategies, volume 1: core techniques and cross-cutting issues,* pp. 29–74. Washington, DC, World Bank. (Available at: http://www-wds.worldbank.org/external/default/main?pageP K=64193027&piPK=64187937&theSitePK=523679&menuPK=64187510&searchM enuPK=64187511&theSitePK=523679&entityID=000112742_20040818172234&se archMenuPK=64187511&theSitePK=523679)

De Fraiture, C., Giordano, M. and Yongsong, L. 2008. Biofuels and implications for agricultural water use: blue impacts of green energy. *Water Policy,* 10 (Supplement 1): 67–81.

den Biggelaar, C., Lal, R., Wiebe, K., Eswaran, H., Breneman, V. and Reich, P. 2003. The global impact of soil erosion on productivity ii: effects on crop yields and production over time. *Advances in Agronomy,* 81: 49–95.

Dixon, J. and Gulliver, A., with Gibbon, D. (2001) *Farming systems and poverty: improving farmers' livelihoods in a changing world.* Rome, Italy/Washington, DC, FAO/World Bank.

Ellis, E. C. and N. Ramankutty. 2008. Putting people in the map: anthropogenic biomes of the world. *Frontiers in Ecology and the Environment,* 6(8):439-447 doi:10.1890/070062.

Ellis, F. 2000. *Rural livelihoods and diversity in developing countries.* Oxford, UK, OUP.

Eswaran, H., Lal, R. and Reich, P. F. 2001. Land degradation: an overview. In: Bridges, E. M., I. D. Hannam, L. R. Oldeman, F. W. T. Pening de Vries, S. J. Scherr, and S. Sompatpanit (eds.) *Responses to Land Degradation.* Proc. 2nd. International Conference on Land Degradation and Desertification, Khon Kaen, Thailand. New Delhi, India, Oxford Press.

European Commission. 2010. EU Water Framework Directive. (Available at: http:// ec.europa.eu/environment/water/water-framework/index_en.html)

Fairtrade. 2011. Fairtrade International. (Website: http://www.fairtrade.net/)

Fan, S., Omilola, B. and Lambert, M. 2009. *Public spending for agriculture in Africa: trends and composition.* Regional Strategic Analysis and Knowledge Support Systems (ReSAKSS) Working Paper No. 28. Washington, DC, IFPRI. (Available at: http://www.resakss.org/index.php?pdf=42375)

FAO 1976. *A framework for land evaluation. FAO Soils Bulletin,* 32. Rome, FAO. (Available at: http://www.fao.org/docrep/x5310e/x5310e00.HTM)

FAO 1996. *Control of water pollution from agriculture.* Irrigation and drainage paper 55. Rome. (Available at: http://www.fao.org/docrep/W2598E/W2598E00.htm)

FAO 2000. *The elimination of food insecurity in the Horn of Africa. A strategy for concerted government and UN agency action.* Summary report of the inter-agency task force on the UN response to long-term food security, agricultural development and related aspects in the Horn of Africa. Rome. 13 pp. (Available at: http://www.fao.org/docrep/003/x8530e/x8530e00.htm#TopOfPage)

FAO 2002a. *Land tenure and rural development.* FAO Land Tenure Studies 3. Rome. (Available at: ftp://ftp.fao.org/docrep/fao/005/y4307e/y4307e00.pdf)

FAO 2002b. *Land-water linkages in rural watersheds.* Land and Water Bulletin 9. Rome. (Available at: ftp://ftp.fao.org/agl/aglw/docs/lw9e.pdf)

FAO 2002c. *Gender and access to land.* FAO Land Tenure Studies 4. Rome. (Available at: ftp://ftp.fao.org/docrep/fao/005/y4308e/y4308e00.pdf)

FAO 2003. *Legislation on water users' organization: a comparative analysis.* Legislative Study 79. (Available at: http://www.fao.org/DOCREP/006/Y5049E/Y5049E00.HTM)

FAO 2004a. *Decentralization and rural property taxation.* Rome, FAO Land Tenure Studies 7. Rome. (Available at: ftp://ftp.fao.org/docrep/fao/007/y5444e/y5444e00.pdf)

FAO 2004b. *Land and Water.* Legislative Study 79. (Available at: http://www.fao.org/DOCREP/006/Y5049E/Y5049E00.HTM)

FAO 2004c. *Water charging in irrigated agriculture. An analysis of international experience.* Rome, FAO Water Report 28. (Available at: ftp://ftp.fao.org/agl/aglw/docs/wr28e.pdf)

FAO 2006a. *Integrated Agriculture-Aquaculture.* FAO Fisheries Technical Paper 407. Rome, FAO.

FAO 2006b. *World agriculture: towards 2030/2050. Interim report. Prospects for food, nutrition, agriculture and major commodity groups.* Rome, FAO. (Available at: http://www.fao.org/fileadmin/user_upload/esag/docs/Interim_report_AT2050web.pdf)

FAO 2006c. *Livestock's long shadow.* Rome, FAO. (Available at: http://www.fao.org/docrep/010/a0701e/a0701e00.HTM)

FAO 2006d. *Stakeholder-oriented valuation to support water resource management processes. Confronting conceptions with local practice.* FAO Water Report 30 . Rome, FAO. (Available at: ftp://ftp.fao.org/agl/aglw/docs/wr30_eng.pdf)

FAO 2006e. *Modern water rights: theory and practice.* FAO Legislative Study 92. (Available at: ftp://ftp.fao.org/docrep/fao/010/a0864e/a0864e00.pdf)

FAO 2007a. *Irrigation management transfer: worldwide efforts and results.* FAO Water Reports 32. Rome, FAO. (Available at: http://www.fao.org/docrep/010/a1520e/a1520e00.htm)

FAO 2007b. *Land evaluation: towards a revised framework.* FAO Land and Water Discussion Paper 6. Rome, FAO. (Available at: ftp://ftp.fao.org/docrep/fao/011/a1080e/a1080e00.pdf)

FAO 2007c. *Food insecurity, poverty and environment global GIS database.* FAO Environment and Natural Resources Working Paper 26. (Available at: http://www.fao.org/geonetwork/srv/en/main.home?uuid=0dc30f20-851b-11db-b9b2-000d939bc5d8)

FAO 2007d. *Remediation of arsenic for agriculture sustainability, food security and health in Bangladesh.* FAO Working paper. Rome, FAO. (Available at: http://www.fao.org/nr/water/docs/FAOWATER_ARSENIC.pdf)

FAO 2007e. *Modernizing irrigation management – the MASSCOTE approach.* FAO Irrigation and Drainage Paper 63. (Available at: http://www.fao.org/nr/water/docs/masscote/technical/Masscote.pdf)

FAO 2008a. Financial mechanisms for adaptation to and mitigation of climate change in the food and agriculture sectors. High-Level Conference on World Food Security. (Available at: ftp://ftp.fao.org/docrep/fao/meeting/013/k2516e.pdf)

FAO 2008b. *Global review of good agricultural extension and advisory service practices.* Rome, FAO. (Available at: ftp://ftp.fao.org/docrep/fao/011/i0261e/i0261e00.pdf)

FAO 2008c. *Scoping agriculture-wetland interactions.* FAO Water Reports 33. Rome, FAO. (Available at: http://www.fao.org/nr/water/docs/WaterReports33.pdf)

FAO 2009a. *State of the world's forests 2009.* Rome, FAO. (Available at: http://www.fao.org/docrep/011/i0350e/i0350e00.htm)

FAO 2009b. *The state of food and agriculture 2009.* Rome, FAO. (Available at: www.fao.org/docrep/012/i0680e/i0680e.pdf)

FAO 2010a. *The state of world fisheries and aquaculture.* Rome, FAO. 197 pp. (Available at: http://www.fao.org/docrep/013/i1820e/i1820e00.htm)

FAO 2010b. FAOSTAT database. (Available at: http://faostat.fao.org/)

FAO 2010c. AQUASTAT database. (Available at: www.fao.org/nr/water/aquastat/main/index.stm)

FAO 2010d. *Global forest resources assessment 2010.* FAO Forestry Paper 163. Rome, FAO. (Available at: http://foris.fao.org/static/data/fra2010/FRA2010_Report_en_WEB.pdf)

FAO 2010e. Global survey of agricultural mitigation projects. 30 pp. (Available at: http://www.fao.org/docrep/012/al388e/al388e00.pdf)

FAO 2011a. *The state of food and agriculture 2010-11. Women in agriculture: closing the gender gap for development.* Rome, FAO. (Available at: http://www.fao.org/docrep/013/i2050e/i2050e00.htm)

FAO 2011b. Land tenure. (Available at: http://www.fao.org/nr/tenure/lt-home/en/?no_cache=1)

FAO 2011c. *State of the world's forests 2011.* Rome. (Available at: http://www.fao.org/forestry/sofo/en/)

FAO 2011d. *Climate change, water and food security.* FAO Water Reports 36. Rome, FAO. (Available at: http://www.fao.org/nr/water/jsp/publications/search.htm)

FAO 2011e. Multiple use of water. (Website: http://www.fao.org/nr/water/topics_irrig_mus.html)

FAO and FIVIMS 2003. Poverty mapping, chronic undernutrition among children: an indicator of poverty. Food Insecurity and Vulnerability Information and Mapping Systems, Rome. (Available at: http://www.fivims.org/index.php?option=com_content&task=blogcategory&id=37&Itemid=56)

FAO and WFP 2010. *The state of food insecurity in the world. Addressing food insecurity in protracted crises.* Rome, FAO. (Available at: http://www.fao.org/docrep/013/i1683e/i1683e.pdf)

FAO/ICLARM/IIRR 2001. Integrated Agriculture-Aquaculture: a primer. FAO Fisheries Technical Paper 407. Rome, FAO. (Available at: http://www.fao.org/docrep/005/y1187e/y1187e01.htm)

Faurès, J-M., Svendsen, M. and Turral, H. 2007. Reinventing irrigation. In: Molden, David (ed.). *Water for food, water for life: A comprehensive assessment of water management in agriculture.* London/Colombo, Sri Lanka, IWMI/Earthscan. pp. 353–394.

Fischer, G., Van Velthuizen, H., Shah, M. and Nachtergaele, F. O. 2002. Global agro-ecological assessment for agriculture in the twenty-first century: methodology and results. (Available at: http://www.iiasa.ac.at/Admin/PUB/Documents/RR-02-002.pdf)

Fischer, G., Tubiello, F. N., Van Velthuizen, H. and Wiberg, D. A. 2007. Climate change impacts on irrigation water requirements: effects of mitigation, 1990–2080. *Technological Forecasting and Social Change,* 74(7): 1083–1107.

Fischer, G., Hizsnyik. E., Prieler, S. and Wiberg, D. 2010. *Scarcity and abundance of land resources: competing uses and the shrinking land resource base.* SOLAW Background Thematic Report TR02. Rome, FAO. (Available at: http://www.fao.org/nr/solaw/)

Foster, V. and Briceño-Garmendia, C. 2010. *Africa's infrastructure: a time for transformation.* Washington, DC, World Bank. 355 pp. (Available at: https://www.infrastructureafrica.org/aicd/flagship-report)

Frenken, K. 2010. Sources of water for agriculture. SOLAW Background Thematic Report TR03. Rome, FAO. (Available at: http://www.fao.org/nr/solaw/)

Garduno, H. and Foster, S. 2011. *Sustainable groundwater irrigation: approaches to reconciling demand with resources.* GWMATE Strategic Overview Series No. 4. Washington, DC, World Bank.

Garrity, D. P., Akinnifesi, F. K., Ajayi, O. C., Weldesemayat, S. G., Mowo, J. G., Kalinganire, A., Larwanou, M. and Bayala, J. 2010. Evergreen agriculture: a robust approach to sustainable food security. In: Africa. *Journal of Food Security,* 2: 197–214.

GEF 2011. Projects and funding. Global Environment Facility. (Website: http://www.thegef.org/gef/gef_projects_funding)

GEO 2010. Group on Earth Observations. (Website: http://www.earthobservations.org/)

Geodata Institute 2010. *Where are the poor and where are the land and water resources.* SOLAW Background Thematic Report TR14. (Available at: http://www.fao.org/nr/solaw/).

Giordano, M. A. and Wolf, A. T. 2002. The world's international freshwater agreements. In: UNEP (ed) 2002. *Atlas of international freshwater agreements,* pp. 1–8. UNEP, Oregon State University and FAO. (Available at: http://www.transboundarywaters.orst.edu/publications/atlas/atlas_pdf/2_WorldsAgreements_atlas.pdf)

Grepperud, S. 1994. *Population–environment links. Testing a soil degradation model for Ethiopia.* Divisional Working Paper No 1994–46. Environment Department, Washington, DC, World Bank.

Grey, D. and Sadoff, C. 2006. The global water challenge: poverty growth and international relations. Paper presented at Global Issues Seminar Series. Washington, DC, World Bank.

Gross, R., Schultink, W. and Sastroamidjojo, S. 1996. Stunting as an indicator for health and wealth: an Indonesian application. *Nutrition Research,* 16(11–12): 1829–1837.

Halwart, M. and Van Dam, A. (eds) 2006. Integrated Irrigation and Aquaculture in West Africa: Concepts, practices and potential. FAO Fisheries and Aquaculture Paper. Rome, FAO. (Available at: http://www.fao.org/docrep/009/a0444e/a0444e00.htm)

Hamilton, K., Sjardin, M., Shapiro, A. and Marcello, T. 2009. Fortifying the foundation: State of the voluntary carbon markets 2009. Washington, DC/New York, New Carbon Finance/Ecosystem Marketplace. (Available at: http://www.ecosystemmarketplace.com/documents/cms_documents/StateOfTheVoluntaryCarbonMarkets_2009.pdf)

Hardin, G. 1968. The tragedy of the commons. *Science,* 162: 1243–1248.

Heath, H. and Binswanger, H. 1996. Natural resources degradation. *Environment and Development Economics,* 1 (1): 65–84.

Hellegers P. J. G. J., Perry, C. and Nasser, A. 2011. Incentives to reduce groundwater consumption in Yemen. Irrigation and Drainage. 60: 93–102.

Hoekstra, A. Y. 2010. *The relation between international trade and freshwater scarcity.* Economic Research and Statistics Division Working Paper ERSD-2010-05. Geneva, WTO. (Available at: http://www.wto.org/english/res_e/reser_e/ersd201005_e.pdf)

Hoekstra, A. Y. and Chapagain, A. 2007. Water footprints of nations: water use by people as a function of their consumption pattern. *Water Resource Management,* 21: 35–48.

Hoogeveen, J., Faurès, J-M. and Van De Giessen, N. 2009. Increased biofuel production in the coming decade: to what extent will it affect global freshwater resources? *Irrigation and Drainage,* 58: S148–S160.

Huang, Q., Rozelle, S., Lohmar, B., Jikun Huang and Jinxia Wang. 2006. Irrigation, agricultural performance and poverty reduction in China. *Food Policy,* 31(1): 30–52.

Huang, J., Xiaobing Wang, Huayong Zhi, Zhurong Huang and Rozelle, S. 2011. Subsidies and distortions in China's agriculture: evidence from producer-level data. *Australian Journal of Agricultural and Resource Economics,* 55(1): 53–71. (Available at: http://onlinelibrary.wiley.com/doi/10.1111/j.1467-8489.2010.00527.x/pdf)

Hussain, I. 2007. Pro-poor intervention strategies in irrigated agriculture in Asia: issues, lessons, options and guidelines: Bangladesh. *Irrigation and Drainage,* 56 (2–3): 119–126.

Hussain, I. and Hanjra, M. A. 2004. Irrigation and poverty alleviation: review of the empirical evidence. *Irrigation and Drainage,* 53(1): 1–15.

IBRD 2011. Rising global interest in farmland. Can it yield sustainable and equitable benefits? (Available at: http://siteresources.worldbank.org/INTARD/Resources/ESW_Sept7_final_final.pdf)

IEA 2009. *World energy outlook 2009.* International Energy Agency. Executive summary. (Available at: http://www.worldenergyoutlook.org/docs/weo2009/WEO2009_es_english.pdf)

IFPRI 2009. 'Land grabbing' by foreign investors in developing countries: risks and opportunities. (Comprehensive table: http://www.ifpri.org/sites/default/files/bp013Table01.pdf)

IIASA/FAO 2010. Global Agro-Ecological Zones (GAEZ v3.0). Laxenburg, Austria/ Rome, Italy, IIASA/FAO.

IPCC 2007. *Climate change 2007: Impacts, adaptation and vulnerability.* Contribution of Working Group II to the Fourth Assessment Report of the Intergovernmental Panel on Climate Change. Parry, M. L., Canziani, O. F., Palutikof, J. P., van der Linden P. J. and Hanson, C. E. (eds), Cambridge, UK, Cambridge University Press, pp. 273–313.

Irz, X., Thirtle, C. and Wiggins, S. 2001. Agricultural productivity growth and poverty alleviation. *Development Policy Review,* 19(4): 449–466.

Jua, Xiao-Tang, Guang-Xi Xing, Xin-Ping Chena, Shao-Lin Zhangb, Li-Juan Zhangc, Xue-Jun Liua, Zhen-Ling Cuia, Bin Yinb, Peter Christie, Zhao-Liang Zhub, and Fu-Suo Zhanga. 2009. Reducing environmental risk by improving N management in intensive Chinese agricultural systems. *Proceedings of the National Academy of Sciences,* 106(9): 3041–3046. (Available at: http://www.pnas.org/ content/106/9/3041.full.pdf+html)

LADA 2010a. Land degradation in drylands. (Available at: http://www.fao.org/ nr/lada/)

LADA 2010b. *National land degradation assessment Senegal and review of global socio-economic parameters in the LADA data base.* SOLAW Background Thematic Report TR19 – prepared by the Centre for World Food Studies (SOW-U), Free University (VU), Amsterdam. (Available at: http://www.fao.org/nr/lada/index. php?option=com_docman&task=doc_download&gid=685&Itemid=165&lang=en)

Lipper, L., Dutilly-Diane, C. and McCarthy, N. 2010. Supplying carbon sequestration from West African rangelands: opportunities and barriers. *Rangeland Ecology and Management,* 63(1): 155–166 (Available at: http://www.bioone.org/doi/ pdf/10.2111/REM-D-09-00009.1)

Lipton, M. 2007. Farm water and rural poverty reduction in developing Asia. *Irrigation and Drainage,* 56: 127–146.

Llamas, M. R. and Custodio, E. (eds) 2003. *Intensive use of groundwater: challenges and opportunities.* Lisse, Balkema Publishers.

Lundqvist, J., De Fraiture, C. and Molden, D. 2008. Saving water: From field to fork – curbing losses and wastage in the food chain. SIWI Policy Brief. Stockholm International Water Institute. (Available at: http://www.siwi.org/documents/ Resources/Policy_Briefs/PB_From_Filed_to_Fork_2008.pdf)

Mainuddin, M. and Kirby, M. 2009. Spatial and temporal trends of water productivity in the lower Mekong River Basin. *Agricultural Water Management,* 96(11): 1567–1578.

Mateo-Sagasta, J. and Burke, J. 2010. *Agriculture and water quality interactions.* SOLAW Background Thematic Report TR08. Rome, FAO. (Available at: http://www.fao.org/nr/solaw/)

McCay, B. J. and Acheson, J. M. (eds) 1987. *The question of the commons: the culture and ecology of communal resources.* Tucson, AZ, University of Arizona Press.

MEA. 2005. Millennium Ecosystem Assessment. (Available at: http://www.maweb.org/en/index.aspx)

Meinzen-Dick, R. 2007. Beyond panaceas in irrigation institutions. *Proceedings of the National Academy of Sciences,* 104(39): 15 200–15 205.

Molden, D. (ed.). 2007. *Water for food, water for life. Comprehensive assessment of water management in agriculture.* Colombo/London, IWMI/Earthscan. (Available at: http://www.iwmi.cgiar.org/assessment/)

Molden, D., Oweis, T., Steduto, P., Bindraban, P., Hanjra, M. A. and Kijne, J. 2010. Improving agricultural water productivity: between optimism and caution. *Agricultural Water Management,* 97(4): 528–535.

Molle, F. and Berkoff, J. 2006. *Cities versus agriculture: revisiting intersectoral water transfers, potential gains and conflicts.* IWMI Comprehensive Assessment Research Report 10. Colombo, Sri Lanka, IWMI Comprehensive Assessment Secretariat. (Available at: http://www.iwmi.cgiar.org/assessment/files_new/publications/CA%20Research%20Reports/CARR10.pdf)

Molle, F. and Wester, P. (eds) 2009. *River basin trajectories: societies, environments and development.* CAB International. Wallingford UK: CABI; Colombo, Sri Lanka: International Water Management Institute (IWMI) 311 pp. (Comprehensive Assessment of Water Management in Agriculture Series 8).

Morris, B. L., Lawrence, A. R. L., Chilton, P. J. C, Adams, B., Calow, R. C. and Klinck, B. A. 2003. *Groundwater and its susceptibility to degradation: a global assessment of the problem and options for management.* Early Warning and Assessment Report Series, RS. 03-3. Nairobi, Kenya, United Nations Environment Programme.

Morris, M., Kelly, V., Kopicki, R. J. and Byerlee, D. 2007. Fertilizer use in African agriculture. Directions in development agriculture and rural development 39037. The World Bank, Washington, 144p.

Mukherji, A., and Shah, T. 2005. Groundwater socio-ecology and governance: a review of institutions and policies in selected countries. Hydrogeology Journal, 13: 328–345. (doi: 10.1007/s10040-005-0434-9)

Mundy, M. 1995. *Domestic government: kinship, community and polity in North Yemen.* London, IB Tauris.

Nachtergaele, F. Biancalani, R. and Petri, M. 2010a. *Land degradation.* SOLAW Background Thematic Report TR06. Rome, FAO. (Available at: http://www.fao.org/nr/solaw/)

Nachtergaele, F., Bruinsma, J., Valbo-Jorgensen, J. and Bartley, D. 2010b. Anticipated trends in the use of global land and water resources. SOLAW Background Thematic Report TR01. Rome, FAO. (Available at: http://www.fao.org/nr/solaw/).

Nachtergaele, F. O., Petri, M. and Biancalani, R. 2011. Land degradation. Chapter 3. In: Lal, R. & Stewart, B.A. (eds) *World soil resources and food security.* Advances in Soil Science. Boca Raton, CRC Press.

Neely, C. and Fynn, A. 2010. Critical choices for crop and livestock production systems that enhance productivity and build ecosystem resilience. SOLAW Background Thematic Report TR11. Rome, FAO. (Available at: http://www.fao.org/nr/solaw/

Nkonya, E., Cenacchi, N. and Ringler, C. 2010. International cooperation for sustainable land and water management. SOLAW Background Thematic Report TR16. Rome, FAO. (Available at: http://www.fao.org/nr/solaw/)

Nori, M. and Neely, C. 2009. The tragedy is on, the tragedy is over: pastoral challenges and opportunities for conservation agriculture. *Proceedings of the IV World Congress on Conservation Agriculture, New Delhi, 4–7 February 2009.* (Also available at: http://www.achmonline.org/Resource/Conservation%20Agriculture,%20Nori%20and%20Neely.pdf)

OECD 2010a. *Sustainable management of water use in agriculture.* Paris, OECD.

OECD 2010b. Database on aid activities. Paris, Organisation for Economic Co-operation and Development. (Websites: http://www.oecd.org/dataoecd/20/29/31753872.htm; ODA data: http://stats.oecd.org/Index.aspx?DatasetCode=CRSNEW)

Oldeman, L. R., Hakkeling, R. T. A. and Sombroek, W. G. 1990. World map of the status of human-induced soil degradation. An explanatory note. Global Assessment of Soil Degradation (GLASOD) Working Paper 90/07. Wageningen, ISRIC. (Available at: http://www.isric.org/isric/webdocs/Docs/ISRIC_Report_1990_07.pdf)

Perry, C., Steduto, P., Allen, R. G. and Burt, C. 2009. Increasing productivity in irrigated agriculture: Agronomic constraints and hydrological realities *Agricultural Water Management,* 96: 1517–1524.

Pimentel, D., Harvey, C., Resosudarmo, P., Sinclair, K., Kurz, D., McNair, M., Crist, S., Shpritz, L., Fitton, L., Saffouri, R. and Blair, R. 1995. Environmental and economic costs of soil erosion and conservation benefits. *Science,* 267(5201): 1117–1123.

Pretty, J., Toulmin, C. and Williams, S. (eds) 2011. Sustainable intensification: increasing productivity in African food and agricultural systems. *International Journal of Agricultural Sustainability (special issue),* 9(1): 5–24.

Robins, N., Clover, R. and Singh, C. 2009. *A climate for recovery. The colour of stimulus goes green.* HSBC global research, London.

Rockström, J., W. *et al.* 2009. Planetary boundaries:exploring the safe operating space for humanity. *Ecology and Society* 14(2): 32. (Available at: http://www. ecologyandsociety.org/vol14/iss2/art32/)

Rosegrant M. W. and Svendsen M. 1993. Asian food production in the 1990s: irrigation investment and management policy. *Food Policy,* 18: 13–32.

Sadoff, C. and Grey, D. 2005. Cooperation on international rivers: a continuum for securing and sharing benefits. *Water International,* 30(4): 420–427.

Sadras, V. O. and Grassini, P. 2010. *Status of water use efficiency of main crops.* SOLAW Background Thematic Report TR07. Rome, FAO.

Salman, M., Koohafkan, P. and Casarotto, C. 2010. *Investments in land and water.* SOLAW Background Thematic Report TR17. Rome, FAO. (Available at: http://www.fao.org/nr/solaw/)

Savory, A. and Butterfield, J. 1999. *Holistic management: a new framework for decision making.* Washington, DC, Island Press.

Schmidhuber, J., Bruinsma, J. and Boedeker, G. 2009. Capital requirements for agriculture in developing countries to 2050. In: *How to feed the World in 2050.* Proceedings of an expert meeting, Rome, FAO. 24–26 June 2009. (Available at: ftp://ftp.fao.org/docrep/fao/012/ak542e/ak542e09.pdf)

Scoones, I. 1995. *Living with uncertainty: new directions for pastoral development in Africa.* London, Intermediate Technology Press.

Settle, W. and Garba, M. 2011. Sustainable crop production intensification in the Senegal and Niger River basins of francophone West Africa. *International Journal of Agricultural Sustainability (special issue),* 15: 171–185.

Shah, T. 1993. *Groundwater markets and irrigation development: political economy and pratical policy.* Bombay, India, Oxford University Press.

Shah, T. 2009. *Taming the anarchy: groundwater governance in South Asia.* London/Washington, DC, RFF Press.

Shah, T. and Singh, O. P. 2004. Irrigation development and rural poverty in Gujarat, India: a disaggregated analysis. *Water International,* 29(2): 167–177.

Shamsudduha, M., Taylor, R. G., Ahmed, K. M. and Zahid, A. 2011. The impact of intensive groundwater abstraction on recharge to a shallow regional aquifer system: evidence from Bangladesh. *Hydrogeology Journal,* 19: 901–916. (doi: 10.1007/s10040-011-0723-4)

Sheldrick, W. F., Syers, J. K. and Lingard, J. 2002. A conceptual model for conducting nutrient audits at national, regional, and global scales. *Nutrient Cycling in Agroecosystems,* 62(1): 61–72.

Siebert, Stefan, Döll, Petra, Feick, Sebastian, Hoogeveen, Jippe and Frenken, Karen. 2007. Global map of irrigation areas version 4.0.1. Frankfurt am Main, Germany and Rome, Italy. Johann Wolfgang Goethe University and FAO, Rome, Italy.

Siebert, S., Burke, J., Faurès, J-M., Frenken, K., Hoogeveen, J., Döll, P. and Portmann, F.T. 2010. Groundwater use for irrigation – a global inventory. *Hydrology and Earth System Sciences,* 14: 1863–1880. (Available at: http://www.hydrol-earth-syst-sci.net/14/1863/2010/hess-14-1863-2010.html)

Simondon, K. B. 2010. Review on stunting: clarification and use of the indicator for the assessment of poverty. United Nations System Standing Committee on Nutrition, Task Force on Assessment, Monitoring and Evaluation (Draft). SOLAW Background Thematic Report TR14.

Simpson, B. W. and Ruddle, L. J. 2002. Irrigation and pesticide use. pp. 193–198. In: Bruce R (ed). *Best practice irrigation in sugarcane production. Short course.* Course manual. Townsville, Qld, CSIRO. (Available at: http://www.clw.csiro.au/publications/consultancy/2002/BestPracticeIrrigationinSugarcaneProduction.pdf)

Smaller, C. and Mann, H. 2009. *A thirst for distant lands: foreign investment in agricultural land and water.* Foreign Investment for Sustainable Development Program, Winnipeg, International Institute for Sustainable Development (IISD). (Available at: http://www.iisd.org/pdf/2009/thirst_for_distant_lands.pdf)

Smith, L. E. D. 2004. Assessment of the contribution of irrigation to poverty reduction and sustainable livelihoods. *Water Resources Development,* 20(2): 243–257.

Smits, S., Renwick, M., Renault, D., Butterworth, J. and van Koppen, B. 2008. From practice to policy: background paper for the International symposium on multiple-use water services, Addis Ababa, Ethiopia, 4-6 November 2008.

Steduto, P, Hsiao, T. C. and Fereres, E. 2007. On the conservative behaviour of biomass water productivity. *Irrigation Science,* 25: 89–107.

Tanji, K. K. and Kielen, N. C. 2002. *Agricultural drainage water management in arid and semiarid areas.* Irrigation and Drainage Paper 61. Rome, FAO. (Available at: ftp://ftp.fao.org/agl/aglw/docs/idp61e.pdf)

Tennigkeit, T. and Wilkes, A. 2008. An assessment of the potential for carbon finance in rangelands. Nairobi, Kenya, World Agroforestry Centre, ICRAF. (Available at: http://www.fao.org/fileadmin/templates/agphome/scpi/cgwg/ICRAF_WP68.pdf)

Tennigkeit, T., Kahrl, F., Wölcke, J. and Newcombe, K. 2009. *Agricultural carbon sequestration in Sub-Saharan Africa: economics and institutions.* Washington, DC, World Bank. (Available at: http://africacarbonforum.com/2009/docs/presentations/Day2/timm%20tennigkeit.pdf)

TerrAfrica 2009. Country Support Tool. For scaling-up sustainable land management in sub-Saharan Africa - Field Application. (Available at: http://knowledgebase.terrafrica.org/fileadmin/user_upload/terrafrica/docs/topic_page/Country_Support_Tool_2_.pdf)

Thirtle, C., Irz, X., Lin, L., McKenzie-Hill, V. and Wiggins, S. 2001. *Relationship between changes in agricultural productivity and the incidence of poverty in developing countries.* DFID report No. 7946, 27/02/2001. London, DFID. (Available at: http://www.odi.org.uk/events/documents/2334-background-paper-colin-thirtle-relationship-between-changes-agricultural-productivity-incidence-poverty.pdf)

Tiffen, M., Mortimore, M. and Gichuki, F. 1994. *More people, less erosion: environmental recovery in Kenya.* Chichister, UK, John Wiley.

Tilman, D., Socolow, R., Foley, J. A., Hill, J., Larson, E., Lynd, L., Pacala, S., Reilly, J., Searchinger, T., Somerville, C. and Williams, R. 2009. Beneficial biofuels – the food, energy, and environment trilemma. *Science, 325,* 270–271.

Tubiello. F. and van der Velde, M. 2010. Land and water use options for climate change adaptation and mitigation in agriculture. SOLAW Background Thematic Report TR04A. Rome, FAO. (Available at: http://www.fao.org/nr/solaw/)

Tubiello, F. N., Soussana, J. F., Howden, M. and Easterling, W. 2007. Crop and pasture response to climate change; fundamental processes. *Proceedings of the National. Academy of Sciences,* 104: 19 686-19 690.

Tubiello, F., Schmidhuber, J., Howden, M., Neofotis, P. G., Park, S., Fernandes, E. and Thapa, D. 2008. *Climate change response strategies for agriculture: challenges and opportunities for the twenty-first century.* Agriculture and rural development discussion paper 42. Washington, DC, World Bank.

Turral, H. and Burke, J. 2010. *Sustainable crop production and intensification in irrigated cropping systems.* Land and Water Division, Rome, FAO.

UNCCD 2007. *High-level round table discussion on desertification and adaptation to climate change.* Conference of the Parties, Eighth session, Madrid, 3–14 September 2007. (Available at: http://www.unccd.int/convention/menu.php)

UNCTAD 2006. *FDI from developing and transition economies: implications for development.* World Investment Report 2006. New York and Geneva, UN. (Available at: http://www.unctad.org/en/docs/wir2006ref_en.pdf)

United Nations 2009. *World population prospects: the 2008 revision population database.* New York, UN Population Division.

UN-REDD 2011. The United Nations Collaborative Program on Reducing Emissions from Deforestation and Forest Degradation in Developing Countries. (Website: http://www.un-redd.org/)

Uphoff N. Kassam, A. and Harwood, R., 2011. SRI as a methodology for raising crop and water productivity: productive adaptations in rice agronomy and irrigation water management. *Paddy and Water Environment,* 9: 3–11.

Von Braun, J. and Meinzen-Dick, R. 2009. *'Land grabbing' by foreign investors in developing countries: risks and opportunities.* Policy Brief 13. Washington, DC, IFPRI. (Available at: http://www.ifpri.org/sites/default/files/publications/bp013all.pdf)

Wang, Jinxia, Jikun Huang, Zhigang Xu, Rozelle, S., Hussain, I. and Biltonen, E. 2007. Irrigation management reforms in the Yellow River basin: implications for water saving and poverty. *Irrigation and Drainage,* 56: 247–259.

Wani, S. P, Sreedevi, T. K, Rockström, J. and Ramakrishna, Y. S. 2009. Rainfed agriculture: past trends and future prospects. In: Wani S. P. (ed). *Rainfed Agriculture: Unlocking the potential,* pp. 1–35. Wallingford, UK, CAB Intl. (Available at: http://www.iwmi.cgiar.org/Publications/CABI_Publications/CA_CABI_Series/Rainfed_Agriculture/Protected/Rainfed_Agriculture_Unlocking_the_Potential.pdf)

White, R. P., Murray, S. and Rohweder, M. 2000. *Pilot analysis of global ecosystems: grassland ecosystems.* Washington, DC, World Resources Institute. (Available at: http://www.wri.org/publication/pilot-analysis-global-ecosystems-grassland-ecosystems)

Whittington, D., Xun Wu and Sadoff, C. 2005. Water resources management in the Nile Basin: the economic value of cooperation. *Water Policy,* 7: 227–252.

WHO-FAO-UNEP 2006. WHO Guidelines for the safe use of wastewater, excreta and greywater. Volume 4. Excreta and greywater use in agriculture. World Health Organization. Geneva.

Wichelns, D. 2010. An economic analysis of the virtual water concept in relation to the agri-food sector, background reports supporting the OECD study (2010). *Sustainable Management of Water Resources in Agriculture.* Paris, OECD. (Website: www.oecd.org/water)

Winpenny, J. 2010. Global trends in financing water. In: Ringler C *et al.* (eds). *Globalization, Trade and Global Change,* pp 143–167. New York, Springer.

Winpenny, J., Heinz, I. and Koo-Oshima, S. 2010. The wealth of waste. FAO Water Report 35. (Available at: http://www.fao.org/docrep/012/i1629e/i1629e.pdf)

World Bank 2003. Implementation completion report for the Loess Plateau project. Report # 25701. Washington, DC, World Bank. (Available at: http://www-wds.worldbank.org/external/default/WDSContentServer/WDSP/IB/2003/05/01/000160016_20030501180454/Rendered/PDF/257011CN1Loess1d0Rehab0Project01ICR.pdf)

World Bank 2005. *Shaping the future of water for agriculture: a sourcebook for investment in agricultural water management.* Washington, DC, World Bank. (Available at: http://siteresources.worldbank.org/INTARD/Resources/Shaping_the_Future_of_Water_for_Agriculture.pdf)

World Bank 2006. *Directions in development. Reengaging in agricultural water management. Challenges and options.* Washington, DC, World Bank. (Available at: http://siteresources.worldbank.org/INTARD/Resources/DID_AWM.pdf)

World Bank 2007a. *Agriculture for development.* World Development Report 2008. Washington, DC, World Bank. (Available at: http://siteresources.worldbank.org/INTWDR2008/Resources/WDR_00_book.pdf)

World Bank 2007b. *Emerging public-private partnerships in irrigation development and management.* In: Dargouth, S. *et al.* Water Sector Board Discussion Paper Series No 10, May 2007. Washington, DC, World Bank. (Available at: http://siteresources.worldbank.org/INTWSS/Resources/WS10_txt.pdf)

World Bank 2007c. *Investment in agricultural water for poverty reduction and economic growth in Sub-Saharan Africa: synthesis report.* Report No 43768 (2008-01-01). Washington, DC, World Bank. (Available at: http://www-wds.worldbank.org/external/default/WDSContentServer/WDSP/IB/2008/05/29/000334955_20080529023517/Rendered/PDF/437680SR0white10water0200801PUBLIC1.pdf)

World Bank 2007d. China second Loess Plateau watershed rehabilitation project; first and second Xiaolangdi multipurpose project; and second Tarim Basin project. Project performance assessment report. Report # 41122. Washington, DC, World Bank. (Available at: http://www-wds.worldbank.org/external/default/WDSContentServer/WDSP/IB/2007/10/31/000020953_20071031102004/Rendered/PDF/41122.pdf)

World Bank 2008. *Poverty analysis in agricultural water operations.* Water Working Notes No 16. Washington, DC, World Bank. (Available at: http://www-wds.worldbank. org/external/default/WDSContentServer/WDSP/IB/2008/06/18/000333037_20 080618031322/Rendered/PDF/442260NWP0WN1610Box327398B01PUBLIC1.pdf)

World Bank 2009a. *Environmental flows in water resources policies, plans and projects: findings and recommendations.* Report No 48743. Washington, DC, World Bank. (Available at: http://www-wds.worldbank.org/external/default/ WDSContentServer/WDSP/IB/2009/06/04/000334955_20090604063828/ Rendered/PDF/487430PUB0envi101Official0Use0Only1.pdf)

World Bank 2009b. *World Development Report 2010.* Washington, DC, World Bank. (Available at: http://econ.worldbank.org/WBSITE/EXTERNAL/EXTDEC/ EXTRESEARCH/EXTWDRS/EXTWDR2010/0,,contentMDK:21969137~menuPK :5287748~pagePK:64167689~piPK:64167673~theSitePK:5287741,00.html)

World Bank 2010a. Deep wells and prudence: towards pragmatic action for addressing groundwater overexploitation in India. Washington, DC, World Bank. (Available at: http://siteresources.worldbank.org/INDIAEXTN/ Resources/295583-1268190137195/DeepWellsGroundWaterMarch2010.pdf)

World Bank 2010b. *Managing Water Scarcity.* A background paper for the MNA study on Peace, Stability and Development. Washington, DC, World Bank.

WWAP 2009. *United Nations World Water Development Report 3: water in a changing world.* Paris/London, UNESCO/Earthscan. (Available at: http://www.unesco. org/water/wwap/wwdr/wwdr3/)

Yetim, M. 2002. Governing international common pool resources. *Water Policy,* 4(4): 305–321.

Index

A

Acacia albida (Faidherbia albida), 142–143
acquisitions, large-scale
  of croplands, 105–106
  status and trends, 7
  and sustainable intensification, 12
adaptation to climate change, 14, 170–172, 175
administration institutions. *see* institutions
agricultural policy, 77
agricultural production
  challenges of, 14–15
  core land and water indicators, 243–248
  and greenhouse gases, 118–119
  and intensification, 10–12
  land and water degradation, 112–119
  land suitability, 246
  population growth, 52–53
  statistics, 3
  systems at risk, 8
  water pollution, 117–118
  see also irrigated agriculture; rainfed agriculture
agroforestry management practices, 149, 150–151, 159–160, 173–174
algal blooms, 118
allocation systems, 72–76, 186–191
ammonia fertilizer, 165
Andhra Pradesh Farmer Managed Groundwater Systems (APFAMGS) project, 190
aquaculture, 50–51, 105
aquifer health, 155
aquifer-based systems, risks to, 223
  see also irrigated agriculture
arable land in use, 243–244
  see also agricultural production
arsenic contamination, 168
'at risk' systems, 9, 123–132, 221
autonomous adaptation, 170

B

Bill & Melinda Gates Foundation, 208
biodiesel, 106–107
biodiversity, 47, 142, 213
bioethanol, 106–107

C

carbon sequestration, 49, 184, 211–214
carbon trading, 96

Caribbean, loss of natural forests in, 109
cereals, impact of climate change, 122, 248
Chicago Climate Exchange (CCX), 215
children, stunting among, 65
China
  Mekong river basin, 162–164
  watershed rehabilitation, 89
Clean Development Mechanism (CDM), 96, 211
climate change
  adaptation, 14, 170–171
  and agriculture, 169–170
  anticipated impacts of, 120–123
  impacts of, 248
  mitigation, 14, 171–172
  patterns of, 8
coastal alluvial plains, risks to, 131–132, 223–224
communal tenure systems, 73–74
conservation agriculture, 149–150
consumption. *see* demands
controlled grazing, 152
Convention on the Law of Non-Navigational Uses of International Watercourses, 76
country groupings, 235–236
country programmes, for sustainable land management policy, 239–242
crop and livestock systems, 151
crop residues, 144
crop water productivity, 162–164
  see also water productivity
croplands, large-scale land acquisitions of, 105–106
CULTAN method, 165
cultivated land. *see* land resources

D

degradation
  status and trends, 4
    see also land degradation
delta systems, risks to, 131–132, 221, 223–224
demands
  future perspectives for, 7–8, 52–53
  production response, 52–53
densely populated highlands in poor areas, risks to, 125–127
desalinated water, 40, 155
desertification, 95, 153, 174
developing countries
  future perspectives for, 8

integrated crop-livestock systems, 151

integrated pest management (IPM), 166–168

intensification
   and agricultural production, 10–12
   environmental risks associated with, 164–169
   future perspectives for, 8
   irrigated agriculture, 54
   and poverty, 69
   role of knowledge, 199–200

intensive temperate agriculture systems,
   risks to, 128–129

international cooperation
   enhancing, 209–215
   investments, 209–215, 230
   land and water management, 92–99, 204–205
   reforming, 229–233
   requirements for, 12–14
   role of knowledge, 231–232

International Land Coalition, 204

international partnerships, land and water
   management, 200–209

Inventory of land and water systems at risk, 232

investments
   challenges, 5–7
   developing national frameworks, 196
   gaps in, 97–99
   international cooperation, 209–215, 230
   land and water management, 90–92
   milestones and achievements, 94–96
   need for, 228
   requirements for, 12–14

irrigated agriculture
   in Africa, 224
   current status, 35–43
   expansion rate, 40
   externalities, 237–239
   impact on water-related ecosystems, 115–117
   implications for, 54–56
   irrigation management agencies, 84–86
   land productivity, 43
   modernization, 194–196
   and poverty, 69–70
   productivity and production gaps, 43–45
   resources in, 35–45
   risks to, 223
   water resources constraints, 42–43
   water sources, 40–41, 154–156

irrigation systems
   impact of climate change, 123
   management agencies, 84–86
   modernizing, 156–159
   status and trends, 4

islands, risks to, 131–132

K

knowledge gaps
   response to, 12, 199–200
   and sustainable land management policy, 229

L

Lake Chad Basin Sustainable Development
   Program (PRODEBALT), 207

land acquisitions
   of croplands, 105–106
   status and trends, 7
   and sustainable intensification, 12

land and water management
   access to resources, 4, 65–69, 186–191, 226
   allocation systems, 72–76
   core indicators, 243–248
   distorted incentives, 88
   international agreements, 204–205
   regional cooperation, 203
   status and trends, 3–5
     see also sustainable land management (SLM)
       policy

land cover types, 245

land degradation
   agricultural production, 112–119
   Brazil, 174
   cost of, 186
   definition of, 108
   impacts and causes, 108–120
   and poverty, 65–69
   status and trends, 113
   Land Degradation Assessment in Drylands
     (LADA), 108–112

land policy, 77–78

land reform and redistribution, 188

land resources
   assessment of, 26
   current status, 21–25

land suitability, 58–59, 246

land tenure systems, 72–74, 186–188

land use planning, 83–84

landslides, 174

large contiguous surface irrigation systems in dry
   areas, risks to, 130

large-scale land acquisitions. *see* acquisitions,
   large-scale

Latin America, loss of natural forests in, 109

less and least developed regions, 236

liquid biofuels, 106–107

livestock production, 104–105, 151, 152

low-income food deficit countries (LIFDC).
   see developing countries